# Chase Your Shadow

## ALSO BY JOHN CARLIN

Knowing Mandela

Playing the Enemy: Nelson Mandela
and the Game that Made a Nation

# Chase Your Shadow

*The Trials of Oscar Pistorius*

## John Carlin

HARPER LUXE

*An Imprint of* HarperCollins*Publishers*

HarperCollins books may be purchased for educational, business, or sales promotional use. For information, please e-mail the Special Markets Department at SPsales@harpercollins.com.

Originally published in the United Kingdom in 2014 by Atlantic Books, an imprint of Atlantic Books Ltd.

FIRST HARPERLUXE EDITION

HarperLuxe™ is a trademark of HarperCollins Publishers

Library of Congress Cataloging-in-Publication Data is available upon request.

ISBN: 978-0-06-237051-8

14 ID/RRD  10 9 8 7 6 5 4 3 2 1

# 1

*The race is not to the swift, nor the battle to the*
*strong . . . but time and chance happeneth to them all.*

ECCLESIASTES 9:11

Balancing on the stumps of his amputated legs, gripping a black 9mm pistol with both hands, he fired four shots through a door in the upstairs bathroom of his home. Behind the door was a small toilet cubicle. A person was inside.

Bewildered and in shock, he staggered towards the door, tried the handle. It was locked. Seconds later, 'Oh my God! What have I done?'

His ears so deafened by the sound of the gunshots that he could not hear his own screams, he rushed down a narrow corridor to his bedroom, holding onto the sides of the walls to keep himself from falling over. He opened a sliding door in the bedroom that gave onto an outside terrace and shouted, 'Help! Help! Help!' At his bedside were his prosthetic legs. He pulled them on, ran back to the bathroom and attempted without success to kick the door down. His screams ever more frantic, he returned to the bedroom, grabbed a cricket bat he kept in case of attack by an intruder, ran back to the bathroom and bashed at the door with desperate fury. A wooden panel gave way, allowing him to reach a hand through and undo the lock. And there he found her, his girlfriend, crumpled on the floor with her face on the toilet seat, her blue eyes vacant, blood pumping from her arm, her hip and her head. She was not moving but maybe, he yearned to believe, she still breathed. Almost fainting from the rotting metal stench of her wounds, battling to get a purchase on her soaked, slippery frame, he eased her off the toilet seat and, with a hand on her head, oozing blood, placed her down on the bathroom's white marble floor, sobbing and screeching, beseeching God to let her live. He found a towel, knelt over her, tried hopelessly to staunch the blood pouring out of the wound on her hip and stared, howling in despair, at her shattered skull and lifeless eyes as the truth began to sink in that not even God could repair the impact of a bullet to the brain – nothing could amend the irreversible immensity of this horror.

The date was February 14, 2013, Valentine's Day. The time he fired the shots, between 3.12 and 3.14 in the morning. The place, his home at Silver Woods Estate, a heavily guarded residential compound in the eastern suburbs of Pretoria, the capital of South Africa. He, Oscar Pistorius, the 'Blade Runner' – at twenty-six, a world-famous athlete, the first disabled runner to compete in the Olympic Games, 'the fastest man with no legs'. His victim, Reeva Steenkamp, a twenty-nine-year-old model and aspiring reality TV star, unknown outside South Africa, whom he would propel, in death, to global fame.

At 3.19 he made the first phone call, to his neighbor and friend Johan Stander, the manager of Silver Woods. The phone records would show later that the call lasted twenty-four seconds. 'Johan, please, please come to my house,' he cried. 'I shot Reeva. I thought she was an intruder. Please, please, please come quick.' Then he phoned the emergency services, but they told him he should try and get her to a hospital himself. And then he phoned the estate's security guards. He made the three calls in the space of five minutes.

With immense effort, grunting, sobbing and gasping for air, he lifted up her drenched body, carried her out of the bathroom and down a passageway towards a set of grey marble stairs, her head hanging limply on his left shoulder. The gun he had fired did not have normal bullets in the magazine. If they had, she might have survived. But he had used dumdum bullets that, instead of simply penetrating their target, expanded on impact.

When he was halfway down the stairs with the dead or dying woman in his arms a security guard called Pieter Baba came in through the front door, joined moments later by Stander and Stander's adult daughter, Carice. Standing there too, was a young man from Malawi called Frankie Chiziweni who lived on the premises, downstairs, and worked for Pistorius as a gardener and housekeeper.

Through his tears he saw the four of them staring up at him, their hands covering their faces, muffling their gasps. He howled at them for help, but for a shocked instant they stood rooted where they were, not wanting to believe what their eyes were seeing. But, yes, that was Oscar Pistorius, the national hero, their gentle, well-mannered friend; that was Reeva, the smiling, warm photographic model that all four of them had seen visiting the estate in recent months. She was in T-shirt and shorts, her long legs dangling from his arms. He wore only a pair of shiny basketball shorts which reached down to his knees, covering the tops of his skin-colored prostheses with their plastic calves, feet and toes. Blood trailed behind him on the staircase, trickled down his back. Blood on her clothes, her matted blonde hair, on his shorts, his legs, his bare torso and shoulders – streams of it.

Stander, the oldest of the four, was the first to collect himself, calling out that an ambulance was on its way and urging Pistorius to lay Reeva down on a rug by a sofa in the sitting room, near the front door. He dropped to his knees, lowered her delicately onto the ground and screamed that he wanted that ambulance now, as he scrutinized her bruised face for some sign of life. He put a finger between her lips, trying to prise open her mouth, as if that would make her breathe. With his other hand he covered the wound on her crushed right hip, where the bleeding was heaviest. The gestures were as futile as they were desperate. There was no sign of breathing, no end to the haemorrhage. Carice Stander placed a towel on Reeva's hip, asked him if he had some rope or some tape to staunch the blood in the third wound, on her left arm, conspiring with him in the frantic, make-believe struggle that they could do something, anything, to bring her back to life. Ten minutes had passed since he had fired the shots. Her eyes were closed and she made no sound.

He fingered the inside of her wrist, searching for a pulse, finding none. 'Please, God, please, let her live, she must not die!' he prayed. 'Stay with me, my love, stay with me!'

Two minutes after the others a fifth witness entered the house, a doctor called Johan Stipp, who lived a hundred yards away and had been woken by the sound of the shots.

'What happened?' the doctor asked.

'I shot her. I thought she was a burglar. I shot her,' he cried, still with his fingers in her mouth, trying to force a way in between her teeth, which were clenched shut.

Dr Stipp was a radiologist and no expert in an emergency, but he went through the motions of checking for signs of life, expecting to find none for he saw that the top of her skull had cracked open and brain tissue was leaking out of it. He felt her wrist: no pulse. He opened her right eyelid: no contraction of the pupil. She was brain-dead, mortally wounded.

An ambulance arrived at 3.43. Two paramedics walked into the house and confirmed the doctor's diagnosis, pronouncing her dead.

Sobbing, beyond hope of God's mercy now, he retreated up the stairs. Carice Stander panicked. She realized the gun must be up there and feared he would do what she herself might have done in his place.

She followed him upstairs, trying to think what she could do to try to stop him from shooting himself – but there was no need. He just stumbled about the corridor that led to his bedroom, in a haze of tears. A part of him longed for death. Whether it came to that or not, he would first need understanding and forgiveness from someone close to him, someone who would spread the word. He sought that now, not in his family, who would be sure to be on his side, but in a friend called Justin Divaris, the person who had introduced him to Reeva. Pistorius went to his bedroom, got his mobile phone and called Divaris. It was five to four in the morning.

'There has been a terrible accident. I shot Reeva,' he told Divaris, who could not make out, or could not believe, what he was saying. He asked him to calm down and repeat himself. 'I shot Reeva. It was an accident.' How badly had he shot her? 'I've killed her. I've killed my baba,' he wept. 'God take me away.'

When the call ended the police arrived. A white colonel in plain clothes walked in, accompanied by black uniformed officers, followed at 4.15 by Hilton Botha, a police investigator. Botha took charge of the crime scene, ordered the house to be sealed and instructed a police photographer to get to work. The photographer took pictures of the dead woman, covered in towels, from all angles, then full-body shots of Pistorius in his sodden basketball shorts, the bereft look in his eyes at odds with the muscular power of his blood-smeared shoulders. Botha, more accustomed to visiting crime scenes in poorer neighborhoods, was struck by the marbled spaciousness of his home, the expensive-looking ornaments and paintings, the shelves stacked with athletics trophies, the contrast between the pristine orderliness of Pistorius's home and the grisly spectacle presented by his victim.

After the photographer had gone upstairs to take pictures of the bedroom and the bathroom where he had shot Reeva, Pistorius slipped off to the kitchen, alone for a moment, to sob and retch and vomit. A policeman followed him and asked him why he was throwing up. It was the smell of the blood on his hands, he replied. Could he wash them? The policeman said he could, and he turned on the tap and washed away for the last time all physical connection with the woman he had loved, gazing at the red liquid swirling down the kitchen sink.

The romance had begun barely three and a half months earlier on a lovely spring day. Justin Divaris, the friend he had phoned forty minutes after the shooting, had introduced them to each other. Divaris owned the South African dealerships for Rolls-Royce, McLaren and Aston Martin. Pistorius and Divaris had struck up a mutually useful relationship. Pistorius was crazy about cars, and Divaris gave him the keys to some of the more extravagant models in his showroom, on one occasion a white Rolls-Royce, to run around in at weekends. In exchange he would play the role of 'ambassador' for Divaris's brands, sprinkling some of his celebrity gold dust over the fashionable events Divaris would host when he launched a new car. The most prized guests were those who were able to pay for an Aston Martin cash-down. The adornments at these feasts were young women in high heels and short dresses, whom Divaris's people would recruit for the night from Johannesburg and Cape Town model agencies. Reeva was one of those models. She was eye-catchingly beautiful and she inevitably attracted Divaris's attention. Reeva also liked cars, and it was on November 4, 2012, at the Kyalami motor-racing track, twenty minutes' drive from Pistorius's home and half-way between Pretoria and Johannesburg, that Divaris brought the two of them together for the first time.

For Pistorius it was love at first sight. As he would testify in court later, he was 'bowled over'. Three years older than he, Reeva was strikingly beautiful, lithe and self-confident – worldly in a way that the much younger girlfriend with whom he had broken up with only weeks earlier, after eighteen months together, had not been. She felt an immediate attraction to him too. He had more star quality than anyone in South Africa save for Nelson Mandela, yet he had a winning shyness about him, an old-fashioned courteousness and an unusually soft and gentle voice. And he was handsome. Six-feet tall on the prostheses hidden under his jeans, he had a gymnast's body, high cheekbones and kind, smiling eyes.

When he invited her to attend a red-carpet South African Sports Awards ceremony that very evening she assented without a second thought, phoning a close woman friend as soon as she could get away, to tell her the mind-boggling news that she had a date with the famous Blade Runner. Just how famous she would find out later that evening when the two of them became the magnet for all the photographers' attention – she in a short, tasseled, cream dress and high heels; he, celebrated in magazines as South Africa's best-dressed man, wearing a sharp dark suit, white shirt and black tie. More engrossed in one another than with the crowd attending the glittering event, that night the two of them stayed up talking until three in the morning.

Now, three and a half months later, it was five in the morning on Valentine's Day, of all days. The ambulance had come and gone, taking Reeva's body away, and his home, cordoned off with yellow tape, was flooded with police. He was not handcuffed, but there was no possibility of escape. If there was one thing he would not be able to do, given that everyone in South Africa knew his face, it was to slip away unseen. Botha, the policeman in charge, said he should go into the garage and not move from there.

What happened during the next few hours would remain for him a tear-stained blur. His lawyer, a large man called Kenny Oldwadge, arrived. His older brother Carl was the first family member on the scene. Then an uncle, Arnold Pistorius, and then his younger sister, Aimée, appeared at the garage door, his gasping cries like knives to their hearts. Arnold, the stiff-backed family patriarch, stood back as Aimée and Carl wrapped his trembling body in their arms. Pistorius regarded Aimée, who was twenty-four, as his closest friend. Carl was usually more emotionally awkward, the burly, rough and tumble playmate who had watched over him when he was a child in the schoolyard. But they were all broken now, sitting silently by his side, taking turns to put their arms around him as he sobbed.

The policemen let an interval pass, then told Pistorius the time had come to go away with them. He put on a grey tracksuit top with a hood and slid into the back of a police car. They drove him to a nearby precinct and led him into an office where he was informed that criminal procedure dictated he should go to hospital for tests. Then a short, bald man wearing civilian clothes appeared and introduced himself as the head of the South African Police Service's forensic psychology section.

Colonel Gerard Labuschagne had learned of the shooting from the news broken by a South African paper at 8.03, nearly five hours after it had happened, via Twitter. The post had read: 'Oscar Pistorius shoots his girlfriend dead in his house.' Labuschagne responded with the same disbelief and stupefaction as the rest of the public. By 9 a.m. images of the Blade Runner's home turned into a crime scene, juxtaposed with a photograph of him smiling and arm in arm with Steenkamp, were appearing on TV and computer screens in every corner of the globe. Labuschagne made a call to a superior and received an order to rush to the police station. He had judged, and his superior had agreed, that, in the absence of any eyewitnesses, a reading of Pistorius's psychological state immediately after the shooting might yield some clue as to what exactly had happened that night. Hilton Botha, a policeman for twenty-four years, had already made up his mind that it was an open and shut case – he had seen dozens like it and was sure it was murder, deliberate murder following a lovers' argument.

Labuschagne, aware of Pistorius's claim that he had imagined he was firing at an intruder, anticipated that when the trial came the athlete would lodge what the courts called 'a psychological defense'. There was always the prospect of a confession. How long could he carry on insisting on the implausible story that he imagined a burglar had locked himself in the toilet? But, short of that, Labuschagne wanted to observe Pistorius as closely as he could in the immediate aftermath of the shooting. The news that the suspect was about to be taken to the hospital would give the psychologist the opportunity to observe him over the course of several hours, to try and gain a sense of whether he was telling the truth or not.

Content to watch him out of the corner of his eye, asking nothing, Labuschagne accompanied Pistorius to the police car that would take him to the hospital. He sat in the front next to the driver, Pistorius in the back with another policeman, keeping his head down to avoid being seen. Neither of them spoke, save once when Labuschagne, trying to win his confidence, called out a warning for him to duck down because he had spotted a vehicle in the rear-view mirror that seemed to be carrying news photographers.

The car dropped them off at the hospital that serviced the township of Mamelodi – a place the police would never have taken a white man under apartheid, the system of racial discrimination that had lasted half a century, ending twenty years earlier when Nelson Mandela was elected South Africa's first black president.

Mamelodi was a poor and densely populated residential area on the periphery of Pretoria, which had been blacks-only by law under apartheid and remained blacks-only in practice now. The politics of South Africa had changed utterly since Nelson Mandela's election as president in 1994 but Mamelodi remained poor, as did hundreds of townships like it. Addressing poverty and inequality was the task of Mandela's heirs in government now, an incremental exercise plagued by official incompetence and the apparently inevitable corrupting effects on a political party, the African National Congress, that had been in power for twenty consecutive years. The verities of Mandela's time, when the political and moral questions had been indistinguishable, had given way to the muddle of day-to-day governance in a country whose challenges were no longer unique in the world. But, while dissatisfaction with the party that had liberated black South Africa grew, Mamelodi and places like it had more access to electricity and running water than before. Also, a black middle class, a concept unimaginable in the apartheid days, had emerged and now consisted of some six million people out of a total South African population of fifty million. The power of the apartheid state had been deployed to defend a system in which black people could not vote, in which they were told where they could and could not live and what hospitals, buses, trains, parks, beaches, public toilets or public telephones they could and could not use. The principle had always been to keep the races apart so as to guarantee white people a superior standard of living. But now some members of this new black middle class lived in Silver Woods as neighbors of the country's most celebrated white man; at least three of them would turn out to have been woken by the sound of gunfire in the dead of night and would later appear as witnesses for Pistorius's defense at the murder trial. One thing that had changed unambiguously and for the better during the twenty years of democracy had been the racial climate, one example of which had been that the Blade Runner was, or had been, as much of a hero among the people of Mamelodi as anywhere else in South Africa – the greatest national hero for South Africans of all races since Mandela himself.

Had he visited the township twenty-four hours earlier it would have been cause for exuberant celebration. But the police kept his visit to the hospital at Mamelodi quiet, sparing themselves the commotion and him the distress of a potentially mixed welcome.

Labuschagne and the man who, like Mandela in his day, had suddenly become South Africa's most famous prisoner spent nearly three hours together at the hospital, most of the time alone – the police colonel on a chair, the prisoner on a medical bed – in a small consulting room. A doctor eventually came in and took scrapes from under Pistorius's nails, examined his body for scratches and bruises. Then more waiting for blood and urine tests, to all of which he numbly succumbed. As it turned out, all the tests drew blanks. No alcohol, no illegal drugs, no physical evidence of a fight. Nothing here that could be used in court against him, making it all the more urgent that while Pistorius's state of mind was still raw from the shooting, Labuschagne should try and identify something of value for the prosecution case. Labuschagne's problem was that the lawyers had already intervened to the point of forbidding the police from asking him anything about the events of the night. In fact, apart from the first fraught exchanges with the police at dawn, never at any point did he submit to police interrogation of any kind.

Labuschagne, casting about for a way to break the ice, mentioned that they had both happened to go to the same high school in Pretoria. He spoke about sport, asked him about his running in what turned out to be a vain effort to stem his weeping. But the attempt at conversation yielded, at best, monosyllabic replies, until one question elicited a burst of anger. Labuschagne asked him if he wanted anything to eat.

'How do you expect me to eat now?' he shouted back. Pleased with the outburst, eager to elicit more of the same, Labuschagne repeated the question moments later. Was he sure he did not want to eat something? Back came the same exasperated response, followed by wails that echoed down the hospital corridors, reaching the ears of his family members Aimée and Arnold who were on their way to the room where he was being held. Escorted by uniformed police who had warned them they could not have any physical contact with him, they had come to bring him some fresh clothing. The police were opposing bail and he would need clothes for the following night, which he would be spending in a cell, and for the next morning when he would appear before a magistrate to be formally charged. The encounter with his relatives was as brief as it was sombre, their faces funereal. The three of them left and he returned to his bed, more shattered than before.

Towards 4 p.m. Labuschagne and two other policemen drove him back to the police station. There he had his first meeting with his attorney, Brian Webber, whom he had known since the age of thirteen, having gone to school with Webber's son. He had stayed overnight at the Webbers on various occasions and the two boys had remained close friends throughout their teens. Webber had always been fond of Pistorius and, in later years, had taken pride in his athletic achievements. For the lawyer, fighting a losing battle to preserve some modicum of professional detachment, this first encounter was heartbreaking, all the more so once he took in the tiny holding cell, reeking of urine, where his son's old pal would have to spend his first night of captivity.

Labuschagne went to bed that night in some frustration, having derived little of value for the prosecution case. The suspect's emotional state was entirely consistent, he concluded, with that of someone whose life had abruptly gone to pieces. Nothing he had said or done had offered any clue as to whether he had knowingly murdered Reeva Steenkamp, as the police contended, or whether the shooting had been, as Pistorius had claimed in the very first phone call he had made, a terrible accident.

# 2

*Unexpressed emotions will never die. They are buried alive and will come forth later in uglier ways.*
SIGMUND FREUD

O scar Pistorius was born on November 22, 1986 with a condition called fibular hemimelia. As mysterious as it was rare, the disease had no traceable genetic link to his parents. The fibula, the thin bone that runs between the knee and the ankle alongside the more prominent tibia, was missing in each of his legs, which were consequently unusually short. The ankles were only half formed; the heels faced not down but sideways, parallel to the Achilles tendons; the insteps were not convex but concave, in the shape not of an arch, but of a boat. Instead of five toes, he had two. His devastated parents saw right away that no human being could ever stand, let alone walk, on feet as narrow and twisted as these.

Sheila Pistorius was born Sheila Bekker, a fairly common surname among the 40 or so per cent of the white South African population who defined them-selves – in a country where everyone felt historically compelled to have some sort of tribal affiliation – as 'English-speakers'. Sheila did not work outside the home. Henke Pistorius, her husband, was a business-man, an erratic one prone to dramatic ups and downs, but at the time of Oscar's birth he was doing well, providing his family with the abundant material com-forts of white, upper middle-class life in apartheid South Africa. They lived in a large home, high up on a ridge in the suburb of Constantia Kloof, in rich, dynamic Johannesburg, forty miles south of Pretoria, the SouthAfrican capital.

Henke belonged to the majority white grouping in South Africa, the Afrikaners, who had their own language derived from the Dutch colonists who had begun settling in the Cape in the seventeenth century. He took pride in his people's history. He liked guns, as many Afrikaners did, and was given to making solemn pronouncements before his Calvinist God. A defining moment in Afrikaner history, as every

Afrikaner child learned at school, was the Day of the Vow. On December 16, 1838, Afrikaner trekkers who had emigrated from the Cape, outraged, among other things, by the British colonial rulers' abolition of slavery, had fought a decisive battle against a large army of Zulu warriors. Vastly outnumbered, the trekkers had made a vow that, in return for God's help in obtaining victory, that date would be honored by them and their descendants as a holy day of worship. The trekkers were victorious, 470 of them armed with guns defeating a Zulu army of ten thousand, armed only with spears.

It was in the spirit of that historic vow that Henke made a vow of his own within minutes of his son's birth. Just prior to the birth he had told the obstetrician that he did not mind if it was a boy or a girl so long as the child had ten fingers and ten toes. Now, having been the first to identify the feet's deformity, Henke ceremonially held up the infant with both hands and declared, before mother, doctor and nurses: 'This is my son Oscar and I declare before God that I shall love him and stand by him for the rest of my days.'

In practical terms, standing by their son meant Sheila and Henke Pistorius had to make a choice between amputation of his legs and corrective surgery. They consulted eleven doctors in South Africa and overseas. Some argued for surgery on both legs; some proposed amputation of the right foot and surgery on the left. It was the advice of one particular South African doctor that tipped the balance in favor of double amputation below the knee.

The doctor's name was Gerry Versfeld. Had Henke and Sheila Pistorius not chanced upon Dr Versfeld, a white man who at the time worked in a hospital in Soweto where only black patients were admitted, they might have lacked the confidence to go along with the most drastic option of all. Had the paths of Dr Versfeld and his infant self never crossed, the chances were that Pistorius would never have known what it is to run, would never have found fame, wealth and glory, and would never have met Reeva Steenkamp. The choice the parents made would plot the course of his life.

Pistorius had always been grateful to Dr Versfeld, the orthopaedic surgeon who carried out the operation. He had climbed so high thanks to him, and for all the head-turning acclaim he received he never forgot the man whose appearance in his life a few months after he was born had compensated so amply for the freak deficiency of his genes, directing him towards global stardom when he achieved the miracle of running in the Olympic Games.

He had had a lucky escape. If his two lower limbs had not been removed when he was very young he would have had to suffer a multitude of surgical procedures during his childhood, through to his late teens. Doctors would have had to lengthen his legs and subject him to a series of delicate and complex procedures to try and remold the mangled mess of his feet. He would have been looking at eight to ten operations over a period of sixteen to eighteen years. Even then, the finished product would have been well short of perfection. The surgeons would never have been able to recreate the arch of the feet, or do much to diminish their clawed rigidity. The sinewy energy of his youth would have been trapped inside a severely impaired body. He would have moved about the home as old people do – able to get up to go to the bathroom, to fetch things from the kitchen, and little more. He would never have been able to run. Covering 200 meters, the distance at which he won his first gold medal in 21.97 seconds, would have taken an age. His legs would have had no spring, no push-off, as Dr Versfeld put it, when he hit the ground. All his concentrated effort would have been invested in laboriously lifting up one foot, then the other. When he was older he was able to picture it. He had come across individuals born with conditions similar to his in just one leg. They had been visibly, inescapably handicapped. He, on the other hand, had always been secure in the knowledge that when he wore long trousers few could guess that there was anything wrong with him.

His gratitude towards Dr Versfeld was enriched by mutual affection. The professional relationship between the doctor and the Pistorius family grew into a close friendship. He and his wife became regular dinner guests at the Pistorius home, where they never ceased to celebrate the choice they had made.

The alternatives had been limited and the implications lifelong. Taking the surgical route would have let his parents cling to the hope that future advances in medicine would one day yield a wonder remedy or, failing that, would at least allow the possibility of deferring amputation to a later date. Opting for amputation right away meant forcing themselves to visualize their child pinned to an operating table to have his tiny limbs sawn off. They would be condemning him to the status of an amputee, dependent on artificial legs, for the rest of his days. They might one day be held to account by a mutilated son who might never forgive them for what they had done.

The choice was between letting the surgeons play God and playing God themselves.

Dr Versfeld never wished to claim any credit for the choice Pistorius's parents made. Whenever they thanked him, he always insisted that all he had done was to provide information; responsibility for the final decision had rested with them. Dr Versfeld was a mild, self-deprecating man, tall and slender, serenely confident in his professional abilities. The young Pistorius would have heard him scoff over dinner at his family home at the notion that he had become a surgeon out of some solemn sense of vocation. 'It's all because as a boy my hobby was woodwork,' Dr Versfeld would smile. 'At school my best subject was geometry. And then I did medicine, so it was almost a natural consequence that I should become an orthopaedic surgeon. In my woodwork I had to drill holes and cut things very accurately, measuring angles. And now that's what I do for a living.'

But his face would turn grim as he recalled his feelings when the time came to operate on the eleven-month-old infant. He would confess later that he had struggled to preserve the mechanical detachment his profession required.

'Keeping my emotions in check was not an easy job. It was not nice at all, but your head told you it was the right thing and you had to ensure the head won. But even so, it was a wrenching experience to chop off the limbs of a very little boy.'

Nor was his job technically easy. It was not a question simply of sawing through a bone and discarding everything below it. Dr Versfeld judged that one part of the damaged foot had to be preserved in order to help the boy retain some degree of mobility when he was not wearing the prosthetic legs on which he would depend for most, but not all, of his waking moments for the rest of his life. That part was the heel pad, 'nature's cushion', as Dr Versfeld described it, 'very specialized tissue consisting of compact fat globules'. The objective was to salvage both heel pads – weight-bearers, like the knee – and attach them to the bottom of the truncated tibia so that, rather than being dependent solely on his prosthetics for movement, he would be able to walk short distances on his stumps. A clean cut at the bottom of the tibia without the heel pad would have made it impossible for him to get about – the skin there, lacking those fatty globules, is very fine and would have torn too easily. Lacking that support, it would have been impossible for him even to stand up without losing his balance.

In order to be able to retain those fatty skin flaps, Dr Versfeld had to cut very close to the heel bone. Using only hand instruments and the naked eye, it required all his concentrated expertise to get the whole heel out, free it from the Achilles tendon, disarticulate the ankle, remove the ligaments, and then join the heel flaps to the bottom of the tibia. The procedure – an agony for the waiting parents – lasted four hours, two for each leg. And though the ligaments, the ankle, the entirety of the tiny, twisted, concave foot were thrown, as Henke Pistorius would indelicately put it afterwards, 'into the dustbin', he would be able to move nimbly enough about the home on the stumpy ends of his short, thin, tapered legs.

Pistorius's childhood would have been very different had it been decided to delay the amputation. Eleven months was the age chosen because it is around this stage that a child typically begins to take its first steps. Three months afterwards, the Pistorius parents took their son to the consulting room of Trevor Brauckmann, the prosthetics specialist in Pretoria who built and fitted his first artificial legs. The child studied the wooden pair that Brauckmann gave him with curiosity, submitted with still keener interest to seeing his stumps fitted into the legs' deep sockets, steadied himself by holding onto a set of parallel bars, then let go and started stumbling delightedly around the room, reveling in his new-found self-sufficiency, like any infant taking its first steps. His parents had arrived for the appointment with confused feelings of hope and self-accusation, but left overjoyed at the cheerful abandon with which their child had taken to these strange new appendages.

In the coming years he learnt to run and to play out-door games side by side with his boisterous older brother, Carl, encouraged always by his mother who taught him to refuse to behave as if he were in any way impaired. It served him well. Had she not instilled in him this mental habit he would have lacked the gumption to imagine himself competing against the world's fast-est runners. Looking back on his childhood, he vividly recalled playing soccer on stony fields, riding mountain bikes with his big brother, climbing trees and falling off them battered and bruised, a proud little tearaway – but he tried to repress the memory of the painful sores and blisters on his stumps, so painful that there were stretches of several months when he could barely move, let alone walk, and had to stay quietly at home under his mother's care, unable to join his friends at school.

Those unhappy episodes gave steel to his charac-ter, injected a resilience in him that Dr Versfeld cel-ebrated when he traveled to Athens in 2004 to see him run in his first Paralympics race, cheering him on when he won that first gold medal, taking pride in the seventeen-year-old prodigy's achievement, deriving satisfaction from the modesty with which he responded to his triumph and to the many more that would follow.

Nothing prepared the doctor for what was to happen nine years later. Never had he detected a suggestion in anything his most famous patient had said or done during the twenty-six years he had known him that could have predicted a moment of such lethal loss of control. That person, he would tell friends, was a stranger to him. It made no sense at all.

Opting for amputation over surgery had made sense at the time, but it would turn out to be a sort of Faustian pact. Pistorius would achieve all his heart desired, but there would be a price to pay. Had Sheila and Henke Pistorius taken the route that some other doctors had suggested he would have become an entirely different person, his life would have taken an entirely different course, what happened would not have happened. Wheelchair-bound, the recurrent operations he would have been subjected to as he grew up would have meant far longer absences from school, drastically altering his personality. His mother would have struggled to persuade him that he was just another normal boy. She might have had to give up on the attempt altogether, resorting to more painstaking, less convincing means to build up his sense of self-worth. His schoolmates, seeing him wheeled into class, or at best limping badly, would have responded to him with pity, if he was lucky, or with sniggering contempt if he was not. He might have had the fortitude finally to emerge strong and wise from his predicament, but the chances are that along the way he would have felt himself to be a scorned outsider; his impulse, to hide away from the world.

That was his impulse now, after the shooting. All the misery and shame he had been spared as he grew up hit him in one concentrated bolt, at the age of twenty-six, in the early hours of Valentine's Day in 2013. His love affair with the beautiful and worldly Reeva Steenkamp, in whose fashionable circles he would have been unlikely to have moved had he not found fame and fortune, was an achievement that told the world he had won life's race. Ending Reeva's life, and in the same instant annihilating his own, had condemned him to the shadow existence he had fought so hard to avoid – inspiring compassion in some, derision in others, and ripping forever from his grasp all that he had striven with such fierce resolve to win.

# 3

*One that loved not wisely but too well.*

SHAKESPEARE, *OTHELLO*

His bed in the police cell was a blanket on a cement floor. Not that it mattered very much. He would not have slept that first night on any surface. Ever since he was a little boy he had lived in fear of criminals, now he knew what it felt like to be one. Worse was to come the next morning, Friday, February 15, when he was driven in a police convoy to a court in the center of Pretoria where he appeared before a magistrate who confirmed what he knew was coming. It took no more than five minutes for the magistrate to announce that the state would be charging him with premeditated murder. At the word 'murder', he broke into wild sobs.

His sister, Aimée, who was sitting directly behind him with his uncle and other family members, put her hands to her face and wept. As for bail, the state opposed it and a hearing would be held at which a different magistrate would decide the matter the following Tuesday.

The name of the bail magistrate was Desmond Nair. Of Indian descent, which would have precluded him from occupying any judicial post under apartheid, he was highly experienced and respected. Magistrates and judges possess enormous power in South Africa, where the jury system does not exist. In theory they are supposed to perform their roles with the coldest impartiality, but that does not stop both defense and prosecution lawyers from paying close scrutiny to their backgrounds in the hope of finding some vulnerability that might help swing a verdict. Pistorius's defense lawyers clutched at what they thought might be grounds for optimism in a remarkable case from 2011 in which Nair had presided over the bail hearing.

At the center of that case was an Afrikaner rugby player called 'Bees' Roux, who was arrested and charged with murder for beating a black policeman to death. At a pre-trial meeting, attended by Roux and his lawyer, as well as the state prosecutor and the brother and wife of the victim, Roux expressed sincerest regret and explained what had happened. He had imagined that the policeman, whom he had encountered at night, had planned to rob him, possibly kill him. An exceptionally large man, Roux struck the policeman with force, knocking him unconscious. He sought to revive him, Roux said, but it was too late. In tears, Roux apologized to the policeman's relatives and implored their forgiveness. They granted it. First the brother, also weeping, embraced Roux; then the policeman's widow made a short dignified speech in which she thanked Roux for his candor and said that she did indeed forgive him. The prosecutor proposed a deal. Roux would plead guilty to culpable homicide, the South African legal term for unpremeditated manslaughter, he would pay the family of the dead policeman compensation and receive a suspended sentence of five years in jail. The presiding magistrate concurred, and Roux was a free man.

Would Nair, seeing the possible parallels between the two cases, show similar leniency over Pistorius's bail application? His lawyers tended to think so. There was another, more personal, reason that might help their cause, too. Research by the defense had revealed that Nair was in the midst of his own family tragedy. His first cousin had recently killed her two children, then herself, with poison. Pistorius's team hoped that at the Tuesday hearing Nair's private suffering would sharpen his compassion for the fellow sufferer who stood before him with sorrow written all over his face, and that Nair might rule in his favor.

But Tuesday was still several days off, and as Pistorius was led out of the courtroom where he had just been charged with murder and into the police car that would take him to another police station, in the middle-class and previously all-white Pretoria suburb of Brooklyn, his thoughts dwelt on the horror of what he had done, but also on those that might lie ahead. He would be spending at least the next four nights in a cell; if he were denied bail, it would be for every night until the trial was over, whenever that might be; and if in the end he were found guilty, he would be spending much of the rest of his life in a dank and dangerous prison with some of the worst criminals in the world for company. Should he be found guilty as charged, of premeditated murder, the sentence would be twenty-five years, minimum.

The scrum of TV cameras outside the courtroom, mobbing the car that drove him back to his police cell, brought home to him how fascinated the world was with the prospect of a figure as heroic as he had been falling so low. The mystery behind Reeva's death made the drama all the more compelling. Had the story of what happened at his home in the early hours of Valentine's

Day been cut and dried, had it been beyond dispute from the beginning that he had killed Reeva Steenkamp either deliberately or accidentally, interest in the case would not have been so great or so enduring. What was to keep the story bubbling, month after month, all the way through to the eventual verdict, was that the events of that night remained so open to speculation. Endless debates would be held at dinner tables across the globe on the question of whether he had wanted to kill her or not.

His fame and her beauty – but especially his fame, because people felt they knew enough about him to venture informed opinions – enlivened the debate. But the fact that two other contemporary cases had whipped up the public imagination to a similar degree, even though the protagonists had been unknown when their stories broke, revealed the powerful attraction that unresolved mysteries exerted, with or without the celebrity factor. One was the case of Madeleine McCann, the little British girl abducted in Portugal in 2007, never to be seen again. The other was that of Amanda Knox, the American accused by the Italian authorities of the murder of a British woman, Meredith Kercher, also in 2007. In both instances, millions of people felt entitled to pronounce with assurance about what had happened on the nights in question.

One camp in the McCann case held that the parents, both of them doctors, had accidentally killed their child by giving her an overdose of sleeping pills, then disposed of the body and pretended to the world that she had been abducted by a criminal. Similarly, some observers of the Knox case said that the American woman, far from being innocent as she claimed, had participated in a satanic game of group sex that had led to her friend Meredith's grisly death. Others maintained with equal conviction that the McCanns and Knox were telling the truth and had been grievously traduced.

Carefully selecting the copious evidence provided by the news media to corroborate their views, what people on each side were doing would reveal more about themselves, their prejudices and motivations, than about what really happened, the truth of which was known only to the strangers in whose personal dramas they chose to involvethemselves.

Another controversial case with which analogies were drawn was the celebrated O. J. Simpson murder trial in America. Global interest was also enormous, and the core allegation in both stories was a riveting one: famous athlete kills beautiful woman he loved. The majority view in the US, even before the trial began in Los Angeles in 1995, was that Simpson was guilty of the murder of his ex-wife, Nicole Brown. But there the similarities ended. The Simpson case followed the classic lines of a whodunit. A body had been found and it was up to the cops to discover the identity of the killer. Simpson was accused of murdering his ex-wife; the job of the police and prosecution was to prove he had done it.

In Pistorius's case the who, the when, the where and the how were not in dispute. And, thankfully for South Africa – even if it were no consolation for him – there was no racial element involved. In the Simpson case the accused had been black, the victim white, and American opinion divided accordingly. In the Pistorius case there was no clear division of opinion or splitting of sympathies along racial lines. As Justice Malala, a well-known black political commentator wrote, 'For us South Africans, it is impossible to watch Oscar Pistorius run without wanting to break down and cry and shout with joy.' Knowing this used to fill Pistorius with joy too.

One thing he had been proud of as a South African was that admiration for successful national sportsmen, not just for him, was color-blind. Blacks and whites and all shades in between had taken the rugby players Francois Pienaar (white) and Bryan Habana (mixed-race), and the cricketers Hashim Amla (Indian and Muslim) and Makhaya Ntini (black), to their collective hearts. Sport, as Pistorius recalled Mandela saying, was a great breaker of racial barriers. No one wished to be cut out of the celebrations when the national team won. All those sportsmen had inspired all their compatriots, just as he had done.

What made Pistorius stand out from all the others was that because of his unique physical condition he exemplified the country's continuing task of overcoming the hard legacy of the past. Every South African shared in his triumphs, seeing them as occasions to applaud what all races liked to see as the indomitable national spirit. Everyone had wanted to identify with him because he fed South Africans' self-image as a never-say-die people. The Afrikaners, whose forebears had ridden north from the Cape in the early nineteenth century to conquer a hostile land, never ceased to remind themselves and anyone else who would listen that the word 'survivors' best defined who they were. But the truth was that all South Africans were survivors. Survivors are, by definition, pragmatists. This shared characteristic was the chief reason why, unlike other warring peoples who had proved unable to rise above past grievances, black and white South Africans were able to agree to abolish apartheid and to make peace. They see themselves as problem-solving people, and it was this can-do attitude that gave rise to a uniquely South African expression, which the Afrikaners invented but all other races incorporate into daily conversation, 'We'll make a plan.' Pistorius, whose life story it seemed to sum up, used it all the time. It meant, 'We'll overcome this obstacle. We'll think of something. We'll get to our destination.'

By triumphing on the world stage he had shown people everywhere that South Africans were indeed made of sterner stuff. He had set an example to all: if he could make a plan, if he could soar in the face of the cards life had dealt him, anybody could. He held up a flattering mirror to South Africans, reflecting back the image they wished to see of themselves at their best.

Not anymore. Now he reflected South Africa at its worst. Though people knew him only through the media, and knew less of Reeva Steenkamp and nothing at all of what had passed between them on the night she died, many had made up their minds that he was a monster who had killed her knowingly, not in a panic but in a rage, and they clamored for a punishment to fit the crime, one that would send a message that women had endured enough.

The figures showed how much. South Africa was tenth in the world murder rankings by country, with forty-five killings a day on average in 2013, and undisputed global champion when it came to violence against women. Every four minutes a South African woman or girl – often a teenager, sometimes a child – was reported raped, and every eight hours a woman was killed by her male partner. (The phenomenon has a name in South Africa: 'intimate femicide'.) On the face of it, as many South Africans saw it, Pistorius had swelled those statistics. There was no shortage of opinion pieces in the press during the weeks and months that followed the shooting framing his case in the context of generalized gender violence.

He hated that. He hated the unfairness of people assuming he was guilty before he had had a chance to tell his story in court, and it mortified him that they were choosing to portray him as a woman-hater. All the more so as Reeva herself had been an advocate for women's rights, speaking out against abusers and rapists. He had always supported her – had shared in her outrage and horror at one very recent crime, one so savage that it was singled out by the president, Jacob Zuma, in his annual state of the nation address.

On February 3, 2013 a seventeen-year-old girl called Anene Booysen from a poor rural township near Cape Town was raped, mutilated and left for dead at a construction site near a bar where she had spent much of the night with friends. A doctor who had tried to save her life was quoted in the press as saying that after raping her the attacker had opened up her stomach and ripped out her intestines. Pistorius and Reeva had discussed the case, the two of them as appalled as anybody else in South Africa. Reeva was moved to make her feelings public on Instagram. 'I woke up in a happy safe home this morning,' she wrote. 'Not everyone did. Speak out against the rape of individuals in SA. RIP Anene Booysen. #rape #crime #sayNO.' She had spent part of February 13 polishing up a speech she was due to give two days later to students at a school in Johannesburg in memory of Anene Booysen and in honor of the 'Black Friday Campaign for Rape Awareness'.

It might have seemed hard to square the idea of a woman with this kind of social conscience planning to share a bed with a monster that very night. Yet that was how many people chose to view it – most vocally the Women's League of South Africa's ruling African National Congress, Mandela's party. Pistorius had spotted members of the League outside the magistrate's court where his bail application was being heard, calling for his head. 'Real Men Don't Rape And Kill Women', one placard read; 'Pistorius Must Rot In Jail', another. Lulama Xingwana, South Africa's Minister for Women, Children and People with Disabilities, joined the campaigners, stridently declaring that he should be denied bail.

The same government minister went so far as to blame Reeva's death on the culture of the Afrikaners, 'Young Afrikaner men', she said, were 'brought up in the Calvinist religion believing that they own a woman, they own a child, they own everything and therefore they can take that life because they own it'. She did apologize and retract her remarks afterwards, having perhaps understood, as other black women might have reminded her, that it was a shared problem, that no male sector of any racial group in South Africa could claim a monopoly on virtue in the treatment of women.

Some comments by Henke Pistorius did not help the cause very much either. Speaking to the press the day after his son shot Reeva Steenkamp, he said that the African National Congress had failed to protect white people from crime, hence the need for people like him to arm themselves. The racist undertones, revealed in the insensitivity shown by his failure to realize that black people suffered more from crime than white, caused a public furor – and still more embarrassment, if that were possible, for his son. Henke then made matters worse by stating, with ludicrously bad judgment in the circumstances, 'As a family, we value life much too much to produce guns at every opportunity we can use them. I have been in positions where I could use a gun but we have been brought up in a way that we value the lives of others very highly.'

The snorts of those who had made up their minds that Henke's son had attached so little value to Reeva's life that he had deliberately killed her resounded across the land. They may not have known Reeva, but they took her death personally. Her fate symbolized everything that South African women found terrifying about the country they lived in – a culture of violence where men were desensitized to the harm they caused others, even if those others were supposedly their friends or loved ones; where notions of masculinity were so perverted that hitting and raping women was seen almost as a cultural norm, not least by members of the police force; and where guns and other lethal weapons were favored instruments of everyday persuasion. Men seemed to get away with murder in South Africa, and now this high-profile case offered an opportunity not to be missed to send a message to male society at large. The women who thought this way wanted revenge; they wanted Pistorius to burn on the pyre as an example to all men with misogynist malice in their hearts.

Yet the truth was that long before prosecutors pushed for the state's revenge in the murder trial, even before the bail hearing, Pistorius's punishment had already begun. In the cell at Brooklyn police station where he was locked up after his first court appearance he slept once again on the floor. Aimée, Carl and his uncle Arnold came to offer their moral support, but their visits were cause for grief as well as comfort. The contrast between the carefree times they had shared a few days before and his circumstances now brought home how completely the landscape of their lives had changed.

He was no longer the miracle runner whose future blazed bright. He was a sobbing child in the body of a muscled athlete, who had committed a crime for which there was no possibility of redress. Not on this earth, at any rate. Uncle Arnold, who turned to God in times of hardship, found a church minister to visit Pistorius in his cell. Bible in hand, the minister spent hours by his side, reading from the scriptures, dwelling on God's inscrutable mercy. Hearing the priest reciting the hypnotic biblical phrases brought some respite, but not enough to allow him much sleep during the six days and nights he would remain in that cell. He barely ate, and he suffered from chronic headaches. He was in no fit condition, emotional or physical, to consult with his lawyers, who in order to prepare their case for bail needed from him a cogent narrative of the events he was battling so hard to keep out of his thoughts.

At least they were not strangers. Brian Webber was one; the other was Kenny Oldwadge, who had represented him on the previous two occasions when he had got into trouble. Problematic at the time – trifles in comparison with what he faced now. Once, in 2009, he had crashed a speedboat into a wooden pier, but the damage was almost all self-inflicted, for he had broken his jaw and a pair of ribs and spent two days unconscious, needing 180 stitches to his face. Another time a drunken woman at a party at his home had tried to sue him after he smashed a door in her face. In both cases Oldwadge saved him from criminal prosecution. He considered Kenny and Brian to be friends as well as legal hired hands. He was right to think so. The two lawyers arrived at Brooklyn police station as if for a funeral.

The thought did not occur to Pistorius – as it would to others later, when the trial began – that he might have done better to enlist the help of lawyers who could view his predicament in a colder, more professional light. Back in that cell he was relieved that it was Kenny and Brian, and not persons unknown, who were ministering to his needs. An affidavit had to be prepared if he was going to get out on bail, and every detail had to be re-created and set down on paper. He had not slept for two nights and he was confused, uncertain where he was. The task was made all the more complicated by the fact that there was no table to write at in the cell, nor anywhere to sit down. For the two lawyers, who between them had accumulated more than forty years in the profession, it was the most emotionally excruciating and technically complicated encounter they had ever had with a client. He wept and vomited throughout. But somehow, torn between their professional duty and their personal distress, they succeeded in extracting from the chaos of his mind what seemed like a coherent narrative of the sequence of events at his home that night, which they hoped would convince magistrate Nair to set him free.

Early in the morning of Tuesday, February 19 his cell door was opened, and minutes later he found himself being driven once more in the back of a police vehicle through the streets of Pretoria, towards the court where his bail application was to be heard.

Photographers would be waiting for him, battalions of them. Nothing new there. In that other life, which felt every day more like a distant dream, they had followed him wherever he went. He would arrive in a chauffeur-driven sponsor's car at a hotel in London or Paris or some other foreign city, knowing that when he stepped out there they would be scrambling to snatch a picture of him. He had responded to it all with confusion and delight at first, after he won that first Paralympic gold in Athens, but by the time the crowning triumph at the London Games had come along the experience of being mobbed by the media was as routine for him as it was for the most famous soccer players or Hollywood stars. He had learned how to prepare his face for the cameras as circumstances required. He had his PR people around to help him, but, as they themselves would tell him, he was a natural, smiling grandly, striking noble poses or brooding handsomely, like a trained model. When he had to talk in public, he knew when to be self-effacing, when to be gracious, when to be appropriately grateful. His fellow athletes, who did not know of his anxious preparation for such encounters, were in awe of the seemingly effortless ease with which he presented himself to the world.

He was far more insecure than he let on, however, to the point that he would sometimes endure moments of befuddlement as he waited to appear on the media stage, wondering who this character called Oscar Pistorius that he played really was. From childhood he had been building a shell around himself, learning to put on a brave face to the world. He felt braver, the shell felt stronger, when he had a woman by his side. First it had been his mother, a far greater presence in

his life than his father, and then, from the age of sixteen, he acquired the habit of falling serially in love.

**Nandi came** first, the girl of his dreams. She was attractive, wise for her age, loyal – and she would always
remain loyal. Years later, after his fall, she would not
say a word against him. But success changed him and
she moved on. He was heartbroken for about a month
and then Vicky took her place. He fell truly in love
with her too, and proved it to her one Valentine's Day
when he went to her house, hung two hundred bal-
loons on the trees and garden fence, and wrote 'I love
you, Tiger' with a can of spray paint on the tarmac of
the road outside her gate. (His very first romantic encounter, at the age of eight, had also been a Valentine's
Day moment, when he gave a rose to a little girl at his
school.) When Vicky went, Jenna took over. Then
more women, some older than himself, some younger.
Then Samantha, with whom he remained for eighteen tumultuous months; and then, when he had just
turned twenty-six, Reeva, who he was instantly convinced would provide his final port of call, banishing
all who had gone before her to the shadows.

The only woman Pistorius could turn to now, as
he prepared for the ordeal of the bail hearing, was
Aimée, the one enduring soulmate during his decade of

turbulent loves. She would be sitting there in court, as would his brother, Carl. But Carl had a reckless streak. Like Pistorius himself, he was prone to shifting moods, one minute calm and polite, the next in a state of high exuberance. He was loyal but not as dependable as Aimée, the steady sibling. More considered and mature than her brothers, she was the baby of the three but a pillar of strength. There was no guile in Aimée, no hidden subtexts. With the other women in Pistorius's life it had always been complicated, all-or-nothing infatuation; the love he and his sister felt for each other was easy, affectionate and unconditional.

Yet neither the comfort of her presence in court nor any trace of the skills he had previously exhibited in his public appearances would enable him to compose his features for the ordeal ahead, as the police car slowed down outside the court building and he saw the mob that awaited him. The shell he had labored so long to build around himself cracked and the cameras, tributes once to the adulation he inspired, flashed in cruel mockery of the champion he had been.

With shame and dread he stepped out of the vehicle, as the policemen either side of him carved a path through the scrum of photographers battling to get a clear shot of him. Once inside the courtroom there was nowhere to hide. His body language laid bare his desolation. Acknowledging his family's presence with a sad nod, he shuffled in, head bowed, a shrunken husk of the athletic phenomenon who had amazed the world. For a decade he had been inspiring awe, now he evoked pity or contempt. The brutal question on the lips of many was whether he felt more sorry for what he had done to Reeva Steenkamp, or for what he had done to himself.

The state prosecutor at the bail hearing, Gerrie (pronounced 'herrie') Nel, had no doubt what was the answer to that question, and he did not shrink from letting Pistorius know it. Nel's job was not to feel his pain but to compound it, portraying him before magistrate Nair as a callous, self-engrossed glory-seeker, amply capable of premeditated murder.

There had been an age of innocence when Pistorius's idea of a menacing rival was a young Brazilian double amputee who presumed to challenge his status as the planet's fastest Paralympic runner. Now the foe was Nel, and what was at stake was not the outcome of a 200 meter sprint but whether he would spend the next quarter of a century behind bars. Nel, who would be the prosecutor at the murder trial too, was a man who could have made five times more money had he opted to become a defense lawyer in private practice. Some of his fellow lawyers said he lacked the self-assurance to operate on his own, without the weight of the state behind him; others said that he was driven by a zeal to uphold the rule of law on behalf of the South African state. Whatever the case, he was dogged and he was plucky. In his role as state prosecutor he had faced down threats from powerful people in government and from gangland criminals with contract killers on their payrolls.

Nel, dressed in the black robes of his profession, stood before the similarly attired Desmond Nair, and proclaimed the state's certainty that the accused had known exactly whom he was shooting at when he fired his gun. It was common cause, he said, that the victim had died 'of multiple gunshot wounds', that he had fired four bullets through a locked bathroom door, three of which had struck Reeva, one in the hip, one in the right arm, one in the head. Where the state differed from the defense was in the contention that it was premeditated murder. Premeditated did not have to mean that he had meticulously planned to kill Reeva Steenkamp; all the state had to do, Nel contended, was to prove that he had resolved to do away with her life prior to pulling the trigger.

If Nel's purpose was in part to obtain a reaction from the man in the dock, he succeeded. Battling as he had been to keep his features stonily composed, Pistorius winced at that first mention of the charge that he had knowingly killed Reeva; then he covered his face with his hands and his shoulders heaved.

Nel seized his chance. 'It is a possibility,' he said, casting a wry glance at the gallery, 'that after shooting someone, one starts to feel sorry for oneself.' Aimée put her hand to her mouth and shook her head, dismayed by Nel's pitilessness. But the prosecutor pressed on. It was possible the accused felt sorry, he said, because he was thinking, 'I am going to jail and my career is gone.'

There was method in Nel's heartlessness. He did not want the public, much less the magistrate, to sympathize with the fallen hero. He wanted them to despise him.

Pistorius had gone into the bail hearing knowing that people would find his version of events difficult to believe. He could see how people might think that in his place they would lie. His lawyers were well aware of how hard it would be to convince the public, never mind a magistrate, that he was telling the truth. The pressure was on him to provide a plausible alternative or, as some chose to see it, to fabricate a good story. The tone and content of the affidavits presented to the magistrate had to be carefully judged. A British media adviser had warned his lawyers not to 'over-egg' his case. At the adviser's prompting, the initial idea of including in the affidavit mention not only of his immense love for Reeva, but of his desire to marry her, was removed. It was true, he insisted to his lawyers – but they had judged the public mood and, by extension, what that of the magistrate was likely to be. The mention of marriage plans might have elicited howls of derision from the courtroom, which was packed with news reporters and members of the public, while adding nothing of material substance to the evidence the magistrate would need to consider.

Everyone in the room heard his sobs as Oldwadge began reading the affidavit.

'By about 10 p.m. on 13 February 2013 we were in our bedroom. She was doing her yoga exercises and I was in bed watching television. My prosthetic legs were off. After Reeva finished her yoga exercises she got into bed and we both fell asleep. We were deeply in love and I could not have been happier.

'I am acutely aware of violent crime being committed by intruders entering the home with a view to commit crime, including violent crime. I have received death threats before. I have also been a victim of violence and of burglaries before. For that reason I kept my firearm, a 9mm Parabellum, underneath my bed when I went to bed at night.'

He said he woke up in the early hours of February 14, remembered he had left a fan outside on a balcony next to his bedroom and went to fetch it, walking on his stumps. On closing the sliding doors behind him he heard 'movement' in the bathroom, down a corridor from the bedroom.

'I felt a sense of terror rushing over me. There are no burglar bars across the bathroom window and I knew that contractors who worked at my house had left the ladders outside. Although I did not have my prosthetic legs on I have mobility on my stumps. I believed that someone had entered my house. I was too scared to switch on a light. I grabbed my 9mm pistol from underneath my bed. On my way to the bathroom I screamed for him/them to get out of my house and for Reeva to phone the police.

'I fired shots at the toilet door and shouted to Reeva to phone the police. She did not respond and I moved backwards out of the bathroom, keeping my eyes on the bathroom entrance. It was pitch dark in the bedroom and I thought Reeva was in bed. When I reached the bed, I realized Reeva was not in bed. That is when it dawned on me that it could have been Reeva who was in the toilet.'

Had he been an ordinary member of the public, had he been able to put some distance between himself and his predicament, he might have considered his story – as so many did – hard to believe. Quite apart from his failure to register whether his girlfriend was lying next to him when he rushed from his bed, gun in hand, to the bathroom, who could possibly believe that he had imagined a burglar would choose to hide in a toilet? What would a burglar have hoped to find in a toilet that was worth stealing? It was surely ridiculous to expect people to believe that he could have been so stupid – and the jokes, mostly of the 'he hasn't a leg to stand on' variety, came thick and fast. A photograph posted on social media of a bathroom door with the message 'Using toilet – Please don't shoot' scrawled on it went viral. It was the kind of thing he too would have laughed about, and maybe even sent out on his Twitter account, had it been some other celebrity at the center of the drama.

His lawyers, though, were not amused at the obligation to set out the core elements of their case at the bail hearing. Pistorius's desperation to avoid spending the months – or, as it turned out, one year – prior to the trial behind bars forced them to come up with a vividly detailed description of what he said had happened that night. That included the irreversible acknowledgment that he had indeed fired the bullets that killed Reeva, leaving his defense no option but to acknowledge that he had meant to shoot someone, while arguing that he had not meant to shoot her. He was locked into that version, with little room for maneuver once the trial began, and with ample time for the prosecution to deploy police detectives to pick holes in it. Barry Roux, the veteran trial lawyer who led his defense team at the bail hearing and would do so again at the murder trial, lamented the necessity of showing his hand so early on, but recognized there was no choice.

What Pistorius did not know was that South African lawyers not involved with the case, but as riveted by it as the general public, believed it would be impossible for him eventually to avoid serving time in prison, even if he was released on bail now. Under South African law to be acquitted of premeditated murder still left open the possibility of being found guilty of another, lesser charge. The judge would have the discretion to convict him of a lower category of murder, for which the sentence would also be jail. Or, what many lawyers believed would be the best option for him, to find him guilty of culpable homicide, or manslaughter, for which the range of sentencing possibilities was wide. He could be lucky in such an instance and get out on a suspended sentence, or unlucky and be ordered to serve fifteen years.

Spared these gloomy reflections during the bail hearing, there came a moment in court when his defense team was presented with an unexpected gift. It came in the shape of Hilton Botha, the first police investigating officer to arrive at his home after the shooting. Botha was a blunt and hardened detective who had shown no sympathy for him as he knelt by Reeva's body, wailing at the horror of what he had done. Now Botha received his comeuppance in court. He was supposed to have been there to further the prosecution's case against bail; in the event, he ended up undermining it.

Stirring memories of the O. J. Simpson case in the minds of American reporters present, it emerged that Botha had made a mess of the scene he had found at Pistorius's home, stomping all over the place with apparent scant regard for safeguarding evidence and generally revealing himself, in the face of questioning by Barry Roux, to be an unreliable witness as well as a less than competent investigator.

Botha had initially declared in court, led by Nel, that the fatal shots had been fired downwards into the bath-room door, which would have meant that Pistorius had had his prosthetic legs on, contradicting his account that he had been on his stumps. But when Roux put it to Botha that he had no evidence to support the contention that he was wearing his legs, Botha backed down and admitted that this was so.

Botha said a female witness had heard an argument between two people at Pistorius's home between two and three in the morning on the night in question, before the shooting happened. Under cross-examination by Roux, Botha conceded some uncertainty as to whether the witness had been 300 or 600 meters away at the time. Botha also agreed that the witness would not be able to know if the voices she heard belonged to Pistorius and Steenkamp. As for another claim made by Botha, that he had found steroids at Pistorius's home on the morning of the shooting, Roux convinced the court that there was no basis for it, that what he had thought were performance-enhancing drugs had in fact been innocuous herbal remedies.

Roux's case centered on demolishing the state's case, but he also came up with a useful piece of counter-evidence in the shape of a female witness who knew Reeva well. This witness cast doubt on the state's argument for premeditated murder by saying that her friend had been 'very much in love' with the accused.

Nel fought back, telling the court that it was an indisputable fact that Pistorius had killed somebody and, questionable witnesses aside, that it seemed inexplicable that he would not have checked to see whether Reeva was in bed prior to seizing his gun from under it, that he would not have called out her name at the first sign of danger, or that she would not have screamed after he fired the first of the four bullets, alerting him to the fact that she was in the toilet. Nel added a populist touch to his arguments when he said that if Pistorius were granted bail it would be a slap in the face for South African women who had been victims of crime. He counseled the magistrate not merely to pay 'lip service' to the national cause of reducing crime against women, but to be seen to take tough action against it.

In the event, the magistrate paid little heed to this appeal, limiting himself to the evidence he had heard. In a two-hour reading of his judgment, he set out the arguments for and against bail, offering no clue as to what his verdict would be right up until the end. The tension was excruciating. Pistorius would not be able to cope with jail, living alongside murderers. Even if they didn't get to him first, how would he be able to carry on living with the memory of what he had done with no aunt or sister or cousin or grandmother to comfort him?

On the magistrate droned, one moment raising Pistorius's hopes, dashing them the next. Nair acknowledged the flaws in the police handling of the case but noted also the 'quite pronounced improbabilities' of the bail applicant's account of what had happened. He had a list of difficulties, as he put it, with that version; but neither, on the other hand, was the prosecution's case watertight. There again, it would be unreasonable to expect the state to have 'all the pieces of the puzzle now'. As to the possibility of Pistorius jumping bail and fleeing the country, Nair judged it to be limited because of his national and global fame and his physical impairment. Nor did Nair believe he presented 'a threat to the public'.

Whereupon, he finally declared on February 22, eight days after the shooting, that Pistorius would be granted bail pending payment of 1 million rand (US$100,000) and his handing over his passport and any guns he might own (other than the one with which he had shot the victim, which was in the possession of the police). On meeting these conditions, he would be free to go home – or, as it turned out, to the home of his uncle Arnold. The Pistorius family members embraced each other, then reached out to hug him.

He sobbed with relief, but on the streets of South Africa the magistrate's decision was greeted with outrage by many. It reeked of preferential treatment – rich boy's justice. It felt like an insult to the many thousands – 46,000 was the official figure for the whole of South Africa – who lay in filthy jails pending trial, many of them either on charges far more innocuous than his or where the evidence of guilt was substantially less. A case in point, as one newspaper pointed out, was that of a fifty-year-old black paraplegic called Ronnie Fakude, who had spent two years in prison awaiting trial not for murder but for fraud. He continued to wait as the Pistorius bail verdict was delivered, able to move only by dragging himself around a crowded cell on his hands.

South African columnists had a field day. Justice and equality were the legacies Nelson Mandela had bequeathed to the country; the favorable treatment received in a law court by a rich and famous white man had put those principles to the test and found them wanting. Justice in South Africa, as a judge had once said of justice in Britain, was open to all men, like the doors of the Ritz Hotel. Pistorius had found himself the best team of lawyers that money could buy and that, aided and abetted – in a view widely held – by an impressionable magistrate, had won him an unde-served freedom.

Pistorius himself was in no state to dwell on such considerations. For him and his family Barry Roux was the hero of the hour. He had confirmed his reputation as one of the top criminal defense lawyers in South Africa by the meticulous doggedness with which he had successfully pursued what seemed to many of his peers to be an unwinnable cause. But Roux pressed on. He lodged an appeal against the conditions set and, still more surprisingly, won again. A second court lifted the restriction on leaving South Africa and revoked a ban imposed by magistrate Nair on drinking alcohol, deeming it to have been 'unreasonable and unfair'.

A further victory came when Hilton Botha was removed from the case after it emerged that he had been charged with attempted murder relating to an incident in 2011 in which he and two other police officers had allegedly fired on suspects inside a minibus. The state's case was, for now, in disarray.

Pistorius had won round one of the legal battle and now, instead of wearing a green prisoner's uniform, he would be in his own clothes, eating his own food, sleeping in his own bedroom at his uncle's place – for he could not bear to go back to live in his own home. His family would be there to comfort him when images of Reeva stormed his guilty mind – but he would seek comfort, too, in the ghostly presence of another woman, one who had shaped his character, leaving a deeper imprint than Reeva or any other of his lovers had ever done: his mother, Sheila. Tattooed in Roman numerals on the inside of his right biceps were the date on which she was born and the date on which she died.

# 4

*If a man has been his mother's undisputed darling*
*he retains throughout life the triumphant feeling, the*
*confidence in success, which not seldom brings actual*
*success along with it.*

SIGMUND FREUD

From the start, Sheila Pistorius had had no intention of enrolling her son in any kind of special school for children with disabilities. Pistorius spent his primary years at a regular school, and when adolescence beckoned she presented him with the challenge of attending Pretoria Boys High School, where the best and the toughest went.

It was a school that produced champions, high achievers, many of whom would excel in later life in sports, politics, business and the law. A South African institution established in 1901 and famed throughout the land, Pretoria Boys High had been conceived in conscious imitation of the strict and venerable British public school model, and for most of its years it had been a whites-only institution. But around the time of Nelson Mandela's release from prison the school began admitting black children and soon acquired a reputation for enlightenment, so much so that at Mandela's presidential inauguration in May 1994, an event that drew heads of state from all continents, its students were invited to serve as waiters.

In 2000, when Pistorius was thirteen and a year away from starting high school, he and his mother had a meeting with the headmaster, Bill Schroder. Schroder was a giant of a man, in whom benevolence and toughness impressively combined. He took a paternal interest in his boys while also presiding over a regime where old-fashioned caning continued as a punishment of last resort. He took the school's founding motto *Virtute et Labore*, virtue and work, seriously and held firm in his defense of the values those words embodied.

But during that meeting, held in the sanctum sanctorum of his study, Schroder felt unusually ill at ease. Sheila Pistorius, then forty-two years old, was an attractive woman with a big smile and an ebullient personality. Schroder, more accustomed to inspiring awe than succumbing to it, vividly recalled the encounter years later. He had met more parents than he could remember, but this one, he said, 'was THE most amazing woman – quite remarkable, with a special light about her'.

The school buildings and grounds were unlike anything Pistorius had ever seen or imagined. A forbidding stone archway at the entrance, a Victorian-style red-brick main building, Latin inscriptions on walls, names engraved on wood of the alumni who had fallen in the two world wars, a hundred acres of land with rugby and cricket fields where some of the finest South African sportsmen had honed their talents. It was a scarily imposing scene when glimpsed through the eyes of a child, and all the more so when across a desk there sat a formidably large man of authoritarian demeanor. Yet the boy appeared quite at ease, listening quietly as Schroder and his mother discussed his future prospects, his academic strengths and weaknesses, the sports he would play.

Mention of sports reminded the headmaster of the reason why he felt less comfortable than he usually did at these meetings. He could no longer avoid broaching the question that had been in his mind from the moment mother and son had entered the room. Pretoria

Boys had never admitted a boy without feet before – not, at any rate, during the decade that Schroder had been in charge. Pistorius would start out as a day student, but it was possible, his mother said, that in due course he would become a boarder (the school offered both options) and that prospect rendered the matter all the more delicate. It would be a heavy responsibility for the school, one that would ultimately fall on the headmaster's shoulders. Unable to restrain his concern any longer, Schroder asked, 'Yes, but . . . is he going to cope?'

Sheila Pistorius looked baffled. She exchanged glances with her son, who shrugged. 'I don't think I follow,' she replied. 'What are you saying?' Schroder mumbled something about the boy's condition, his, umm . . . prosthetic legs. 'Ah,' Sheila Pistorius smiled. 'I see. But please don't worry. There's no problem at all. He's absolutely normal!' She explained that she understood very well that Pretoria Boys was a famously athletic school and that, far from being a cause for concern, it was a large part of the reason why her son wanted to be taught there. She listed some of the sports and outdoor activities he had engaged in from early childhood: cricket, rugby, soccer, mountain biking and wrestling, for which he had won several competitive medals. As for getting about, going to the bathroom at night and that sort of thing, no worries there either. He took off his artificial legs when he went to bed but, Sheila explained, was perfectly capable of walking short distances on his stumps. The boy nodded reassuringly. Schroder looked at him and looked at his mother. Had he detected any edge of anxiety in her voice, or any sign of misgiving in him, he might have hesitated. But he did not. Relieved and satisfied, he bade farewell to them both. The boy would fit in well. He looked forward very much to welcoming her son as a student in the next school year, in January 2001.

There had been an alternative to Pretoria Boys, another reputable high school in the city called the Afrikaanse Hoër Seunskool (Afrikaans Boys High School). There was huge rivalry between the two, in particular when it came to rugby, and the Afrikaner one was where his father, Henke, had studied. Pistorius, who spoke Afrikaans, chose the one where English was the language of instruction, which happened also to be the language he spoke with his mother.

His parents had divorced when he was six. Henke left home and went to live seven hundred miles away in Port Elizabeth – as chance would have it, the city on South Africa's south-eastern coast where Reeva Steenkamp grew up. As the family told it, Henke did not abide by his pledge always to stand by his son as enthusiastically as he had declared he would on the day he was born. He did not disappear. Not at first. He would see his three children once every two weeks, and they enjoyed their outings with him. But money was a problem. The family's sole breadwinner until the marital break-up, Henke did not meet all his financial responsibilities afterwards. Often because he was not able to. Henke made a living chiefly out of agricultural lime mining, but he was a volatile administrator, one day up, the next down, opening and closing companies with a frequency that exasperated the rest of his family – especially his three brothers, who were all steadily successful businessmen.

Sheila and the children were obliged to move to a smaller home and she to find work for the first time in her life, as a school secretary, disrupting their domestic stability and giving her less time to attend to the child who needed the most care. The quality of the medical attention he received suffered too. She could no longer afford to pay for her son to attend a private prosthetist, sending him instead to a public hospital to have his legs adjusted to fit his growing bones. They had been a comfortably-off white family in a country where to be born white had always been a guarantee of material security. But after her husband left, Sheila Pistorius had to make every penny count.

It was lucky for her, as it would be for her son twenty years later, that the extended Pistorius family had money and were prepared to part with it to help their own flesh and blood. The home they moved into was bought not by Henke, but by his wealthy brother Arnold. Pistorius's paternal grandmother helped out with money too. They would struggle, but they would not starve. Sheila had so little faith in her husband that, with what turned out to be eerie foresight, she approached Arnold and his wife one day and asked them, please, in the event that she should die, to take care of her children. They assured her they would. When the time came for Pistorius to go to Pretoria Boys High it was Arnold, not Henke, who paid the bills.

She thanked her brother-in-law, but most of all she thanked God. A devout and active Christian, she sang in her church choir, traveled to Jerusalem to visit the holy sites, and taught her children to love and trust the Lord. Life could be hard and cruel at times, as Jesus had found, but God the Father was benevolent, He had a plan. 'Things happen for a reason,' she would tell her son. There was a divine method and a deeper truth behind the apparently random suffering one had to endure. God was her rock and she was her son's, and he absorbed her teachings, attending church services and praying daily as a boy and for the rest of his life.

She was the center of his childhood universe, instilling in him the conviction that he might be different from other people but he could do anything, she told him, to which he set his mind and body. It was to her, not to his father, that he would later attribute his fierce drive to succeed.

While he saw his father less the older he became, his mother was the one who taught him not to feel self-pity, not to show weakness when he was teased, as sometimes happened at primary school, about his artificial legs. She also instructed him to brush off the curious remarks of strangers with jokes, saying his feet had been bitten off by a great white shark, or pointing out the advantages of having artificial legs. You could slam a nail into them, as he sometimes did to shock unsuspecting new acquaintances, and it did not hurt.

Sheila practiced what she preached, refusing to make any distinction between her treatment of her disabled son and her other children. Hence the story he would tell journalists a hundred times when he became famous of how in the morning, when he was preparing to go to school, she would tell him to put on his legs in exactly the same tone of voice as she would order his elder brother to put on his shoes. That he should consider that story to be the most eloquent illustration of an upbringing during which he was encouraged to deny the limits of his condition says much about the centrality of his mother in his life, and how assiduously she sought to make amends for having brought him into the world not fully formed. But limits there were, and during those periods, sometimes lasting for months, when as a small child the cracks and blisters on his stumps were too painful for him to go to school, it was she who nursed his wounds and comforted him, sitting by his side with his head on her chest, stroking his hair.

Sheila's refusal to let her son's disability hold him back physically or mentally was the engine behind his remarkable triumphs on the running track. She never imagined that he would become world-famous, but she did know that the funny little wooden legs he wore when he was small would inspire curiosity and sometimes mockery. In her determination that he should never feel awkward or ashamed, that he should always stand proud, she drummed one lesson into him. Never, ever forget, she would tell him, that people regard you the way you regard yourself. He listened well and acted on her words. What she failed to foresee was that by hiding the truth from himself and others he might gain in self-image in the short term, but might lose out by failing to face up to the truth of his disabled body, hampering his capacity to develop as an emotionally healthy human being. It sometimes meant pushing himself harder than he really wanted to; it meant smiling and looking strong when inside he felt sad or weak. His success in concealing his vulnerabilities from others built up the outer layers of his self-esteem, but he paid a price in terms of the turmoil generated by the impossibility of reconciling the person he wished to be with the one he was. The striving always to be regarded as normal, at peace with his disability, contained an element of self-delusion, causing him anxiety and stress.

But the tension between his two evolving personas was not something a child so in thrall to his mother would have been consciously aware of, and he absorbed her lessons, doing as she did when people asked her how she coped with having a son with no feet – denying that there was a problem, always putting on a brave face.

Sheila Pistorius played the part convincingly. As her son would only fully understand in adulthood, there was a dark side to her own life that she tried hard to hide, the consequence of the anguish she suffered in an unhappy marriage and, later, as a single mother raising three children with barely enough to make ends meet. Among friends and acquaintances she was resolutely good-humored, revealing little of this inner grief. Everybody viewed her in the same light as the headmaster of Pretoria Boys High. Other teachers there who

met her were left marveling at how 'alive, compassion-
ate and genuine' she was, 'how bubbly and cheerful'.
Her son would describe her in just such terms when the
time came for journalists to write profiles of him.

Maybe he really did continue to believe into adulthood that all had been well at home; maybe the habit
of denying uncomfortable truths had become second
nature to such an extent that he failed to register that
his mother often drank herself to sleep. She was an
intermittent and solitary alcohol abuser who found
relief from the pain she feared to confront not only in
God but in the bottle. Sometimes she drank so much
that she would fail to wake up in the night when her
two younger children cried out for her. In such circumstances Carl, the eldest of the three, would take charge
and play the role of father, hiding their mother's condition from his siblings.

Pistorius was able to persist in seeing in his mother
not the wreckage of a life of misfortune or bad choices
but a hardy survivor and a moral guide. The lessons
she imparted to him all boiled down to the same thing,
which he set out in the introduction – on the very first
page, in the very first words – of his autobiography,
*Blade Runner*, written five years before he shot Reeva
Steenkamp, at a time in his life when his overriding
preoccupation was to run as fast as he could. Sheila

wrote a note for her son when he was five months old which she intended him to read when he was an adult. The note, as set out in his book, said: 'The real loser is never the person who crosses the finishing line last. The real loser is the person who sits on the side, the person who does not even try to compete.'

She would remain the voice of his conscience for the rest of his life and it was uncanny that she should have come up with a metaphor so prescient – and unspeakably sad that she should not have lived to see her son run and compete and cross the finishing line in first place, all over the world.

She spent the last fifteen years of her life trying to ensure his life would not be the vale of tears it seemed predestined to be, but she could not spare him the tragedy of her own death.

Eight years after her divorce, eight years of maternal self-sacrifice and constant struggling to make ends meet, Sheila Bekker fell in love with and married an airline pilot. Pistorius had had mixed feelings when the relationship began a year earlier, but he grew to like and trust his mother's suitor and felt that if she was happy with him, he should be too. The wedding took place in November 2001. Within a month she fell ill. The doctors found that she had a severely damaged liver, but they got the precise diagnosis wrong. They thought she had hepatitis and prescribed medicine accordingly. She reacted adversely to the drugs, was hospitalized and rapidly declined. Henke's reaction revealed that he had his faults but that he was not an ogre, that, as some of the female members of his family in particular would say, there was a loveable and decent side to his nature. His relations with his ex-wife had always remained superficially cordial. He had abandoned her and she had been deeply hurt, but for the sake of the children, as she would tell herself, she never let any ill feeling show. Now that Sheila badly needed help, Henke sought to provide it, turning to his old friend Gerry Versfeld for advice. They discussed the possibilities of a liver transplant and Dr Versfeld put him in touch with experts in the field. But it was too late.

When it happened it came as a surprise, for, true to character, she had not told her children how ill she was. Pistorius was in the middle of a history lesson in his second year at Pretoria Boys High, on March 6, 2002, when Bill Schroder came into the classroom and told him to come out immediately and meet his father at the school gates. He and his brother, Carl, jumped into Henke's Mercedes and he drove off at speed, more distraught than they had ever seen him, to the hospital. They made it to her bedside with ten minutes to spare. Other family and friends were already in attendance.

But it was a wake more than a farewell. She died without recognizing them, in a coma, tubes riddling her body, at the age of forty-four.

Pistorius was fifteen and it was as if he had lost a part of himself. Grief-stricken, and for the one and only time in his life questioning his faith in God, he briefly sought relief in marijuana. He was rudderless and, for all practical purposes, an orphan. The spasm of paternal attentiveness when the emergency had arisen remained just that. Until he started running seriously two years later he saw his father at most once every six months. Going to live with him was not an option; boarding school now became the closest thing to a home. In the holidays he would stay with his mother's sister, his aunt Diana, or with his uncle Arnold's family who had adopted his younger sister Aimée as their own. Aimée had moved in with her father in Pretoria after her mother died, but that had lasted barely two months. Unhappy sharing a roof with her father, she conveyed a discreet message to her uncle Arnold and his wife, Lois, through their daughters, that she would like to come and live with them. They agreed and she became a member of their family, a fifth daughter. She was still living with them when Reeva died.

Aimée and Carl cried at their mother's funeral, but their brother did not. After he returned to school following her burial he told very few of his classmates what had happened. But the next morning he woke up in floods of tears. Losing one's mother at fifteen is sad enough in any circumstances but for Pistorius she had been his life's crutch and moral example. She had shaped his personality, his strengths as well as his weaknesses, and even when she was no longer present she would continue to steer the course of his life to a degree that would only become fully apparent much later, after the next great disaster struck.

There was another side to her character, apart from the drinking, that Pistorius preferred to forget but that left a deep imprint on him. Sheila was terrified of crime. She lived in fear of an intruder breaking into her home, often jumping up in bed when she heard a sound in the middle of the night, then rushing to the phone to call the police. She would wake up her children, take them into her bedroom, lock the door, and wait until the police arrived. Her fears were not unfounded. When Henke left, the family had moved not just to a smaller home but to a rougher neighborhood. There were several break-ins at her home, to which she responded by taking an ominously extreme precaution. Every night she went to bed with a loaded pistol under her pillow.

# 5

*Stone walls do not a prison make.*
RICHARD LOVELACE,
*TO ALTHEA, FROM PRISON*

Caged inside the home of his rich uncle Arnold during the year-long wait for his murder trial, the sounds, images and smells of that night tormented Pistorius. He would gladly have given up all the riches and every last ounce of the glory he had earned to turn the clock back and undo what he had done, but it was irrevocable. He had fired those gunshots; he could not unfire them.

There were occasional moments of respite from the horror of memory, when he was able to shut off the screams inside his head and repress the nauseating stench of blood in his nostrils, but the remorse never left him. He had one consolation: knowing that his family understood, forgave and would stand by him, no matter what. His uncle Arnold and his wife Lois, their four daughters and sons-in-law, other uncles and aunts, Carl, and, most of all, Aimée – they, along with other members of the extended but close Pistorius family, were always ready to sit silently with him, prodding him gently towards the understanding that his old life had gone forever and he had to find the strength to build himself anew.

Before Pistorius, no one could have imagined that a double amputee would rank among the fastest 400 meter runners in the world. Thanks to the celebrity he had gained, the little-known discipline of Paralympic sport, which he had ruled over from the time he won his first gold medal at the age of seventeen, had come to grip the public imagination. Thanks to him, the world at large had learned to regard disabled athletes – and, by extension, all disabled people – with a new respect, and they in turn had begun to view themselves with a new dignity.

Running had shaped his public identity and raised him to impossible heights. But he knew that from now on his fame and reputation would be defined less by his triumphs on the track, or by the good that he had done, than by the tragedy of that night. Reeva's death by his hand had seemed to have destroyed any possibility of ever resuming high-level competition on the world stage. That part of his life was over. What he had to do now was to learn to live with a sorrow that was more implacable than guilt.

He also needed a new purpose in life. One was ready to hand.

Now the shadow of the trial loomed, his task was to prepare himself for it with as clear a mind as he could muster. But in order to manage that he had to imagine an existence beyond the hell he had inhabited since Reeva's death. To that end, Pistorius's lawyers encouraged the family to help him visualize a favorable legal outcome and to start contemplating the outline of his rehabilitation after it. The lawyers admitted they were anxious about how he would perform in court, fearing he might fall apart when the critical moment came to take the stand and face cross-questioning by the state prosecutor. It was impossible for Pistorius to imagine how he would hold himself together in the face of the evidence of what had happened that night, but he owed it to his family to try.

They had all understood immediately that there was no question of him going back to live alone at the home where he had shot Reeva. When his uncle Arnold invited him to stay at his place, where his younger sister had been living for the last ten years, he did not think of turning down the offer.

There he suffered, but in some style. Arnold Pistorius lived in a mansion perched on the hills of Waterkloof Ridge, where the rich people of Pretoria and the foreign ambassadors lived. His home stood out in the stately neighborhood. While other residences were built in a gentle Mediterranean style, with pastel walls and terracotta-tiled roofs, his was a forbiddingly sturdy, red-brick pile, with the air of a military compound. A waterless moat and a sentry box manned round the clock by security guards defended the front of the property. A sign by the entrance gate announced the name of the house, 'Bateleur' – after a breed of African eagle that preys on snakes.

Arnold Pistorius liked to say that he lived in 'an African house'. Originally a church minister's home, he and his wife Lois had spent a decade supervising its reconstruction, carefully selecting the hardiest stone, brick and wood the continent could yield and hiring the finest local craftsmen to assemble it all. On the second floor were the bedrooms, reached by a manorial wooden staircase; downstairs, a large entrance hall, lounge, dining room, study and kitchen. Sculptures large and small of giraffes, elephants, leopards and baboons adorned each room; paintings on the walls depicted scenes from the African bush. High windows on the ground floor at the back of the house looked down onto a large swimming pool in the shape of a cross, and beyond that, across a valley, on a hill three miles away, could be seen South Africa's most imposing architectural landmark, the Union Buildings, seat of state power since 1910.

Arnold's seat of power inside the house was the room in which he conducted his business meetings – a dark study, with brown leather chairs, where he kept a collection of antique guns and, rearing from a wall, a big-game trophy, the head of a black buffalo. For Arnold, it served as a statement of his proud Africanness, of his authority as the ruler of a traditional Afrikaner household, and as a symbol of his material success. In his early sixties, he was a lean, tall, white-bearded man, ramrod straight, who never tired of saying that to be an Afrikaner gave you as much claim to be an African as if you were a Zulu, Xhosa or any other of the darker-skinned peoples who called the southern tip of the continent home. His family had inhabited Africa, he would say, since long before the forebears of most American families had arrived in the United States.

Arnold Pistorius had done well in modern, post-apartheid South Africa. Rather than cower and cringe and consider emigrating to Australia, as some other white people had done when Nelson Mandela took power in 1994, he had seen democracy as an opportunity. Mandela had not sought revenge against the Afrikaners, apartheid's inventors and, for twenty-seven years, his jailers. Mandela had calculated that, in the interests of peace, not only the Afrikaners but white people in general should be allowed to keep their money and, in the interests of prosperity, be encouraged to invest it in the country of their birth. Arnold Pistorius took Mandela at his word. A black aspirational middle class, a concept quite alien during the apartheid years, was newly rising, and Arnold bet that building shopping malls for them would be good business. The bet worked and he made a great deal of money, much of which he invested in game reserves in the Kruger National Park, where the animals evoked in the sculptures of his home ran free.

To his nephew Arnold gave the run of his big home, which included access to an indoor cinema and a spacious gym equipped with all the latest apparatus, where he worked out with frantic enthusiasm. But where he lived now, since what they referred to in the family as 'the incident', was not in the main house but in a large apartment – or 'cottage', as Arnold called it – located at the bottom of a long, steep flight of steps beyond the swimming pool, next to a pond with three resident swans – unfriendly beasts, Arnold would warn visitors, liable to bite anyone who came too close. The cottage, resembling a hotel suite of the type his nephew used to frequent on his triumphant world travels, consisted of a bedroom, a large living room and a bathroom. Within the limits of his uncle's property Pistorius enjoyed five-star luxury and, with the cinema, the pool, the gym and a permanent staff of servants on the premises, five-star amenities. But he was a recluse now, a virtual prisoner. The athletics track at the high performance sports center in Pretoria where he used to train was out of bounds. Before, he had sought public attention; now, he shunned it. Before, the fans mobbed him; too many now would turn their backs on him. But he did need company, constant attention, as if he were a small child again. The three women closest to him provided it: his aunt Lois, Arnold's elegant wife; his cousin Maria, who was four years older than he and lived in the house next door with her husband and child; and, most devoted of all, his younger sister Aimée, whom he had adored from the day she was born, on whose pristine little feet he had fixated when she was a baby and he was just three years old, whose company he craved every waking moment in the first weeks after the shooting. Aimée, worked as an analyst for a South African

investment bank, where she had a reputation for quick-
mindedness and a talent for finance surprising to her
colleagues in one so young.

Good-looking, as both male and female members of
the Pistorius clan tended to be, his sister, cousin and
aunt would take turns to sit silently with him, to talk
when he needed to talk, to hug him when he wept, each
filling the role of his absent mother.

A fourth woman in whom he sought comfort was his
paternal grandmother, Gerti Pistorius, who, as family
photographs of her wedding in 1943 showed, had been
an extraordinary beauty, of Scandinavian descent. Her
husband, who was also still alive, had been a dash-
ingly handsome man. The pair set a family standard
for glamor that their famous grandson had matched.
Gerti Pistorius had always doted on the legless boy
wonder, cherishing the moment years back when he
was very small and had appeared at her home wearing
his artificial legs for the first time shouting, 'Grandma!
Grandma! Look, I've got toes!' She had been as proud
as anybody of his achievements, filling the walls of
her home with photographs of him careering down
the track in his one-piece Lycra suit and carbon-fibre
blades, or posing on the podium with a gold medal
draped around his neck. Always elegantly turned out,
even at the age of ninety, she lived in Pretoria, as she

had always done; but when she saw her grandson now it was not to celebrate but to console.

Occasionally the sense of imprisonment would overwhelm him and he would risk a sortie into the outside world. He would drive to his grandmother's, or to lunch at an Italian restaurant with Aimée or Maria in a small shopping center nearby, a simple place with Formica table tops and plastic chairs, where the staff remained welcoming, ready to shake his hand and to go along with the charade that nothing was amiss. Urged on by his cousins' husbands, muscular men who would sweat alongside him at his uncle's gym, he would sometimes attempt some pretense of normality by eating out at a fashionable place called Koi, his favorite Japanese restaurant in Pretoria. A couple of times during the year's wait for the trial he was unable to resist the temptation to flee his cage and attend a party or visit a bar with the fast set he used to enjoy mingling with in Johannesburg. Each time, however, he regretted it because the news would inevitably reach the media, who would seize on these excursions to portray him as a man cold-bloodedly at peace with the crime he had committed. More often he would go for long drives in the countryside in a white Audi he owned. Driving had always been more than a practical matter. It was a release for his nervous energy. He drove very fast, composed at the wheel, but he never went on these drives alone now; always he had a family member by his side. Sometimes he would pluck up the courage to stop and have a drink or a meal, if the place seemed sufficiently remote and discreet. It was a risk, though. There were times when strangers, spotting him, had verbally abused him.

Whatever Pistorius did, in or out of the house, he was rarely left alone. And while his family tried to keep smiling, and sometimes he smiled back, his gloom was contagious, his presence ghostly, unable to forget for long the misery and disgrace he had brought on the people he loved. They could no more ignore his shame now than they could fail to enjoy his triumphs in the past. He was as needy as a sad little child. They called him not Oscar but 'Ozzie', as his mother had done. Sometimes he would sit on a brown leather chair in the study with the head of the big buffalo, and rest his own head on Lois's or Aimée's chest, lying there quietly, not saying a word, as they stroked his hair. He could not bear to be on his own; nor did those who loved him want him to be alone. God and family – that was the Pistorius family motto.

Arnold Pistorius had assumed the steady, patriarchal role in the family tragedy. Although he was as affected as the others by the disaster of Reeva's death, he sought to rise above his own grief by bringing his upright Afrikaner Calvinism and ordered business mind to bear on his nephew's predicament, identifying priorities and endeavoring to make the best of a cruel lot. In the early days after the shooting he took it upon himself to play the part of family spokesman, striving to get the balance right by expressing condolences to the Steenkamp family, explaining that Pistorius was 'numb with shock and grief', forcefully denying the charge that Reeva's killing had been intentional. 'We have no doubt,' he told a battery of TV cameras, 'that there is no substance to the allegation and that the state's own case, including its own forensic evidence, strongly refutes any possibility of premeditated murder or, indeed, any murder as such.' He had even taken it upon himself to phone Reeva's mother, June Steenkamp, as a preamble to exploring whether his nephew might talk to her personally. But she had not been responsive. 'I've got nothing to say to you, and I don't want to hear anything that you've got to say,' she had told Arnold. 'I'm very sorry that I've troubled you, then,' he replied, before she put the phone down.

Arnold made it a point to be present – and, as he saw it, in charge – whenever Pistorius's lawyers or communications adviser came to the house for meetings. The legal fees were going to cost a fortune, and while Pistorius had sold off racehorses and other assets he owned to make the payments, his income had dried up and part of the financial burden of maintaining him now fell on his uncle. That, for Arnold, was not the most difficult part. He could not help but notice how his nephew's hands would tremble, presaging tears and a withdrawal from his surroundings – how he would sink into a black hole of despair, all too often dragging family members into it with him. His depression had become their depression, for they could not avoid putting themselves in his place, imagining what they would be thinking if they were in his skin. Never mind the money – Arnold's harder, and more delicate, mission was to orchestrate the family's strategy to nurse Ozzie back to a modicum of mental health. That was an urgent priority. It meant protecting him from the temptation to commit suicide.

They were right to worry. Pistorius did entertain taking his own life. He felt worthless. Stricken with guilt, seeing no value in getting out of bed in the morning, lacking incentive or motivation of any kind, the future yawned ahead of him vast and empty, with no prospect of pleasure or joy. He derived no consolation from past glories, which served only to mock his present condition. He was going nowhere. He would be better off dead.

Everybody in the family circle could feel in the weeks after he had ended Reeva's life that his desire to keep on living hung by a thread. The prospect of Ozzie committing suicide was the unspoken fear they all shared. And it was Arnold who took the matter in hand.

Reading up on the subject, he concluded that his nephew was suffering from some variety of post-traumatic stress disorder. He discovered, too, that in the United States, in cases where, for whatever reason, someone had killed a person they loved and then instantly regretted it, statistics showed that 20 per cent ended up taking their own lives. Arnold shared this information with the rest of the family, urging them to be ever attentive to Ozzie's shifting moods and to give him reason to believe that life still had a purpose. That meant reminding him of God and His mysterious ways, and making it manifest to him, every moment of the day, that they were keeping faith with him and continued to love him. As his aunt Lois would say, 'If you've got a purpose in life and you believe in God, it gives you a reason to understand things when they're not going smoothly. Humans make mistakes. None of us is perfect.'

Pistorius believed in God too, but he could not understand why, if there was a reason for everything, as his mother had taught him, God had allowed the death of Reeva and the destruction of the ideal love he remained convinced he had found with her. Wrestling with that question as he waited for sleep, if sleep would come, he woke up every morning in despair. For a second or two, as he rubbed his eyes, he would have no memory of what had happened. Then it would hit him like a hammerblow to the head. How to face the day? How to cope with the nightmare of his waking state?

In the first weeks after the shooting, every hour that went by without the dreaded prospect materializing of him ending his own life was a relief for the Pistorius household. They watched him keenly; they tried to read the expression in his eyes as the household sat down to prayer before dinner, holding hands in a circle, in the traditional Afrikaner way. But the tension was hard to live with, and one day Arnold broke it. He sat Pistorius down and asked him if he saw a purpose in life. Could he look beyond the trial and imagine making amends for what he had done and eventually becoming a stronger, better man? Was he aware of the reserves of moral strength that would be required, far greater than any he had drawn on to break world records or compete in the Olympic Games, in order to rebuild a life that would be worth living? Could he contain his despair? Pistorius understood his uncle's questions and the point behind them. He understood, too, that he had caused his family enough pain already and that to succumb to the selfishness of ending his life would pile an unbearable agony upon them. So, yes, he told Arnold, he did see a purpose in his life. With the help of God, he would dig deep and try to start anew. Arnold chose to believe that he meant it.

But the family never dropped their guard, never stopped keeping a wary eye on him as he padded quietly about his uncle's property, fiddling at his computer or his mobile phone, working out in the gym, trying to maintain concentration as he read biographies, with a Bible always close at hand. All he could watch on TV were emotionally neutral wildlife documentaries; anything else made him sad or scared. Romantic films, with the crushing memories they would evoke, were out of the question and anything with violence in it would make him nauseous.

He always wore glasses now, with black frames. Often unshaven, with a wispy beard, he had visibly lost weight and had a hunched, apologetic air about him. Delicately courteous, almost feminine in his gestures and gentle tone of voice, he came across as studious and withdrawn, more academic than athletic, more like a seminarian preparing for the priesthood than the sleek force of nature the world had named the Blade Runner.

At home with Arnold and Lois he was on his best behavior, properly observant of the religious pieties. The fey Christian was the Pistorius that strangers and older family members saw. He even took to holding regular prayer meetings and Bible study sessions in the lounge of his uncle's home with a visiting pastor and a close circle of friends. But he was not pious in his behavior or repentant in his attitude all of the time. He had moments when, aided by the medication he was taking, he forgot his predicament and behaved like any other twenty-six-year-old, dropping the Christian restraint and peppering his conversation, as he had done all his life since adolescence, with the most ubiquitous and all-purpose of English adjectives. 'Can you believe that fucking guy?' 'Crime in South Africa is fuckin' out of control.' And so forth. But, suddenly, even in the company of those with whom he was most at ease, he would break off in mid-conversation, his expression darkening; a pall would descend on the room and he was once again a broken man. It wasn't hard to guess what Pistorius was thinking. It was not hard to imagine the picture he was forming and the sounds he was hearing, the four shots, the door smashed open with a cricket bat, the spectacle that confronted him.

He had destroyed her life, his life, and their life together. After that first day when they had met and they had spent the night talking until 3 a.m., he had been in no doubt that she was the woman for him. She was beautiful, she was smart, she was sassy, she was kind, she took an interest in social issues. She had all the attributes he looked for in a woman and the idea began rapidly to form in his mind that she was the one he would marry and have children with.

Within a week of meeting her he had to travel to Scotland, to the University of Strathclyde, to receive an honorary doctorate. He had been engaged in a project with scientists there to develop prosthetic legs that would be both practical and affordable for poor amputees in Africa. All he had wanted then, though, was to be close to her. When he could not be with her he would bombard her with messages from his phone. He pursued her during those first weeks with the single-minded energy that he deployed in athletics competition. She was alarmed at first by his zeal, telling friends that his smothering attentions provoked mixed feelings in her. She was attracted to him – she called him 'a rock star' – but feared that in a relationship with him she would not have space to breathe. He was more sure about her at first than she was about him. But within a month she had made up her mind.

She took an interest in his running, accompanying him to the track when he trained; she shared his enthusiasm for fast luxury cars; she prayed with him at mealtimes. They started calling each other by pet names, 'my baba', 'my boo', 'my angel'. She did not move in with him but spent nights at his home when he was traveling, even getting to know some of his neighbors at Silver Woods. When he told her he planned to buy a house in Johannesburg and move there early in the next year the two of them looked at new furniture together. They seemed poised to build a shared future.

One bullet to the brain had put an end to those dreams, replacing them with the nightmare images and sounds that assailed him day and night. Only one recourse was left to him: to try and seek refuge in happy memories. It did him good to remember her alive. Alone in his cottage, he dwelt on their brief time together, daydreaming about the life he had hoped to share with her, the children they might have had. He had loved her then and he loved her now and he would love her all his life. If those who doubted him could only come into his cottage, they would know. When they walked in, the first thing they would see, hanging on the main wall across from the entrance, looking down on the room like the Virgin Mary in a Catholic church, was a large framed photograph of Reeva, a professional black-and-white portrait of her face, smiling, misty, provocative and strangely knowing.

# 6

*He who has conquered his own coward spirit has*
*conquered the whole outward world.*
THOMAS HUGHES, *TOM BROWN'S SCHOOLDAYS*

'Anything you can do I can do just as well' was the
spirit in which Oscar Pistorius started out his
life, aged fourteen, at Pretoria Boys High School. Soon
he would be put to the test.

The new boys were packed off for three days to a
remote farm owned by the school. It was early in the
year, high summer, parched and hot in the South
African Highveld, ideal conditions to test their mettle
with a mile-high climb up a rugged, stony hill.

There was a military quality to the culture at Pretoria
Boys. As one former head boy put it, they strove to break

you down when you arrived and then rebuild you in the school's image of itself as a breeder of champions. It was all about discipline, solidarity, tribal mystique. Among the school's alumni were a number of illustrious judges, politicians and entrepreneurs and, most valued of all, sporting legends who had represented South Africa in international competition, notably in rugby, the sport that best represented the school's manly virtues. The idea the school liked to nurture was that the successes students achieved in later life owed at least as much to the resilience and *esprit de corps* acquired within its walls as to individual ability.

It was impressed upon the staff that they were there to enforce a tradition. If need be, with severity. Failure to doff the school cap in the presence of an adult or to address them as 'sir' or 'madam' meant instant punishment. But the teachers were not entirely without mercy. In Pistorius's case, given his condition, they might have excused him from taking part in the hike up that hill, had he asked. He didn't.

The expedition leader was Paul Anthony, a rugby coach who had spent most of the four decades of his life at the school, first as a student and then as a teacher. Most of the boys made it up and down the hill in reasonable time. But half a dozen labored to make it back. Anthony set off in a van to pick up the stragglers.

'It was my very first encounter with Ozzie,' he recalled. 'I was startled, to say the least, on seeing his wooden legs.' Pistorius was in shorts, sweating profusely and covered in red dust, the color of the Highveld soil. 'His legs were chafed and bleeding at the point where the stumps and the prosthetics met,' Anthony continued. 'I told him to jump into the van. Four or five other boys had already accepted the offer. But he refused. I insisted. I said, "Come on, it's no disgrace. Look at these other guys in here." But he wouldn't budge. He was last in, but he finished the course. I was really, really struck by his tenacity.'

Pretoria Boys was a big school, with more than 1,200 boys. Anthony had no more contact with Pistorius until the following year. When he did, it was in the company of his mother. But he did not make the connection, not even after the meeting was over, between the boy before him and 'the boy from the hill'. Pistorius was wearing long trousers and there was no mention at that time of his artificial legs, either by his mother or by him. Reflecting after the encounter on the influence Pistorius's mother had had on his character, Anthony made a connection between her smiling exuberance and her son's stoical drive. Two months later, when he heard the news of her death, it struck him that there was another quality they had in common. When he had met her he had seen no glimmer of the illness that was eating away at her insides. Oscar and Sheila Pistorius shared a genius for masking pain.

The reason he had met them at the start of the 2002 school year was that Pistorius was about to become a boarder and Anthony was the staff member in charge of the 'house', in the British public-school terminology used at Pretoria Boys, to which the boy would belong. The house was called 'Rissik' and Anthony's title was 'housemaster'. He would play the role of surrogate parent for Pistorius during the two years he remained in that post. As Anthony discovered at lights-out on Pistorius's first night as a boarder, his disability was not going to present any special challenge.

'It was 9.30 and I went around and talked to each kid in bed. I got to Ozzie. He was cheerful. He said it was great to be here. But he had a question. He'd had no time to brush his teeth. Could he go? He jumped out of bed and I was completely taken aback. He was on his stumps, on which he moved nimbly. I just gaped. He came back to bed, as if nothing out of the ordinary had happened.'

Some months later Pistorius went on another school outing, this time to a rock pool where the boys took it in turns to hurl themselves down a slide and crash into the water, repeating the action over and over.

Bill Schroder, the headmaster, was present. Less accustomed than Paul Anthony to seeing Pistorius in action, he winced at the boy's recklessness. 'After they got out of the water they had to clamber up some steep, rocky edges before they could slide down again,' Schroder recalled. 'I said to him, "Don't do it!" He was on his stumps, where the skin was terribly thin, and he could so easily have cut himself badly on the rocks. But he insisted he could do it. He begged me to let him, absolutely determined to be seen to do as the others did.'

'He never let you be in a position where you might feel sorry for him,' Anthony said. 'It was amazing how motivated and confident he was, how completely he put you at ease about the fact he was missing his legs. He had no complex that you could see. He never came across as a kid without legs.'

Whether his companions at school let him forget his disability was another matter. Teenage boys are not ones for tender mercies, and less so at a school where rugged self-reliance was the most prized of virtues and the most despicable sin was to go crying to teacher when you were bullied or abused. By long tradition, Pretoria Boys was a place where if you were fat, if you were thin, if you had a big nose, if you were Jewish or belonged to some other minority, you were not allowed to forget it. You were called names, you were pushed around, and you had to learn to get used to it. As one former student described it, 'you had to earn your stripes'.

While the school would become less harshly militaristic under the reforming hand of Bill Schroder, who was headmaster from 1990 to 2009, the boys did not shrink from reminding the kid with no legs of his singularity. One night a group of his schoolmates played a prank on him intended to ram home the cruel truth that, for all his bravado, he was more vulnerable than the rest of them. He woke up in his dormitory to find flames all around him. Someone was shouting that everybody should evacuate the building. He reached out a hand to grab his prosthetic legs, but they were not where he always left them, at the foot of his bed. He looked up and down, panic-stricken, but could not find them. Recounting the incident in his autobiography, he wrote, 'I was almost in tears, terrified that I was going to be left to die.'

It turned out that the other boys had sprayed the dormitory's steel cupboards with lighter fluid and then set fire to them. They carried on laughing at the fright they had given him long after the flames had died out.

If the incident exposed a brittle pride, or left a lasting trauma, he never let on. Anxious always to be perceived as 'one of the boys', he certainly did not vent his hurt to his housemaster, Paul Anthony, who remained in the dark as to what had happened. If there was one lesson you learned from your peers at Pretoria Boys, it was that in the face of physical or emotional pain, you had to 'man up'. No feeling sorry for yourself, or seeking sympathy, allowed.

Yet after he left school he never stopped mentioning the incident, recounting what happened in detail in interview after interview years later, after he had become famous. What he left out was the part where, in his autobiography, he confessed to having been close to tears and in terror of his life. Even in his book, he ended up by shrugging it all off, presenting himself as a good sport capable of taking a joke. The point was to recall the incident as an example of his capacity to confront his disability and take it in his stride.

Nothing during his schooldays was going to hold him back. Not even rugby, among the most violent and physically demanding of team sports. Pretoria Boys was demanding enough academically, a field in which he muddled along but never excelled, but rugby was where the school's prestige was most heavily invested. It did not matter if you were the school dunce, if you played for the first XV rugby team you were regarded as a god. Pistorius did not make it that high, but, determined to show that he would allow no limits to be placed on his ambition, he played rugby for the school at junior level.

Paul Anthony remembered one time when he watched him play against a school from Johannesburg. He also remembered wondering before the game began what would happen in the event that Pistorius was tackled around the legs. He was. As he raced down the wing with the ball under his arm, a rival player dived into him from the side. To the horror of the tackler Pistorius's legs came off. But he got up and kept going for the line on his stumps.

'The game stopped,' Anthony recalled. 'He slipped his prostheses back on and carried on playing. Ozzie never ceased to astonish. But just as astonishing a thing for me that day was to discover how fast he was.'

Someone else, unconnected with the school, would notice it too. His name was Francois van der Watt and he would play a decisive role in Pistorius's life.

One day during his first year at school, when he was still fourteen, he fell while running and broke his prosthetic legs. He went to his grandmother Gerti, who lived in Pretoria, for help. It was an emergency. He needed a new set of legs immediately. Instead of turning to his usual prosthetics specialist in Johannesburg, forty-five minutes' drive away, she looked in the phone book, found a number in Pretoria and dialled it. The person who answered the call was Van der Watt.

'It was a total chance occurrence. I just happened to pick up the phone,' he recalled. 'There were others working there. I was a junior, just starting out in my first job at a prosthetics consultancy. She described the problem and asked, "Can you help?" I told her to bring the boy in right away.'

A tall, big-shouldered, thick-wristed Afrikaner, Van der Watt had been destined from birth to be a farmer in his home country. Born in 1970, he was raised in the countryside near a town called Bethlehem in the Orange Free State, a landlocked province in the geographical heart of South Africa where apartheid was enforced with special rigor – it was the only region in the country where people of Indian extraction were not allowed to live – during the years when Van der Watt was growing up. Oblivious as most white children – indeed, most white adults – were to the way their darker-skinned compatriots were treated, Van der Watt's memories of those days centered on life on the family farm, not least his father's insistence that he get up at dawn to milk the cows. On finishing high school he was sent to study farming in Bloemfontein, the capital of the Free State. Less wedded to the land than family lore required him, however, he soon found

himself taking an interest in the rather unusual subject studied by his college room-mate, orthodontics
and prosthetics. To his parents' dismay, he abandoned
farming and left for Pretoria Technikon to acquire a
qualification in that field. His success was such that
he would end up moving to the United States, to the
small town of Winnie, Texas, where he lived with his
American wife, two children and two horses, representing a company that manufactured artificial legs. But
his first job – 'sort of part-doctor, part-engineer' was
how he described it – was at the company in Pretoria
that Gerti Pistorius phoned on that fateful day.

'I had a look at his prostheses and saw at once they
were beyond repair,' Van der Watt recalled, sitting in
the lounge of his spacious Texas home. 'They were
old-style, 1950s, wooden, and they were an ungainly
mess.'

He decided he should find a set of new, improved
prosthetics for the boy which would allow him to run
and play. 'He was shy,' Van der Watt recalled, 'but as
I would soon discover he really pushed himself to the
limit.' They had several sessions together until they
found exactly the right fit. Along the way, Van der Watt
had a brainwave.

'It was the year 2000, just before the summer
Olympics and Paralympics. I was intrigued by this

Paralympics thing and I got hold of a promotional video for the games, with music and stuff. I thought Oscar should take a look at it. He had no idea Paralympic sport existed and he sat there watching the video in my office, absolutely absorbed. He was smiling and I could sense a tingle in him. Watching that video sparked new dreams in the boy.'

What he needed now was a pair of carbon-fiber 'Cheetah' blades like the ones the Paralympic runners used. The originals were far too expensive and so Van der Watt, inspired by the boy's zeal, decided to try and build a pair of his own. What he lacked was the knowledge required to work with carbon fiber and to mould the blades to the correct specifications. So he made contact with a man who worked with that very material in the manufacture of airplanes and drew for him on a piece of paper a model of what he wanted, based on the Paralympians' Cheetahs, which had originally been inspired by the shape of the legs of the animal itself.

'The airplane guy made the legs, I built the sockets into which Oscar would lock his stumps, I attached the two and we made a plan,' said Van der Watt, who took a photograph of the fourteen-year-old on the very first day he tried them on. He looked proud as could be. The problem, they would soon find, was that they would have to make not just one pair, but several.

'We went to the track thinking, let's see what happens. Then he ran and broke the first pair in five minutes. I probably made five or six pairs until he stopped breaking them.'

His stumps bled, raw from the friction between the makeshift blades and the thin skin, as he pounded up and down the track. But he never gave up.

His persistence drove Van der Watt on. Man and boy were on a mission – almost a secret mission, for, while Pistorius's mother knew and was immensely grateful to Van der Watt, the school had no knowledge of what they were scheming. Pretoria Boys had its own athletics track, but they conducted their experiments elsewhere. For Van der Watt the frustration of seeing pairs of blades that he had laboriously built break one after another was compensated for by the specialized knowledge he was developing about the mechanics of how they worked – sufficient knowledge for him to be recruited, a decade later, as technical adviser to the US Paralympic team.

The two critical elements in the development of an effective prosthetic blade were, first, the comfort of the socket into which the stumps fitted. 'Think of a shoe,' said Van der Watt, echoing Sheila Pistorius's admonition to her son as he prepared for school in the mornings. 'Think a snug fit, not too loose, not too tight, but just right.' Second, there was the alignment of the base of the blade, identifying exactly the correct angle for it to face, exactly where the maximum downward weight of the body would fall so as to exert optimum forward propulsion, maximizing use of the body's energy. In addition to that, Van der Watt explained, it was important to get the weight and length of the blades just right, each in proportion to the runner's strength and size.

But comfort was the key to everything, he said. 'When you're running you are hitting the ground with two and a half or three times your body weight. You measure that by the force applied on the ground, which bounces back as force on the limb, which then generates the forward running propulsion. If the fit of the prostheses is too loose or too tight, you lose speed and you gain pain.'

It was not until 2001 that they hit upon a pair that did not break and with which the boy was entirely comfortable. He was still playing rugby at school, using his normal everyday prostheses, but every other week he would go to a track to experiment with the home-made Cheetahs. At that stage, fourteen going on fifteen, his goal was not the Paralympics. Van der Watt could see he was fast, but he did not know how fast relative to potential competitors at the highest level of disabled sports. 'To me he was just a kid, shy but a bit of a joker, who laughed a lot, played pranks, put staples into his legs to freak out people who did not know he wore prosthetics,' Van der Watt said. 'I was just doing my job for a nice Pretoria kid, with no plan or bigger goals. I was just helping the kid have a good life.'

He loved running on the blades but his chief obsession remained rugby, the sport you had to play at Pretoria Boys to impress your peers. But something had to give, and it did one day when he was playing against another school soon after he had turned sixteen. Two huge boys on the rival team tackled him at the same time. His artificial legs went flying, but he also hurt his knees badly. As he lay on the ground, a spectator goaded him, barking at him to get up and stop behaving like a girl. He did, and played the rest of the game, but after it was over the truth finally began to sink in that his future might not lie in rugby.

He went to see his trusted doctor, Gerry Versfeld, who prescribed a detailed three-month programme of rehabilitation, the last phase of which involved doing a lot of sprinting to build up the damaged knee. At the start of 2004 he began training at the University of Pretoria with an athletics coach by the name of Ampie Louw.

Louw was a big, bluff Afrikaner, then in his mid-forties, who would make it his chief task over the next ten years to help Pistorius make all the tiny, finely calibrated adjustments necessary to squeeze every possible millisecond out of his natural speed. The fruits of the new training became manifest within a month of the two starting out together, at the end of January 2004, when Pistorius found himself representing Pretoria Boys at a schools athletics event in Bloemfontein.

It was with a mixture of curiosity, bafflement and sniggers among the boys of the rival teams that he appeared on the track for the start of the 100 meters. The general supposition was that Pretoria Boys had chosen him for their team out of kindness. No one expected him to finish anything but last. But he won, the cheers he received providing him with his first intoxicating taste of public glory. More was soon to come.

The final event of the day was the 4×100 meters relay. If Pretoria Boys won, they would lifted the schools trophy. Paul Anthony was not there. He was away with his wife on vacation. But he received a running commentary on the phone from a teacher who was present. 'We were fourth of fifth going into the last, then Oscar got the baton,' Anthony recalled. 'Suddenly my colleague cried out, "Jesus Christ, he's flying!" And, boy, did he! He tore through the rest of the field and he crossed the tape first. We were champions!

'I put down the phone in utter disbelief and I told my wife, "I knew he was quick, but I had no idea how quick. It's unbelievable. It's a fairy tale. Someone has to write about this kid." I mean, my colleague was right: the boy with no legs, he could fly!'

Everything happened extraordinarily fast from that day on. It turned out that the time in which he won the 100 meters, 11.72 seconds, beat the world Paralympic record for double, or 'bilateral', amputees. By nearly half a second.

Rugby was forgotten. The best he could ever hope for in that sport was to be a moderately good representative of his school, and never at the highest level. Throwing himself into running, he found the refuge he craved from the pain of his mother's death, but also a pursuit that turned out to be ideally suited to his temperament. To succeed as a runner he needed to depend on no one and nothing but himself. The more he pushed himself to the limits his unlikely talent would allow, the faster he would go. Here, at last, he was the master of his own fate, able to a degree his mother could not have dared imagine not only to disguise his vulnerability from the world, but to shine bright.

Still only seventeen, with a year and a half of secondary school to complete, he competed in the South African disabled games and, although initially perplexed at finding himself in the company of disabled people, a group to which he had been conditioned to imagine he did not belong, he instantly achieved the qualifying time to represent his country in the 2004 Athens Paralympic Games. Suddenly he was all over the news, he did a TV advertisement, he started receiving sponsorship money, he bought his first car and discovered his love of speed on the road – another pursuit where, regardless of his legless condition, he felt in complete control.

In June, three months before the Athens Games, he contacted Francois van der Watt, who had just moved to the US.

'"I am in the South African team. I need new legs," were his words to me,' Van der Watt recalled. 'So I told him to fly over. He did, I measured him, made the socket, got the alignment right and there he was, with his first Cheetahs. They took him to the next level.'

The Flex-Foot Cheetah had been the Paralympic athlete's brand of choice since the early 1990s, and the one Pistorius would use for the rest of his career. The first time he tried them out competitively was in Oklahoma, where Van der Watt took him to take part in the Endeavor Games for disabled runners. He ran in the 200 meters against the fastest men in the US, and won. The local press were all over him. It was the first time he'd made the news outside South Africa.

'We shared a room in Oklahoma City,' Van der Watt said, 'and what struck me was how focused Oscar was, how determined to do his absolute best. He did not seem overawed at all at the prospect of his first big race outside South Africa. Then I saw how he ran, and how well he handled himself in public with the press, and I knew, right there, what I had always suspected but had not dared fully imagine before. He had enormous potential. He was going to be big.'

How would he do in Athens, though, in a giant stadium before a large crowd? All he had was eight months' athletics experience behind him. He would be competing against veterans, a number of them single-leg amputees, who were five or ten years older than he was. Also, Louw had identified a critical weakness in his technique. He was not fast off the starting blocks – not fast enough to win the 100 meters at this level. Having failed as yet to master the art of the sprinter's classic, crouching start, down on one knee, he lost explosivity by using a standing start, as long distance runners did. In the 100 meters he would be giving too much of an early advantage to his rivals to have any hope of winning. He took part in the race anyway, but Louw judged that the best bet at this stage of his career was the 200 meters, where he would have more time to make up ground lost at the start.

Dr Gerry Versfeld flew to Athens to see him run. Familiar as Dr Versfeld was with being in the company of amputees, he was astonished at the spectacle of so many lean, fit sportsmen and women with missing limbs. 'It was a big eye opener, even for me. It was the first time I saw people with disabilities do such things,' Dr Versfeld said. 'The message, loud and clear, was: these are not crocks, these are people with talent and part of our society.'

It was another doctor who, more than half a century earlier, had hit upon the idea of engaging disabled people in competitive sports. The doctor's name was Ludwig Guttmann, a German Jew who had fled to England early in 1939 to escape Nazi persecution. A brilliant neurosurgeon, Guttmann treated soldiers with spinal cord injuries after the end of the Second World War at Stoke Mandeville Hospital, near London. One day it struck him that a good way to lift his patients' morale would be to persuade them to take part in organized sports. In 1948, on the very same day that the summer Olympic Games began in London, Guttmann launched what became known as the Stoke Mandeville Games. This led twelve years later, in Rome, to the first official Paralympic Games.

Pistorius would become the most celebrated beneficiary of Guttmann's generous legacy. At the

Athens Games of 2004, while still only seventeen, he stole the show. 'His only problem was getting going,' Dr Versfeld recalled, 'but he still managed to get bronze in the 100 meters. Then, in the 200 meters, he also got off to a bad start and was ten meters behind in no time, with four or five other runners ahead of him after the gun went off. But then he built up the most amazing head of steam. He wobbles a bit from side to side when you look at him from the front, but from the side, which was my vantage point, he was poetry in motion. It was the most amazing thing I'd ever seen. I was immensely proud.'

He was the youngest runner in the field, but he won the race and, with a time of 21.97 seconds, set a new world record.

Bill Schroder, his headmaster, was thrilled. Pistorius's triumph was the school's triumph too. But he was also concerned. 'He lost his mother at a very, very impressionable age and then, overnight, he was catapulted into iconic wonderkid national status. He was only seventeen and he was being feted in the newspapers, sought out for interviews by women's magazines. Any boy would become impossible in such circumstances at that age, but then he had no mother. His father, Henke, only started taking an interest in him for the first time that I ever saw after he became famous. Plus he had no legs. I was exceptionally worried about how he'd cope, all the more so as I realized that we in the school were the only ones who might be able to give him his bearings.'

Schroder determined that what he should not do was allow him special treatment. Pistorius thought he deserved it. Suddenly a celebrity inside and outside the school, he was becoming a law unto himself. But Schroder was the law at Pretoria Boys. Inevitably, during his final year at school, after Athens, the two clashed. First, over a sponsored car that Pistorius had received. Schroder ordered him to get rid of it. Pistorius protested at first but then grudgingly acquiesced.

The second time, he informed Schroder that he had to take time off from school to take part in an athletics competition in Finland. Schroder told him he was not going. He replied that he had to, it was an opportunity that might never be repeated to take part, not in a Paralympic event, but in an international able-bodied athletics meeting. The exchange became heated, as Schroder recalled. 'He said, "I must go." I said, if you go, you're not coming back. I told him he had to do all the things the others did, with no special privileges, by tradition of the school. I won and he stayed. But he was enraged with me, I know. I heard that he began speaking of me to people as "Mr Fucking Schroder".'

Apart from the principle, there was a practical reason why Schroder did not want to let him take time off from school. He had a duty to discharge as a dormitory prefect. In a room full of junior children he was the one in charge, his job to double up as mentor and enforcer of discipline. Within the confines of that room he had practically the same measure of authority as Schroder had over the whole school. The difference was that he was only eighteen and there was a risk that he, as anyone else that age might have done, would abuse his power.

After he shot Reeva Steenkamp some said that he had. Word spread among those who chose to believe that he had killed her deliberately that at school, in his capacity as dormitory prefect, he had been a violent bully.

How seriously the accusation was taken depended on whether it was measured by the standards of urban middle-class cohabitation or by the higher threshold of rough behavior tolerated within the walls of Pretoria Boys High. Rumors did reach some teachers that he had a violent temper – that sometimes he 'flipped', as one of them put it – and that he threatened the younger boys. But that was hardly news at Pretoria Boys. Others who had been students there reported that their first years had been 'sheer terror', that the prefects to whom they reported were supposed to play a supportive role but in practice used the younger boys to polish their shoes, to clean their bedrooms, and did not hesitate to punish them if they deemed they had broken a school rule. As one former pupil said, 'You were in constant fear of transgressing the norms; you were the slave class of the boarding and house systems.'

Heavy-handedness was the norm. Bullying went with the territory, and for boarders it was especially tough. It was boot camp, as former students would say, an excellent preparation for military life. Prefects were sergeant majors with license to subject their subordinates to all manner of indignities, not excluding physical violence to a degree that might be judged illegal in civil society. What was considered unpardonable among the boys was to go and tell the teachers when someone had done something to you that you did not like. But while the boarders never 'sneaked' when they were at school, during the vacations some did confide in their parents. Some of them talked about the boy with no legs.

Bill Schroder recalled receiving complaints from 'a couple of parents' about the harsh treatment his teenage prodigy had supposedly been meting out to their children. Schroder said he looked into the complaints against Pistorius but found that he had never been involved with 'any incident bad enough to come to my desk'. Schroder judged it right not to reprimand him for bullying.

A policeman might have thought differently. In the all-male world of Pretoria Boys the students enjoyed a freedom to inflict harm that they might not have found in the world beyond the school walls. The danger was that they would fail to behave within legal limits once they left – as in the case of one ex-pupil who left the school in the 1980s, an especially unruly boy who used to break the unofficial rule that fighting was fine but you did not kick someone when he was down. He ended up killing his girlfriend, an ex-beauty queen, and then himself.

# 7

*There is no greater sorrow than to recall in misery*
*the time when we were happy.*
DANTE ALIGHIERI, *THE DIVINE COMEDY*

The close-up of Reeva looking down from the wall of the cottage at his uncle Arnold's was not the only photograph of her that Pistorius kept. On a table to the right of the framed portrait lay a collage of photos of the two of them in public, playing the celebrity couple, both assuming seemingly natural fashion-model poses. On his laptop computer he kept private photographs showing them in less practiced attitudes, playing the fool or caught unawares staring dotingly at one another. In one black-and-white picture she lay asleep in bed as he cradled her, she safe and innocent in his arms; he, tenderly protective.

He remained a prisoner of his memories and could sleep no better in a plush bed than on the floor of a cell. Not the first night in the cottage, not the second, not for three weeks, until the doctors hit upon the right blend of tranquillizers and antidepressants to ease the torment.

His sister Aimée took on the maternal role now. Carl remained staunchly by his side, but it was Aimée who was able to get inside his disturbed mind in a way no other family member could, making his pain her own, endeavoring with all the sisterly affection she could muster to lighten his burden. She lived with Arnold and Lois in a room on the top floor of the main house. When she was not sitting with her brother for hours on end, she was on standby, ready to rush down in response to the cries of a grown man reduced to the condition of a desperately needy child, still prey to the terror Sheila Pistorius had planted in his mind of an intruder stealing in upon him in the dead of night.

Sometimes Pistorius would call her on his mobile phone when she was sleeping. It might be because the demons in his head were driving him to the verge of insanity; it might be simply because he had heard a strange noise.

One night he succumbed so abjectly to his child-hood terrors that he got out of bed and hid inside a cupboard, from which he phoned his sister for help. She ran down the outside steps, past the swimming pool, to the cottage, coaxed him out of the cupboard and held him tight until the frenzy had passed.

One reason, not immediately obvious to the family, for his inability to fall asleep was that he did not want to fall asleep. The medication he was taking solved one problem but caused another. Sleep was no refuge. The images he battled to keep at bay while he was awake took his unconscious mind by storm in the form of ghastly nightmares. He would wake up panic-stricken, the smell of Reeva's blood overpowering his senses, causing him to retch and vomit.

He had held a memorial service for Reeva in the grounds of his uncle's home twelve days after the shooting, a week after her own family had performed her funeral rites in their home city of Port Elizabeth. If part of his purpose was to exorcize the ghosts haunting him, it proved of little use, but throwing himself into the task of preparing the ceremony did him some fleeting good. He filled the area around the swimming pool with flowers, covered the ground with candles, and hung a large photograph of Reeva from a tree. About twenty people attended, some of them family members, notably his brother and sister, and some of them mutual friends of his and Reeva's who remained loyal to him, such as Justin Divaris, the friend who had introduced them to each other and whom he had phoned forty minutes after the shooting. It was an opportunity for all present to recall Reeva's life.

In the love affair with Pistorius she had played Cinderella to his prince. Her family had inhabited a world far removed from the one he enjoyed of luxury cars, five-star hotels, first-class travel and family mansions. They were a poor white family, a species rarely encountered in the South African narrative as it played in the outside world. Henke Pistorius was a wastrel and Sheila had struggled after her divorce, but Pistorius nonetheless came from aristocratic stock. Reeva had been raised on the wrong side of the tracks.

She was born on August 19, 1983 in lively, cosmopolitan Cape Town, on the Atlantic Ocean, but when she was a small child the family moved to Port Elizabeth, Cape Town's poor relation on the Indian Ocean, a plain, listless city remarkable for the failure of its inhabitants to profit more from their long sandy beaches and fine summer weather.

Barry Steenkamp had made his living as a racehorse trainer. Sometimes he was up and sometimes he was down, like Henke. But unlike Henke, even his highs were very low. Barry had a son by a previous marriage; his wife, June, a daughter. Her parents would describe Reeva, born after both had thought they were past having another child, as their 'late lamb'. The home where the family lived was barely a step up from the type owned by black working families in the segregated townships nearby during the apartheid era. Standing on an unkempt plot of land in a residential area known as Miramar, the little house had grey walls and a zinc roof and suffered from comparison with the large, red-tiled homes in which most of their white middle-class neighbors lived. Fortunately there was a good mixed-race Roman Catholic high school called St. Dominic's Priory a short walk away, and there it was that Reeva studied during her adolescence, excelling through hard work and establishing a reputation as a kind and uncomplicated classmate of whom her teachers always spoke well. She had her first taste of what the future would bring during her teenage years when she made it to the finals of the Miss Port Elizabeth contest. But her ambitions at that stage lay elsewhere. She wanted to study law. Her parents could not pay her university fees, but she pushed herself in her studies and obtained a bursary, completing her degree at Port Elizabeth's Nelson Mandela University in 2005, when she was twenty-two.

Uncertain whether she wanted to make a career in law, she explored possibilities in modeling and had her first break a year after leaving university. After dying her naturally dark hair blonde, she was chosen as the white face – others were the black, Indian and 'colored' faces – of Avon cosmetics in South Africa.

Her one uambiguous passion, having grown up in a horse-racing family, was riding. She would get up early in the morning when she was a teenager and go to Port Elizabeth's Fairview racetrack to exercise the horses her father trained. She was what in racing circles they called a 'work rider'. It was in this closed social world that she met the man who would become her first serious boyfriend and with whom she would remain in a relationship for six years. He was a jockey and his name was Wayne Agrella. He was a diminutive man with a big name in South African racing circles.

They might have married, she might have gone into the law, and together they could have accomplished the dream of dragging her parents out of penury that had driven her through her school and university years. Often she would tell them, 'Don't worry. Give me time. I will look after you.'

A misfortune while she was still in law school made them fear for a while that it would be they who would have to look after her. She fell while riding and broke her back. In what would have been the most perverse of twists, she might have been disabled for life. She lay

in hospital for six weeks nursing two crushed verte-
brae, with her doctors uncertain whether she would
ever be able to walk again.

But she made a complete recovery, graduated and
decided to change her life. She never rode again,
split with the jockey Agrella – the relationship would
be described later on in court as 'emotionally abusive' – decided to go into modeling full-time and
moved to Johannesburg, as ambitious South African
men and women from the provinces – among them
Nelson Mandela in his day – had long done. Her parents, in particular her father, had their doubts about
her renouncing the law, but she appeased them by telling them that they should be patient; she would return
and take up legal practice in due course.

She arrived in the big city, had the word 'Lioness'
tattooed on her ankle, and set out to conquer the
world. Her success did not initially match her ambition. At five foot seven she was short for a career in the
fashion world and, though she did manage to sign up
with an agency called Ice Model and land a few early
photographic jobs, it took her years to reach the point
of being able to spare enough money to alleviate her
parents' growing financial distress. While the man
she and all South Africans knew as the Blade Runner
was already an international star on the way to making

millions, she spent five largely anonymous years in the city in which he had been born experiencing as much frustration as joy.

She had a busy social life, with plenty of dancing in nightclubs; she did some live presenting for Fashion TV South Africa, but complained about the cattiness of her competitors in the modeling world; she struggled to get by and badly missed her parents. She found some salvation in the arms of a businessman called Warren Lahoud, with whom she began a relationship early in 2008 that lasted more than four years. But she had not yet made the yearned-for breakthrough in her career, and in October that year she endured an experience on a visit to Port Elizabeth that would offer an eerie portent of the tragedy that lay ahead. She was alone at home with her mother when thieves ripped the burglar bars from the outside walls and stormed in. As the thieves ransacked their home, the two of them hid for fifteen minutes inside a locked room, silent and frozen with fear. Mother and daughter were so shaken by the incident that they sought professional counseling.

The year 2009 showed little improvement in her fortunes but in 2010 things began to look up: she began appearing in advertisements for Toyota cars, Pin Pop lollipops, Cardinal beer and Hollywood chewing gum. Her dream, though, was to appear on the cover of a

mainstream magazine. She took a step in that direction when she was flown to the island of Bazaruto in
Mozambique to pose as a calendar girl for *FHM* magazine, a monthly publication for men of a type known
in South Africa as a 'lads' mag'. At the end of 2011 she
made her breakthrough. She was chosen for the cover
of *FHM*, where she was described as the 'December
Summer Sizzler'. 'I'm super honored to be on the
cover, especially the December issue, and am excited to
see what lies ahead,' she told the Port Elizabeth *Herald*,
which, echoing the city's pride, described her as 'a
beauty with brains'.

Success at last followed success and in the middle of
2012 she was invited to fly to Jamaica to appear on a
South African reality TV show called *Tropika Island
of Treasure*. Poignantly, and in questionable taste, the
show was broadcast two days after her death. It ended
with a set-piece address to the camera in which she
said, 'You fall in love with being in love . . . I don't have
any regrets, any bitterness . . . the way you go out and
make your exit, it's so important. You've either made
an impact in a positive way or a negative way, but just
maintain integrity and maintain class and just always
be true to yourself.'

Being true to herself included breaking up with
Warren Lahoud, in whose home she had been living.

The news came as a blow to her parents, who regarded him as a decent companion and a 'gentleman', with whom she might have led a safe and contented existence. The better news was that she was now earning enough to send them money to buy food and pay their utility bills. Her parents had been struggling more than ever to get by on their own. Barry Steenkamp was no longer training horses and was making what money he could chopping wood in the bush, heaping the cuttings into little piles and selling them by the roadside to passers-by for lighting fires at barbecues. Her mother, June, baked cakes and made sandwiches which she sold to punters at a sparsely attended racecourse outside Port Elizabeth. (In one of their daughter's last communications with her parents she told them she had made a money transfer equivalent to US$100 so that they could watch the pay TV channel on which *Tropika Island of Treasure* would be broadcast.)

But Reeva was still not making a lot of money. In the months preceding her death, she had been living not in her own apartment but in a room at the home of the parents of her best friend, a make-up artist called Gina Myers, in an unfashionable neighborhood of Johannesburg. But she was starting to aim higher. Her role model, she told her agent, was Cameron Diaz, the Hollywood actress with a reputation for beauty, intelligence and mischievous wit. She started to move in more affluent circles, encouraging her to develop a taste for luxury cars and celebrity men. Rumors abounded of an affair with Francois Hougaard, a well-known professional rugby player with dashing good looks. Her postings on Twitter in the second half of 2012 suggested a flirtation with him.

But then she met the most famous young South African of them all, the rich and debonair Oscar Pistorius, and new vistas opened up. Feted as the country's golden couple, photographs of Pistorius and Reeva appeared all over the newspapers and magazines. Public exposure was what she had wanted and now it was what she had, beyond all previous expectations, to the point that she struggled with being in the public eye. She was continually the subject of unwanted attention, which placed more stress on her than on Pistorius, who had long grown used to it. But it was a price she was willing to pay. He loved her and, as those photographs he cherished of the two of them together seemed to confirm, she loved him.

That thought offered Pistorius as much comfort as it did distress during the memorial he organized for her in the garden of his uncle's home. Weeping most of the time, he was fulfilling what he felt to be his religious obligation, while carrying out his own attempt at catharsis. But while the memorial was a private affair, the public were alerted to the fact that it had taken place by a statement issued from a 'reputation management' firm working on Pistorius's behalf.

Cynics, of whom there were many in South Africa, jumped on this, arguing that his chief purpose had been to convey to the world at large the message that he had loved Reeva and that he could not possibly have killed her deliberately, as the police claimed. Shashi Naidoo, a friend of Reeva's who attended the Steenkamp family funeral in Port Elizabeth, said, 'I think this is a sad attempt to alter public perceptions.' Columnists in the South African newspapers made much the same point.

Pistorius tried to shield himself from what people were saying. Trawling social media on his smartphone and roaming the internet on his laptop had been entrenched habits before the shooting. Not any more. Yet it was impossible for him to shut himself off entirely from the noise he was generating online. All it took was an unguarded remark by a visitor to his uncle's home, or a snippet of overheard conversation, to offer him a glimpse of the outer circle to his private hell, where voices shrieked that he was a liar who should rot in jail.

Many members of the public that had once adored him now regarded him with contempt – precisely the outcome he and his mother had striven so hard to avoid

ever since he first became conscious that he was different from other people. Here, at his uncle Arnold's,
he had found a hiding place from the world's prying
eyes, but the truth from which he could not fully avert
his gaze was that many in South Africa and beyond
refused to believe his version of what had happened
that night – they saw him, in a country rife with criminal violence, as one murderer more.

A honed alertness to how people viewed him had come
with his physical condition, but his vigilance had been
sharpened by celebrity. Living his life in a mirror, ever
attentive to the impression he made on others, he had
cultivated a humble, understated persona in the years
of triumph before he shot Reeva. Guided by professionals at Nike and other sponsors who fed off his success
and had a vested interest in preventing him muffing his
lines, he had learned to keep to a tight script. But that
script had changed now. Before, he had grown accustomed to headlines like 'Big-Hearted Blade Runner
Wins Another Gold'. Now it was 'Famous Athlete Kills
Woman He Loved'. Before, he had been able to shape
how the public viewed him; now that was out of his
hands. He was center-stage, the lights of the world still
blazing upon him, in a classically beguiling drama no
TV reality show could compete with, and bereft of all
possibility of shielding his despair from the world.

But Pistorius had once before had a glimmer of the pillorying he was facing now. It had happened in London, when he was at the peak of his fame, five and a half months before the shooting.

His crime back then, a trifle now, had been to respond rather inelegantly to defeat by a Brazilian runner called Alan Oliveira in the 200 meters final at the Paralympic Games. It was as if he had forgotten for a moment how hard he had worked to portray himself as a measured, even-tempered champion – as if he had omitted to register that he was live on TV, not unloading his rage to sympathetic friends in the locker room. He regretted it at the time and he regretted it still more now, for it was ammunition his detractors were using to back the argument that he had been a fraud all along. 'Oscar Is Not Such A Saint' a headline at the time had read.

He knew he should have kept his mouth shut and congratulated the winner, but he never ceased to believe that his fury had been entirely justified. The runner who had beaten him to the line was a double amputee like himself, but it was true, he was convinced of it, that he had worn artificially long prosthetic blades, providing him with an artificially long stride. Nevertheless, he should have known, clever as he had become in the art of managing his brand, that telling the truth was not always a good idea. 'We're not running a fair race here,' he had told the TV interviewer. 'The guy's legs are unbelievably long.' On he had railed, noting that the last time he had seen Oliveira, a year earlier, he had looked a head shorter. 'Absolutely ridiculous!' he had cried, and stomped off.

Casting his mind back to that time, it had been dismaying to learn later that when the TV had cut back to the studio, the panellists had not known how to react. They appeared not just shocked but embarrassed, in part at the ugliness of the outburst, but also because they, along with every other commentator, had always portrayed Pistorius the way he had portrayed himself, as not just 'the fastest man with no legs', but the nicest. Along with the no less bewildered millions watching on TV, the studio panellists had needed a few seconds to adjust to the evidence that Pistorius the hero had mortal flaws, that the portrait he had painted of himself as a softly spoken, wholesome young man did not correspond as fully as they had wanted to believe to Pistorius the flesh and blood man.

That lapse need not have left any lasting damage. He made amends. The following day, when his temper had eased, he apologized. He won the next race and when he spoke this time it was with his usual practiced grace. The sheen had faded for a day or two, but all was quickly forgotten. He remained the golden boy and when he flew back to Johannesburg adoring mobs were waiting for him at the airport, the episode with the Brazilian forgotten.

But when the news broke of what had happened on the morning of Valentine's Day, the very same fans, in South Africa and beyond, recalled the episode in the rush to try and find a connection between the icon they thought they knew and the gunman who had shot the woman he said he loved.

They needed to make sense of what had happened and the first thing they clutched at was that outburst in London. Did that seemingly out-of-character rant in London reveal a dimension of his personality previously hidden from the world? Could the otherwise mild and gracious Pistorius really have done such a thing? Had he been seething with anger at his limbless condition all along? Who was the real Oscar Pistorius?

In the haste to pass judgment and to adjust to this new horror, that widely remembered outburst of egocentric rage was the one possible clue on offer.

Then, after the police had issued their version of what had happened, and he his, at the bail hearing, the public debate that would continue right up to the murder trial, and beyond, began. The details of his version had been set out in his affidavit in court but the substance of it had been leaked to the press on the very morning of the  shooting.

There could be no dispute as to what had happened materially. The facts were that he had fired the bullets, that he and Reeva had been alone in the house, and that there had been no sign of forced entry. Making his case would be a tough sell in court and it was a tough sell to the public at large. He had his supporters, in all corners of the globe, but the prevailing response to his story was one of scepticism. Who but a madman could imagine that a burglar would choose to lock himself inside a toilet? If Pistorius were not mad, which apparently he was not, he had to be lying, so went the argument.

What became crushingly apparent to Pistorius as he followed the reactions on the internet was that people's shock and horror gave way very soon to a macabre form of gloating. Heartbreakingly for him, the impulse to kick the carcass of the fallen hero was most belligerent in the country in which he was born.

Within twenty-four hours of the shooting advertisers had removed from South African streets the numerous billboards with his picture on them promoting Nike and other big brands. 'A bullet in the chamber' had been the unfortunate caption under the ad used by Nike, who raced to suspend their worldwide contract with him. More compelling evidence

of how far he had sunk in the estimation of his compatriots was the statistical information provided by a
Cape Town company hired to analyze popular perceptions of South Africa for the national tourism board.
By tracking millions of Twitter messages it found that
a week after the shooting opinion in the world at large
was fairly evenly divided, but in South Africa a clear
majority was against him, refusing to believe Reeva's
death had been a mistake.

His family blamed the press. Like Pistorius and his
lawyers, they wondered why they kept using the hurtful, loaded word 'killing' all the time? Why not call
what happened a 'tragedy', a word on which everyone
could agree? The answer lay, he and the rest of the
Pistorius clan believed, in a calculated cynicism.

Pistorius knew about media manipulation; he had
been successfully manipulating them for years. He
knew that in order to build market share many media
bosses believed they had to give the public what they
wanted. As attuned to the public mood as the advertisers who paid their bills, that was what – often by an
unconscious process – they did, and in this case they
needed little time to deduce that their task was to reinforce the anti-Pistorius consensus. Just as before they
had always striven to feed the public's desire to see him
as a hero, now they set about digging up evidence to

support a refashioned and equally unreal understanding of him not as saint, but as demon.

The picture the public wanted duly emerged. They learned from the media that far from the perfect, courtly gent he had always been assumed to be, Pistorius was in fact rude and bad-tempered; he had an unhinged edge to his character, swore violently and flew easily into a rage; he was a wild and promiscuous rabble-rouser, but at the same time perversely possessive of the women who fell into his clutches. Some reports, nourished by a police spokeswoman's statement that there had been 'previous incidents of a domestic nature at his place', even claimed he had left a trail of abusive relationships behind him.

The mother of one ex-girlfriend fueled this novel allegation when she posted a message saying how relieved she had been when her daughter broke up with him, for she had known him to be a reckless lunatic. Trish Taylor, the mother of a recent ex-girlfriend called Samantha Taylor, who would turn state witness against him in the trial, wrote on her Facebook page, 'I am so glad that Sammy is safe and sound and out of the clutches of that man – there were a few occasions where things could have gone wrong with her and his gun during the time they dated.'

The impulse of the news media to follow the public mood rather than fly in the face of it was revealed by their general failure to give anything like the same visibility to a string of messages posted by an earlier girlfriend by the name of Jenna Edkins. On February 15, the day after the shooting, she wrote on Twitter, first, 'I would just like to say I have dated Oscar on and off for 5 YEARS, NOT ONCE has he EVER lifted a finger to me, made me fear for my life.' Then, in response to a storm of hate-filled responses, she wrote, 'All I am saying is let him speak, let his side be heard without jumping to conclusions . . . Love and thoughts to Reeva's family.' After which she added, 'You all have my family's love and support #loveandsupportforoscar.' And finally, 'People must stop jumping on the bandwagon with such hurtful allegations. Os is the loving, amazing inspirational person we know him to be.'

But the bandwagon was rolling and in the general cacophony her messages barely received an airing either in the South African media or abroad. Of far greater interest was a *New York Times* magazine profile headlined 'The Fast Life Of Oscar Pistorius', to which few in South Africa had paid much attention when it was published a year earlier. Now it was being quoted everywhere. The piece, published in 2012, prior to the London Olympics and Paralympics, was balanced and largely complimentary. But selective reading provided useful ammunition for the new Pistorius-bashing battalions.

At the time, Pistorius thought he had done a good job of getting the *New York Times* journalist on his side; only in retrospect did he see that he had tried a little too hard, opened up a little too much. He had allowed the reporter into his life in a way that had now backfired on him. Pistorius had picked up the journalist in his car at Johannesburg airport and driven him to his home at speeds that might have landed him in jail in the United States; he had taken him along to watch him fire guns at a shooting range; he had confided in him about the difficulty he had falling asleep. Those snippets had now been cherry-picked by other newspapers and transformed into evidence that he was a maniacally fast driver and a half-crazed, irresponsible gun nut.

Yet he could not deny there was some truth to the charges. Speed was his thing, he was young, his friend the luxury car dealer Justin Divaris sometimes lent him some of the fastest cars on the market. Driving at night from a club or a restaurant in Johannesburg back home to Pretoria on a practically empty four-lane highway, or out on the straight, flat roads of the South African bush, the temptation was too great. He could not resist putting his foot right down and driving at 140, 150, 160 mph. And he did so without fear of paying any penalties. Fame had given him a sense of entitlement. Matthew Syed, a journalist for *The*

*Times* of London who competed for Great Britain at table tennis in two Olympic Games, spent three days with him in 2007. Syed wrote afterwards that Pistorius had been 'charming and likeable' but when they got into his car he seemed to become another person. 'He drove at double the speed limit while talking on his mobile phone, which surprised me even more,' Syed wrote. 'When I nervously asked why he wasn't worried about the police, he said: "They wouldn't want to touch me."'

As for guns, they were a passion – or rather, had been a passion. He never wanted to hold one in his hand again.

Before, guns had been ever-present in his life. His father loved guns; so did his uncles and his grandfather on the Pistorius side of the family. The Afrikaners had conquered the southern tip of Africa with guns. They were proud of that heritage, the Pistorius clan. It was part of who they were. They were not going to give up the tradition now that things had changed in their country and their people were not the bosses anymore. Besides, he had enjoyed guns. They were beautiful mechanical devices, nice to handle, thrilling to fire. When stressed or sleepless, both of which he was frequently, there was no more cleansing release than going to the shooting range to pump bullets with unerring accuracy into a distant target. One day in 2011 he had been so pleased with himself after a shoot at the range that he posted on Twitter, 'Had a 96% headshot over 300m from 50 shots! Bam!'

A more secret pleasure that he shared with some aficionados was shooting dumdum bullets at watermelons and watching them explode like the heads of the villains in PlayStation games, another pastime he enjoyed.

Pistorius winced at the recollection, but it was not, he felt, as if he had been a crazy, gun-toting loner, as the papers were seeking to portray him now. It was not crazy at all to go about armed in a country where the general perception was that crime was out of control. Like so many others, he saw a justification in carrying a gun with him every time he left his home.

Yet he never felt entirely safe. Among the details from the *New York Times* story that the South African press were omitting to mention was one that shed light on what would be his central contention when the trial began – namely, that he lived in a permanent state of anxiety at the prospect of coming under attack, especially at night. He had told the *New York Times* journalist that the security alarm had gone off in his house the night before he had met him and that he had responded in a panic, grabbing the gun by the side of his bed and tiptoeing fearfully down the stairs.

In another context, the reporter had signalled what a nice guy Pistorius was by noting how 'shockingly unperturbed' he had been in trying everyday situations, such as waiting far too long for a car to pick him up at the airport. His sense of entitlement had its limits: in similar circumstances, the New York Times reporter wrote, prima donna American athletes would have blown a fuse.

Retelling that kind of story was not high on the media agenda now. The chief imperative seemed to be to flesh out the image of Pistorius as a criminal monster, and much of the press in South Africa, where there are next to no prohibitions on what is published about impending court cases, delivered. A cascade of articles appeared under headlines such as 'Not Everyone Surprised By Oscar's Fall From Grace' and 'Fast Cars, Hot Temper, Guns: Finding The Real Oscar Pistorius'. Information spilled out about the pistols he owned, licenses he had applied for to acquire assault rifles and shotguns, more late-night runs to shooting ranges, complete with pictures, and the fascination generally of the male members of his family with lethal weaponry. After it emerged later that between them he, his father, two of his uncles and his grandfather owned fifty-five guns, a South African comedian joked on stage, not entirely in jest, that the Pistoriuses were an 'armed militia' and a menace to the state.

The gag seemed less funny when the news broke, six weeks after Valentine's Day, that Carl Pistorius had also been involved in a woman's death. It had happened five years earlier, but charges had been quickly dropped, citing insufficient evidence. The incident barely made the news at the time, but following his younger brother's arrest the state reopened the case. Carl appeared in court on March 27, 2013 in relation to an accident in which a car he was driving crashed into a motorcycle, killing the woman on it. The charge was culpable homicide, the state's accusation being that he had been driving negligently at the time of the collision. If found guilty he might have faced jail, but a magistrate ruled in Carl's favor, determining that there was no proof that he had either seen the victim's motorbike or could have avoided hitting it. Carl walked free.

But the damage had already been done, for the charges against Carl helped embellish negative perceptions of his famous brother, depicting him as belonging to a family genetically predisposed to trouble. To the stories about the guns and fast cars the South African press added some convincing allegations that he had a habit of partying with members of Johannesburg's criminal underworld, that he hobnobbed with night-club bouncers who sold their services as mafia enforc-ers. And so it went on. The image he had painstakingly constructed lay in ruins, replaced by that of a shame-lessly self-engrossed superstar who placed no limits, legal or otherwise, on the fast life he led.

The police, eager to join battle in the court of public opinion, dug up for the press an incident from Pistorius's past. In 2009 he had been arrested for assault and held overnight at the same Pretoria police station to which he would be first taken after shooting Reeva. The accu-sation was that he had slammed a door on a female guest called Casseby Taylor Memory at a twenty-first birthday party held at his home, injuring her leg. But it had also been reported that the woman, who was nine-teen, had been drunk, and that he had denied assaulting her and had been cleared of all charges. This, it turned out, was the basis on which a police spokeswoman had said on the morning of the shooting that he had a history of 'previous incidents' of domestic violence. No other charges of this kind were pressed against him, but while back in 2009, fresh from his triumphs at the previous year's Beijing Games, the public had been predisposed to take his denial of wrongdoing at face value, now they were inclined towards the sinister possibility that he had taken advantage of his celebrity to escape the rap.

But there was little point in denying that he had a hot-headed streak in him and that he was prone to behavior that might be considered understandable in an adolescent but was rash to the point of imbecility in a well-known individual who needed to be attentive to his public image. It was not in dispute that, a few weeks before shooting Reeva, he had been at a fashionable Johannesburg restaurant called Tasha's fiddling with a friend's Glock pistol that he was hiding under the table. It was lunchtime and the restaurant was packed. The gun went off and a bullet ricocheted off the floor, brushing a friend's leg. Realizing that someone could have been killed, but realizing too the damage to his reputation if the story got out, Pistorius was relieved when the friend who owned the gun offered to take the blame. As it happened, the restaurant owners, who would have been mortified to lose his custom, made light of the incident. But it would come back to haunt him when the prosecutor at the murder trial would cite it as yet another instance of his recklessness with guns.

Before, he reflected, people were prepared to believe the best of him; now they were primed to believe the worst. Those who wanted to believe he was guilty of murder were satisfied that they had found ample corroborating material. One, a well-known journalist, proposed that, far from being riven with regret, Pistorius's true state of mind was, 'Okay. Can we get this over with now, please? I'm Oscar Pistorius, the Blade Runner. Can we move on so I can get back to my running?' The journalist set about expounding her theory – namely, that fame had devoured him to such a degree that he believed himself to be above ordinary human rules; that he had licence to kill.

This, too, was the view of the state prosecutor, Gerrie Nel. Were the judge at his murder trial to share it, Pistorius would be found guilty of murder and go to jail. His response would be that, far from having behaved out of a sense of superior entitlement, he had acted, however recklessly and misguidedly, and how-ever bitterly he regretted it now, out of a fear of crime shared by all ordinary South Africans. His defense would be that he lived in a country where to be para-noid was not only normal, but reasonable.

# 8

*Men's judgements are a parcel of their fortunes.*

SHAKESPEARE, *ANTONY AND CLEOPATRA*

Pistorius discovered in the single-minded pursuit of athletic glory the security that eluded him in all other areas of life. He came to learn too through his world travels that the further away from scary, lawless South Africa he could be, the more peace he found. One such place, in whose cool crisp air he trained with revived vigor, was Iceland, a country on the same ocean as South Africa but, in all other respects, its polar opposite.

Where South Africa was sunlit, lush and endlessly varied in vegetation and fauna, animal and human, Iceland's treeless, monochrome landscape was home to three mammalian life forms: sheep, horses and humans – quite possibly the most ethnically homogeneous humans of any country on earth. In South Africa they had eleven official languages, all ever-shifting, subject to continual cross-pollination. In Iceland they had one language, little changed since the writing of the Norse sagas eight hundred years ago.

Iceland had had a representative parliament in place for a thousand years, South Africa for just twenty. South Africa's population was 50 million, Iceland's, 300,000. The gap between rich and poor in South Africa is among the widest in the world. In Iceland the best-off and the least well-off send their children to the same state-run schools and receive the same quality of public health care. Equality among the sexes is such that Iceland is reckoned by the United Nations to be the best country in the world in which to be a woman. In South Africa women and men live in fear of crime and anyone who can afford to live behind a high wall does so. In Iceland, where serious violence is almost unknown, few people bother to lock their houses or their cars. Forty-five people are murdered each day in South Africa; in Iceland the rate is less than one a year.

Possibly the one and only point of contact between Iceland and South Africa was Pistorius. He traveled to the capital, Reykjavik, four times during his athletic career. The manufacturers of his running blades were based there. Össur was the name of the company, the world leaders in prosthetic legs for athletes. They made the Cheetah blades used by the majority of medal-winning Paralympic runners. Össur sponsored Pistorius, supplied him with free blades and customized them to his exacting specifications.

Able-bodied runners have to take good care of their muscles and ligaments; disabled runners have to ensure the mechanics of their artifical extremities are kept finely tuned. When Pistorius ran he was half-man, half-machine. His Cheetahs were to him what the racing car was to a Formula One driver. Made of silicone, carbon-fibre and titanium, the running blades required as much attention to detail as the weight, suspension or wheel alignment of a Ferrari. This was what he worked on with the technical experts at the Reykjavik headquarters of Össur, a multinational enterprise with offices in the United States, Holland, Sweden and China, as well as a factory in Tijuana, Mexico.

The company was founded in 1971 by Össur Kristinsson, a man who, having been born with one leg, set about his work with a determination that went beyond the mere desire for profit. He dedicated most of his energy to resolving the problem, as old as Long John Silver, of how to minimize the friction at the point where the biological leg ended and the artificial one began. What made him happy and rich was hitting upon the idea of cushioning the tube into which the stump was fitted with silicone rolls. In 1999 the company bought out its chief competitors and went global.

One of the companies that Össur bought was Flex-Foot, a company started by an American called Van Phillips, the inventor of the Cheetah. Like Össur Kristinsson, Phillips's creativity was invigorated by a missing leg, amputated below the knee when he was twenty-one. The revolutionary feature of the J-shaped Flex-Foot Cheetah was that its graphite content provided something all previous prostheses lacked: it absorbed and released energy in a way that translated into a capacity to generate spring. A disabled person using them was able, for the first time, to run and jump.

The intention of Pistorius and other Paralympic athletes who traveled to Reykjavik was to improve their speed by achieving the maximum possible return thrust from each stride. He, the best of them all, was the most demanding of them all, as Össur's two top technicians attested.

Their names were Lárus Gunnsteinsson, the company's senior designer, and Christophe Lecomte, a Frenchman who was the head of research and development. 'I ended up exhausted at the end of each day with him,' Lecomte said. 'He made you think hard but also work hard physically, adjusting the screws constantly to get just the right millimetric alignment. But he worked harder still, testing every variant of the blades on the track or on the belt, although the treadmill was not fast enough for him at top speed. He never seemed to more than jog on it. If a screw came off while he was running or something else went wrong he just kept going, testing, running always flat out. Every millisecond mattered for him.'

Often he broke the blades. The Össur boffins had never encountered any other disabled runner who generated such speed or placed so much weight on the ground with each step. But no effort was too great for Össur when dealing with their star athlete and overnight they would build him new ones, resuming testing again the next morning.

Gunnsteinsson said time was never wasted when Pistorius was in town. Together with Lecomte, they would spend every minute of every working day for four or five days anatomizing the technical minutiae of the blades, exploring with limitless patience and persistence every variation that might give him the tiniest of advantages. 'He was so greedy to run faster, almost boring in his obsessive attention to detail,' Gunnsteinsson said. 'He had a huge hunger. More than any other athlete we've ever worked with. He was so focused: absolute tunnel vision. You could see this was everything to him. This was his life here.'

So much was it his life, so fully was he in the moment, that he seemed to be oblivious to the pain caused by the shearing motion of the blade sockets on the skin of his stumps, especially his left one. The wizardry of Gerry Versfeld, the doctor who amputated his legs when he was an infant, had turned out to have its limits. The most difficult procedure during the surgery had been to lock the heel pad horizontally onto the bottom of each stump so as to provide him with the natural cushion necessary to ease the pain of placing his weight on them. But as he had grown older, the heel pad under his left stump had gradually shifted sideways, returning back towards the vertical position it had been in when he was born. By this stage of his life he had practically no protection for the bone at the end of the stump, the consequence being that after a hard day's training the skin had often peeled away, exposing the thin layer of flesh.

'Our greatest challenge,' said Gunnsteinsson, 'is and always has been to find ways to absorb the shock of the impact of the blade on the track so as to try and minimize the pressure on the stumps. But with Pistorius there was only so much you could do. He ran so much and so hard that the sweat poured down his thigh to where the stump meets the prosthesis, which caused skin to chafe. You add to that the fact that he placed an enormous load on that point, seven to eight times his body weight because of the force he applies on the ground; then you factor in that the skin of the stump is not made to take that sort of impact and what it all meant was that at the end of a day's session his stumps were bleeding, swollen, red and sore. But then the next morning he'd start all over again, at the same rhythm and pace.'

Any ordinary able-bodied athlete suffering injuries on a similar scale would take a rest from training and competiton and wait for the body to heal. In order to try and minimize the consequences of training in an almost permanently injured state, Pistorius made a point of acquiring an unusually detailed understanding of the science of his legs and the mechanics of his running.

'Most athletes you deal with speak one language, you as the prosthetics engineer speak another and your job is to translate what they are saying,' Christophe Lecomte said. 'With Oscar it was different. He understood exactly what we were doing right from when he first came here in 2003. He had an aptitude for it. He got the hang of our language almost immediately.'

Trevor Brauckmann, the specialist who fitted Pistorius's very first wooden legs when he was fourteen months old, and would sometimes accompany him to Iceland, had another way of making the same point. 'With the majority of people I treat, communication is not much more sophisticated than between a veterinarian and a horse. With Oscar, it was as if a doctor were talking to a doctor.'

At the Össur headquarters they would carry out tests on him with electronic sensors, high-speed cameras and a device called an accelerometer, anatomizing the way he ran down to its smallest components. 'He was highly intelligent,' said Gunnsteinsson, 'the one athlete who really understood engineering theory. I think we learnt as much from him as he did from us.'

What Pistorius learnt, he wrote down. He was an obsessive note-taker, chronicling the details of his training sessions, of every race. He would explain why in an interview with the *Financial Times*: 'I suppose it's about control, but about an hour or half an hour after every race, I write down everything about it. What I was thinking, imagining and how I felt. I write down what the weather was like and how training went beforehand. I write down how I got there, including whether the train was late or the traffic was bad. I write down what I ate and how I was feeling and details of any injuries, how much rain there was that day. Every race is won or lost in the head, so you have to get the contents of your head right. Writing things down helps you to control your thoughts.'

Lecomte confessed to being somewhat in awe of Pistorius – because of his furious diligence, but also at 'a basic primitive level'. 'He exudes a physical sense of power, quite different from other people. When he had on his blades and wore his Lycra runner's uniform he was like a large, prowling cat. You felt you were in the presence of a kind of superman,' Lecomte said. And yet, as Gunnsteinsson remarked, it was easy to forget that when he went to bed at night he took off his artificial legs and was transformed into a less than heroic-looking creature, unable to perform basic tasks without difficulty. 'You need to pee in the middle of the night and what happens? You either put on your legs or do it in a bottle.'

The two Össur men suspected that he endured as much pain as he enjoyed adulation, but they said he never let them see any evidence of tension between his public and his private self. 'Other Paralympic athletes we have worked with we have found to be difficult people, angry or arrogant prima donnas, but Oscar, however much stress he was going through in testing, was always respectful, measured and thoughtful,' said

Gunnsteinsson. He and Lecomte were also impressed by the kindness he showed far less accomplished disabled athletes, going out of his way to encourage them and give them tips on how to improve their speeds.

Both he and Gunnsteinsson were prohibited by company rules, they said, to talk about 'the incident'. But what both did say was that they saw no connection between the man they knew and what happened that night at his home. They were flabbergasted. Just as Dr Gerry Versfeld, the man who had undertaken the first engineering work on his legs, had said, the man who fired that gun was not the man they knew.

There were two other people in Iceland who shared the Össur people's stupefaction at the news. Like them, they had known him personally. The same could not be said of most of those around the world who shared their belief in his innocence, or at any rate refused to believe he had intentionally killed Reeva.

He had not been completely abandoned by public opinion. Large numbers of his detractors were blindly convinced that he was guilty as charged of premeditated murder. But a rival camp, made up mostly of women, jumped earnestly to his defense, waging propaganda campaigns on his behalf on the internet and sending him letters declaring their unconditional loyalty. They were in no doubt that what had happened at his home on Valentine's Day was not a 'killing', as the press disgracefully insisted on calling it, much less a murder. It was a tragic accident.

They had no more knowledge of the facts than those who vilified him; the view each side chose to take was entirely a matter of faith, obeying an almost religious impulse to clothe the mysteries of life in reassuring certainty. Both camps were notable for their fervor, but those who supported Pistorius were better organized.

Within days of his arrest, previously unheard-of devotees popped up in Europe, North America and Asia, Borneo not excluded. They called themselves the 'Pistorians', and initially it was on Twitter that they made their presence felt, denouncing those who called him a criminal. 'Call me old-fashioned,' one wrote, 'but I'd rather my boyfriend didn't allow a perceived intruder to enter the house unchallenged.' Comments ranged from the reasonable, 'I support Oscar because I believe in innocent until proven guilty. I feel for the Steenkamps, losing a child. I don't attack people. I am a #pistorian and proud to be one!', to the shrill and accusative, 'She was a bikini model. "Sex sells"!!! I would be really upset if my daughter posed like that.'

Pro-Pistorius zeal reached such a pitch of anti-Reeva sentiment that a point came when the Pistorius family felt compelled publicly to put some distance between themselves and the more extremist devotees by issuing a statement. It read: 'The disregard shown by some – specifically those commenting via social media – for the profound pain that Reeva's family and friends are going through is very troubling.'

Overall, though, the Pistorius family were grateful for the solidarity the Pistorians showed and they agreed with their view that the press were out to get him. This led to a strange contradiction. The Pistorians' ostensible purpose was to get their message out far and wide, but they refused to talk to reporters. One particularly outspoken Tweeter who went under the alias @ LiliTyger, posted, 'Another "journo" sniffing around wanting to do a piece on us – does she really think we'll talk to her?' To which a sister Pistorian added, 'Every 2-bit freelancer wants to make name for themselves out of this story. Go & do your work and stop bugging people.'

From all this scattered noise various websites bloomed, the most visited of which was one titled 'Support for Oscar Pistorius', where bloggers posted mainly in English but also in Spanish, French, Italian, German and Afrikaans. Inspirational quotes popped up there daily, letters written as if to a loved one, poems too. A theological thread ran through many of the bloggers' epistles, with much mockery of the 'non-believers' and invocations made to 'the Lord', who was believed to be unambiguously on their idol's side. A typical extract read, 'Because what happened is ugly and their hearts are malevolent, they want to strip Oscar of his beauty too, attack him in the darkness while he is unable to defend himself. Another cruel irony, for Oscar has never been a man to curse the darkness.Oscar has always had a wider vision than most of us. He has taught us tolerance and acceptance.' Pistorius, exemplar and teacher, belonged to the world of light; his enemies, to the infernal shadows.

Mira, a German woman who put up the 'Support for Oscar' website and selected its content, underlined the chief article of Pistorian faith. 'We, the owners of this blog,' it read, 'are a group of loyal supporters . . . We have not met Oscar, and it is unlikely that we ever will . . . We do this because we respect and believe in him wholeheartedly.'

The Pistorians did more than believe his version of events. They believed *in* him, despite – or perhaps because of – the fact that the vast majority had never spent any time with him and could not vouch for him as a flesh and blood person. Except, that is, for the two women from Iceland. In December 2013 they sent him a message on the 'Support for Oscar' website. Alongside a picture of a little girl and a little boy, the message read, 'Our dearest Oscar, merry, lovely Christmas to you and your loved ones. Much love.'

Ebba Guðmundsdóttir was the two children's mother; Sigga Hanna Jóhannesdóttir, Ebba's mother. Ebba Guðmundsdóttir stood out in a country where women tended to be tall, blonde and blue-eyed. In physical terms, she might have fitted in better in multi-racial South Africa. Her hair was dark brown, her eyes were green, her skin olive-colored, suggesting that there might have been some rare dilution of the Viking Icelandic line somewhere in her family's past. A writer of books and presenter of TV programs on cooking healthily for children, she brimmed with cheerful energy.

Early in 2005, Ebba, then in her late twenties, became pregnant for the second time. Her first child had been a girl and this one, an early scan revealed, would be a boy. Her husband, Hafthor Haflidason, was thrilled. He was a soccer fanatic who made a living as a players' agent working with the big European leagues. The prospect of having a little boy to kick a ball around with him filled him with delight. He and Ebba could not have been happier. Twenty weeks into the pregnancy, she went to the hospital for another scan.

Sitting eight years later in a café in Reykjavik, a capital with the air of a small fishing town, with little houses whose bright colors stood in contrast to the grey vastness of the North Atlantic, she recalled, in perfect English, what happened next.

'The radiologist who did the scan suddenly turned pale,' Ebba said. 'She looked and looked again at the blurred black and white photograph but struggled to make out the shape of the legs, which she said were in a very strange position. She left the room for a second opinion, looking really worried. I began to cry. When she returned she was almost hysterical. She said parts of the legs seemed to be missing.'

It turned out that neither the radiologist nor the doctor she had stepped out to consult had ever come across anything like this before, not even in medical textbooks.

'I could only conclude from what she told me that I was carrying a severely disabled child,' Ebba said. 'Despair is not the word. It is not strong enough.' She began to imagine that maybe there was worse news to come, that perhaps the child would be born with mental problems. 'I went to bed that night sure that my son would be so disabled he would not have a life. I remember thinking I hoped I'd miscarry, that something would happen so my child would just die.'

The next morning she and her husband met with a group of doctors who had been studying the sonogram photo and trawling for information outside Iceland about what condition they might reveal. The problem remained grave, the doctors said, but not as dire as they had initially feared. Everything was as it should be except for one thing. The fibulas were missing from both the foetus' legs. Their child would be born with a condition never encountered before in Iceland: fibular hemimelia.

'We returned home and felt a little better,' said Ebba. 'Not good, obviously, but my darkest thoughts had gone. I no longer wanted to have a miscarriage.' Her husband sat down at his computer and searched the internet to try and find out what the implications of fibular hemimelia would be for their son. Suddenly something caught his eye. He called his wife to come quickly and take a look. It was a photograph of someone they had never heard of who had been born with exactly the same condition as their unborn child. His name was Oscar Pistorius.

'The photograph filled the computer screen,' Ebba said, her face lighting up as she relived the moment. 'It was the most wonderful thing! Oscar was crossing the finishing line, breaking the tape, winning the gold at the 200 meters Paralympic race in Athens. Seeing that picture changed everything! It captured a moment of triumph for him and for us it was the moment we moved not just from despair to hope, but to knowing our son would be just fine. I felt the purest relief and joy. My son would not just be able to walk, he would be able to run!'

The boy, who would be named Haflidi, had a role model even before he was born, his mother having decided there and then that there was more to the youth who appeared on the screen than a miraculous ability to run very fast. 'He was beautiful, smiling and we could see in the picture he was a kind young man, and my husband sent my mum the link and I have loved Oscar ever since and our whole family has too. We became his number one fans, following every race he ran, learning all we could about his life.'

Ebba found her own role model in Pistorius's dead mother. She saw Sheila Pistorius as a pioneer and guide who had marked out the path she herself should follow. Like Sheila, Ebba would never feel sorry for herself or her son; she would always regard him as being capable of anything a child with legs could do.

'I often wanted her to be alive for me during that first year after Haflidi was born because there is no manual for raising a boy like him,' Ebba said. 'It must have been so difficult for her. She had no one to turn to. She lacked completely the example she became for me.' Ebba understood better than anyone could have done how difficult it would have been for Sheila Pistorius to decide on the best medical response to her son's condition during his first year of life. 'There was no internet to find information and she had to go from doctor to doctor, hearing all kinds of different advice. There was even one doctor who told them they should amputate above the knees! They play God, some of these doctors, and it is hard for normal people to know when they are just talking nonsense. Oscar's mother had to have been so strong and so brave to make that decision. In Iceland they certainly had no clue what to do. I saw the result of that one day when I saw a boy who was fourteen and had also been born with a problem in his feet. He had not been amputated and he was clearly handicapped, in a wheelchair. But I had the example of Oscar in front of me and that made it so much easier for me than for his mother. It decided the question for me completely.'

One thing was making the rational choice to amputate; another was dealing with it emotionally. As Haflidi approached the age of eleven months, the point at which – following the Pistorius precedent – the surgery would be carried out, she tried to keep outwardly calm, but inside she was in a state of creeping terror, unable to avoid picturing the moment when her baby would be strapped down unconscious on an operating table with a surgeon sawing off his feet.

And then she discovered that, weeks before the operation was due, Pistorius himself was coming to Iceland.

Ebba wrote him an e-mail introducing herself and telling him about Haflidi. He wrote back swiftly. 'Hi,' he said, 'how can I help you?' He could help, she replied, by coming round to her home for dinner. He said he would be happy to do so.

When he arrived in Reykjavik Ebba's husband went to issue the invitation personally at an indoor sports facility where he was testing his new Cheetahs. Hafthor was ready to be amazed. Since winning Paralympic gold at Athens the young man who had already changed his life had been competing ever more seriously in able-bodied races. Just a few months before he had come sixth in the national South African 400 meters race. But nothing had prepared Hafthor for the spectacle that greeted him. Pistorius and Trevor Brauckmann were kicking a football back and forth. Pistorius was wearing his usual walking prostheses, their metal cores covered in flesh-colored plastic, moulded in the shape of real human legs, complete with 'feet' over which he wore normal trainers. What made Hafthor's jaw drop was that Pistorius was not simply nudging the ball along the ground towards his companion, as he might have done with a hockey stick, but performing tricks.

He would hold the ball on the ground between his two lifeless feet and, with a little backward jump, hoist it in the air behind him and over his head. It was the kind of thing Hafthor would watch his professional players do in training, but he had never imagined that a man born with the same condition as his son might be capable of the same thing.

When Pistorius walked into the house for dinner that evening Ebba said it felt as if she were meeting a rock star. It was the very term Reeva Steenkamp would use to describe him, and the qualities Ebba saw in him that day were also the gentler ones that would persuade Reeva to invest her love in him seven years later.

'He was only nineteen then,' Ebba said, 'but he had a big, confident personality. He laughed a lot but he was also extraordinarily polite, with no pretensions. He held Haflidi in his arms, he played with our daughter Hannah. You could see he was one of those adults who is natural with children. I asked him if he would mind taking off his legs. He didn't. He just took them off with no self-consciousness and let me stare at them. I was fascinated and so happy.'

Pistorius might have suffered a jolt on seeing in the Icelandic baby a vision of himself that he had never beheld before. That was him before the amputation, with the mangled feet and misshapen ankles. But if it was a shock, he gave nothing away. He looked so at ease with his new friends, and held the little child with such manifest delight, that Ebba's infatuation with him only grew. She hung on his words as if they were the Sermon on the Mount. Especially when he talked about his mother, whom he described as his life's guiding light and to whom he said he offered up a prayer before every race he ran. He told them she had made no concessions to his condition, treated him no differently from his older brother or his younger sister, and how grateful he would always be to her for that. He recounted his favorite story about her telling his brother to put on his shoes and him to put on his legs; he spoke about the letter in which she said that the real loser was the one who did not compete. And he shared with them his favorite aphorism, 'You are not disabled by the disabilities you have; you are able by the abilities you have.' He rejected the term 'disabled', he said; he preferred what he saw as the more accurate 'differently abled'.

This was manna from heaven for Ebba. Years later, in that cafe in Reykjavik, she recalled the encounter with rapture. 'The compassion he showed! The empathy! The kindness! Everything I had seen in that first photograph was confirmed, and so much more. In the flesh he exceeded my expectations. And he also drew from me something I did not expect: learning that he had no mum, I felt a strong impulse to mother him myself.'

That dinner, Ebba said, was a defining moment in her life. 'It taught me the very important lesson that I should not be overprotective with my son and, most of all, sealed my peace with Haflidi's condition,' she said. And it gave her a mission: to be for her son what Pistorius's mother had been for him. While not religious in the same intense way that Sheila Pistorius had been, Ebba sounded as if she were channeling Sheila when she said, 'I think there is a purpose for Haflidi in not having legs. We don't want him to have legs! I know that sounds a bit crazy but I want him the way he was supposed to be. Oscar told us that if he had a choice between legs and a Ferrari he'd choose a Ferrari! He has had lots of opportunities on account of having no legs. My son the same, even if he is not yet eight years old. He may not have legs but he has a big heart. You lose something but get something else instead. You can't have it all. If something is missing, you compensate, and people love him so much and are so kind to him.'

Including Pistorius himself, who visited Iceland again in the summer of 2007 and went to dinner with the family again, where he sat with Haflidi, now nearly two, on his lap and spoon-fed him, then posed for photographs with him, the two of them with their prostheses off, the famous athlete happy to play big brother to the kid with the same thin stumps as himself. Haflidi knew he was different from other people, but he was a confident, cheerful little boy, mature for his age, who would stand up before his class at school and give talks explaining his condition. Yet, Ebba said, he also grew up not considering himself disabled. Nor did she consider him so. 'We would tell people, "No, our son is not crippled, no need to be sorry or sad. He will be like Oscar Pistorius – beautiful, brave, perfect." I believe my son will do whatever he likes in life and I owe that belief to Oscar. He showed me that not having legs is no big deal, that if people with no legs can run then they can do anything.'

Haflidi himself showed no interest in athletic competition and always came cheerfully last in school races. But Ebba loved watching Pistorius run. She did so on TV or on the internet whenever she could, and she went to watch him live at the track. In May 2009 she, her husband, their two children and her mother, Sigga Hanna, traveled to Manchester to see him compete in the Paralympic World Cup. Before watching Pistorius race they spent a day touring the neighboring city of Liverpool with him. Anyone who did not know them would have imagined they were all part of the same family. Pistorius walked hand in hand with Haflidi and, all politeness, insisted on carrying Sigga Hanna's backpack. The next day at the running stadium he had another gesture for his Icelandic friends. After winning gold on the track he clambered into the stands where the public sat, sought out Haflidi and hung his medal around the boy's neck. At dinner, Pistorius and Sigga Hanna fought good-humoredly over who should pay and when they stepped out of the restaurant Sigga Hanna declared, only half jokingly, that she would like to adopt him.

Haflidi seemed to have understood the point that if Pistorius was like him and Pistorius could be anything he wanted to be, then so could he. But while Pistorius was special for Haflidi, it was his mother and grandmother who needed him most. The ever-deepening relationship with the South African hero proved of more immediate benefit for the two adults than for the child. He was their crutch more than Haflidi's. 'I sometimes think,' Ebba confessed, 'that Oscar helped me more than he did Haflidi. Oscar gave me moral strength and he and his mother were my guides.'

Ebba's mother, Sigga Hanna, put it more bluntly. At the end of a long dinner at her home in Reykjavik she confided just how important Pistorius had been in her life. 'You have to understand,' she said, 'Oscar is what has saved me from insanity.' What did she mean? 'I mean that when I heard the news after my daughter had that scan I felt despair rise up. Oscar saved me from that.'

Needy of his strength, Ebba and Hafthor decided to relocate their family to South Africa for six months. 'We would never have thought of going there had it not been for Oscar. We wanted to absorb his world,' Ebba said. 'He was very patriotic, always speaking of how beautiful his country was, how much he loved it, how he adored Mandela, whom he said he was so proud to have met once.' When she told him they planned to go to South Africa, his delight was tempered by his knowledge of the dark side of South Africa, of which he rarely spoke to foreigners. He feared that if they came they might fall victim to crime. Seeing that it was entirely due to him that they wanted to spend time in his country, he was alarmed by the responsibility these Icelandic innocents had thrust upon him. They should not base themselves in one of the big cities, he told them, and most certainly not in Johannesburg, where he was raised, or Pretoria, where he now lived. He proposed they choose Stellenbosch, a gentle university town in the Cape winelands, 900 miles south of Johannesburg. That should be safe for the kids, he told them. Ebba and Hafthor did as they were instructed, spending a happy time in Stellenbosch with their two children from October 2010 to April 2011, cementing their bond with Pistorius by experiencing life, albeit a somewhat sheltered version of it, in his home country. Just before Christmas, Ebba and Sigga Hanna, impatient to be with their hero, flew north to see him.

'It was lovely. We ate with Oscar and his lovely girl-friend Jenna at his home in Pretoria,' Ebba said. At which point her voice abruptly trailed off.

'It was the home where the accident happened . . .'

The vivaciousness drained from her eyes and her look darkened as she recalled the moment when she first heard the news.

'It was an e-mail on my phone. I let out a cry and sank to the floor with the phone still in my hand, reading and re-reading the message until the horrible truth of it sank in. I was on my knees sobbing – screaming, I guess – as I repeated over and over and over the same question, "What kind of a destiny is this? . . . What kind of a destiny is this? . . ."'

She sensed she was having a nervous breakdown. 'My body just gave in. My nose was blocked. I suddenly had a high fever. And I cried and cried all day long.'

Not for Reeva Steenkamp, whom she had not known, but for her friend. Pistorius's own mother had been spared the horror of this moment, but Ebba, who in her mind had fused Pistorius with Haflidi, made the anguish Sheila would have felt her own. 'I cried because I was able to put myself inside his skin. I could feel what he was going through, I could feel that he was dying, a slow-motion death that would go on every day, day after day after day, for the rest of his life.'

The drowning sensation she had felt at the moment she learned of her son's deformity returned. This time it was not the photograph of Pistorius but the ghost of his mother who came to the rescue. How would she have responded? By the end of the day Ebba had found her answer. It was not the random chaos of the universe, it was not a blind and brutal destiny that was to blame. Sheila Pistorius had never surrendered to so helpless a thought. No, the mysterious ways of Providence were at work once again.

'He is very strong and something very good will emerge,' said Ebba. 'He is extreme, a man who lives on the extremes, and he will do something extremely good. He will do something special, though he is completely broken now. He destroyed two lives, not one. But some good will come of this. It will require more courage and determination than he has shown ever before as an athlete. He will need a lot of courage to forgive himself and to try to have a good life in spite of it. But I think maybe in a strange way it was supposed to be. Things happen for a reason.'

Haflidi came back from school on the afternoon of February 14, 2013 and found his mother crying. 'I told him he must not be angry with Oscar. He had killed his girlfriend by accident, he thought it was an intruder.' To which Haflidi responded, 'It was an accident, so I can't be angry with him, can I?' Ebba, still crying, wrapped her son in her arms.

There could have been no other explanation possible for Ebba; there could have been no other explanation possible for Haflidi. Some people, millions of them around the world, chose to believe he had deliberately killed Reeva Steenkamp; others chose to believe it had been a terrible mistake. For Ebba and for her mother it was never a matter of choice. Over the course of eight years, from four months before Haflidi emerged from Ebba's womb, they had invested their faith and hope in him. The two Icelandic women needed to believe he was telling the truth about what happened that night. To suspect he might be lying was not an option.

# 9

*Nor is the goddess unknown to me who*
*mixes a sweet bitterness with my love.*
CATULLUS, *POEM 68*

Everything could have turned out so differently for
Pistorius. What if he had not broken his wooden
legs on that particular day when he was fourteen? What
if his grandmother Gerti had phoned the number of
another prosthetics specialist? What if Francois van
der Watt had not happened to be there at that precise
moment to pick up the call or, even, had obeyed his
father's wishes and stuck to farming? What if those two
big players in the rival school team had tackled him less
hard instead of injuring him so badly that he was forced
to abandon rugby for running? His athletic triumphs

and his fame, the money he had made and the beautiful women he had met all had their orgins in a succession of haphazard connections. As had the catastrophe
that would define the rest of his days. He had battled
so hard to shape his destiny and had risen so high – yet
here he was, awaiting trial for murder.

His life's great, most implausible piece of luck had
been to find his métier in running. In other sports
he had played, especially team sports like rugby, he
had depended on others. He was one more cog in
the machine. Here, reliant only on himself, he could
impose a measure of control that was unavailable to
him in any other area of life. Running, the purest form
of athletic competition, eliminated almost entirely the
random elements of fate that had caused so much disruption and unhappiness in his life, from the condition
he was born with, to his parent's divorce, to his mother's death. If he trained right and ate right, he would
improve his times; the harder he pushed himself, the
readier he was to overcome physical pain, the greater
his success would be.

Initially, running had been an escape from his sorrow
at his mother's death; in time it proved an escape from
the turmoil to which he succumbed when he fell in love.
On the track he could empty his head of everything
save the single-minded task of improving his speed or

winning a race. Off the track he fell under the spell again, no longer self-reliant and alone. Someone else entered the equation, a person with her own distinct temperament and history, whom he tried to wrestle into his image of female perfection in the same way he sought to transform his impaired body into a perfect running machine. Rarely less than enraptured, his ceaseless pursuit of the one woman who would make him complete was as consuming as his hunger for sporting triumph.

He bet all on romantic love and disappointment was his reward. One woman left – Nandi, Jenna, Vicki – and another took her place, but the pattern repeated itself time after time. From petulant possessiveness to frantic dependency, to hysterical fear of loss. No one could ever quite measure up. He had moments of light when he saw that he was driving himself – and them – mad, but he could not help himself. Jealousy ate him up and he saw rivals everywhere.

He floundered as other men did, only more so. The love stories of the human race were awash with variations on the same banal themes; but he was a man of extremes who had no legs, which gave a uniquely corrosive character to his insecurities about love and sex. Far more than he let on, he felt embarrassed when people saw him without his prostheses on; when it came to revealing his naked stumps to a girlfriend for the first time he battled to mask his anxiety. With his artificial legs on he was a six-foot athletic Adonis, described in magazines as 'South Africa's sexiest man'; take them off and the transformation was drastic. He was not tall, he was dwarfish; he was not fast, he was slow; he was not brave, he was scared; he was not strong, he was weak, his balance so precarious a child could knock him over. The Blade Runner and the private Oscar Pistorius were in perpetual conflict. Laying himself bare before an attractive young woman made him lacerating aware of the strange and vulnerable figure he cut in the contrast between his powerful upper body and the thin, often blistered stumps where the lower half of his body ended. When a new girlfriend first set eyes on the strange disabled figure he cut, the fear of rejection – possibly of hurt or ridicule – consumed him.

But even if that obstacle were successfully negotiated, there remained another doubt. What if she was with him only for his fame and money?

Whether a relationship was long or short changed nothing. When he was twenty-four he had what another man his age might have regarded as a fling with an older woman, divorced with two children. But that was a high-stakes drama, and proved too much for her. She left him and, inconsolable, he turned to an older male friend for advice. The friend, who knew the woman, told him to forget it. There was no going back. He had been too suffocatingly demanding for her. The answer to his troubles lay not with the women he fell in love with, his friend scolded him, but with himself. He was too young to be enduring so much unnecessary anguish. He should aim for the sky in his running, not in love. Not yet. Love will come, the friend told him, but meanwhile focus on your running, have fun with girls but don't fall for them madly every time. Don't be such a crazy romantic.

But he paid no heed and he kept swinging, in one relationship after another, from wedding-bell bliss to operatic despair.

His friend spoke sense, but lacked the courage to tell him what he really thought. It was banal, he figured, it was crassly obvious amateur psychology, but no less true for that. He was falling in love each time with women whom he saw as a reincarnation of his mother. His frustrations came from their failure to match up to the saintly maternal ideal, his jealousies and possessiveness from the panic that they would abandon him, obliging him to endure again the grief of his life's most irreparable loss.

The last woman on whom Pistorius projected his dreams before meeting Reeva was a sweet and innocent girl called Samantha Taylor, whom he met through Facebook – which her mother Trish would use to attack him after he shot Reeva. They found they shared the same birthday, November 22. He was twenty-five and Samantha was seventeen. On and off, the relationship lasted eighteen months.

It was only after meeting Reeva, after Reeva's death, as the murder trial loomed, that he realized how misguided he had been in falling for Samantha. Not just because she had not been in Reeva's class, but because of what he learned from his lawyers in August 2013, six months before the trial began. They showed him the list of 107 state witnesses who would be testifying against him and Samantha's name was on it. The woman with whom he had once thought he would be spending the rest of his days, as he thought he would later with Reeva, was now assisting the police and prosecution, who sought to see to it that he spent many of the rest of his days in jail.

It was perplexing for him to recall that at the end of September 2012, barely more than a month before meeting Reeva, he had gone on a trip with Samantha to the Seychelles – a free trip sponsored by an airline and a hotel chain – where, under palm trees at the edge of the Indian Ocean, they had declared their feelings for each other – in public, before a TV camera, for a

South African show called *Top Billing* about the lives of the rich and famous. As he gazed into her eyes, she told the interviewer how much 'fun' Pistorius was; how she couldn't keep up with him, he was so full of energy. She gazed into his eyes as he replied, 'Sam's special', 'She's very caring', 'She understands me'. Drinking in each other's amorous burblings, he blushed, she blushed, the interviewer told them they were blushing, and then they blushed some more.

But behind the image of love's young dream that the couple presented for the cameras there had been all kinds of trouble. In the early days it was because he had a divided heart, fearful of letting go his previous passion, Jenna Edkins, afraid of wholeheartedly committing to his new one, Samantha. On discovering he was still seeing Jenna, she sent him a text message threatening to end it all. His reply, also from his phone, was thick with regret. He confessed that he had been 'playing' with her emotions, that he had been 'a coward and lonely' and, yes, he had gone running back to Jenna. But she deserved better, he hated himself, he knew that she, 'Sam', was the only one for him. He swore that he would spend the rest of his days making it up to her, if only she would give him a second chance. Which she did. Whereupon he dropped Jenna and for a while he and Samantha were at peace. 'You're the love of my life', he wrote to her. 'You all I dream of. You all I want. You all I need.' He called her his 'little butterfly'.

What Samantha Taylor found as the relationship unfolded was that Pistorius was like the little girl in the nursery rhyme: when he was good, he was very, very good but when he was bad, he was horrid. He could be kind and gentle, and, as so many people on first meeting him would remark, courtesy itself. But, according to her, he would suddenly snap, becoming enraged with Samantha or with her friends, shouting foul abuse in a manner shockingly disproportionate to the cause. She found that the tiniest things would set him off. If he asked her to take a mug from the sitting room to the kitchen or to make him a cup of coffee and she forgot, or if she wore clothes that he found too provocative when they went out, he would fly into a furious temper. It was about controlling his environment and about controlling her. She claimed that his jealousy was such that when they were apart he would ask her not only to tell him what she was doing and where she was but he sought proof; he asked her to send him photographs of herself to his phone so he could confirm that she was not lying. She – convinced that despite it all she was in love with him, fixing her heart on the enchanting side of his two extremes of personality – would do as she was asked. But sometimes she did emerge from the fog of infatuation and wonder what she was doing with him. When he was not in training, Taylor claimed that he would drink too much and he would wave his gun around, causing her to fear he would fire a shot by accident. She felt not physically intimidated but emotionally abused. Advised by her mother and her older sister, Carrie Leigh, who both got to know him well and regarded him with a mixture of fondness and alarm, Samantha would put some distance between her and Pistorius. Whereupon he would call the mother or the sister and, crying on the phone, beg them to intercede with 'Sam' on his behalf. Then the couple would be reconciled again and he would whisper sweet nothings and be gently attentive and Samantha, as she would reassure her family, felt happy and in love once more.

Then they would have another row and he would come back the next day back full of apologies and self-loathing – 'I'm sorry for being a fuck-up', read a typical text message – and more pleas for forgiveness. 'I want to look you in your eyes and tell you I love you so you can see I mean it,' he wrote. Then they would be back together again, and it was 'My baby!' and 'Sammy!' and, in messages sent from some far-flung land, 'I wish I could hold you' and 'I wish you could look into my heart and see how honest and true my love is for you'. Then there was another bust-up and he was sorry again – 'You deserve so much better than me' – but begged to be accepted back into her heart. 'I made terrible choices before I realized I had fallen for you.'

And so on and so forth, until they broke up in the northern summer of 2012 after he went on a date with a Russian supermodel he had met in New York, at which point Samantha ran off to Dubai with someone they both knew called Quinton van der Burgh, driving Pistorius to distraction. Again he saw his mistake, too late he feared. By text message again, he apologized and said it broke his heart to learn she was with Quinton, but now, yes, now, at long last, he was in touch with his true feelings: 'No other girl in the world could replace you . . . I love you with my entire being.'

His honeyed words did the trick and they got back together, which was when they set off on their paid lovers' trip to the Seychelles, where they did their promotional interview, shared a suite with a private pool, walked hand in hand on the white sand, and returned home to Johannesburg, intoxicated with love, until he met Reeva, who promptly became the only girl in the world for him, the one he loved as he had never loved anyone before.

Except that Reeva, like his mother, was now immutable in death and, as he would muse while staring up at the photograph of her on the wall of his cottage, she would always remain his true and unrepeatable one, the incorruptible love whose loss he would never get over. He would have forgotten Samantha entirely were it not for the fact that the clock was ticking down for the trial in which she was giving evidence against him. He might have eliminated from his mind the spats he had had with Reeva, too, were it not that the state prosecutors meant to remind him of them in court. His lawyers told him the prosecution had sent his iPhone and hers to Apple in California to try and get access to messages he had exchanged with Reeva over the internet, on WhatsApp. Finding the text messages between them had been no problem for the prosecution; they got those from the local South African telephone company. Yet they had drawn a blank there, finding nothing that they had written to each other or to other people that might suggest a motive for murder. They did nurture the hope, however, that opening up Apple's virtual cloud archives to get the WhatsApp material would yield what they needed to prove their case that he had killed Reeva intentionally – evidence of an argument between them, just prior to the shooting. To that end, in October 2013, they embarked on what would turn out to be a laborious campaign through the American legal system, for the iPhone manufacturers would not part with the information until they were obliged to do so by law. Pistorius's lawyers were alarmed when they first learned of the prosecution gambit, but he was merely mortified at the prospect of the private exchanges between them being aired in court. He did not believe that anything incriminating would be found.

Overwhelmingly, what the WhatsApp messages contained were gushy messages of love. Pistorous and Reeva competed with each other to see who loved who more. 'I miss you', she wrote. 'I miss you more than you always,' he wrote back. They built up a small encyclopedia of amorous endearments: 'My angel', 'My beautiful', 'My baby', 'My baba', 'My boo'.

The name of the woman of his dreams had changed, but not the sentiments he expressed. He transferred all the tenderness he had felt for Samantha, and more, to Reeva, almost from one day to the next. When Samantha found out in December 2012, a month after Pistorius and Reeva had met, that the relationship was turning serious, she sought revenge in the South African press. 'Oscar has such a way with women,' she was quoted as saying. 'She's probably not the only one he's got . . . Oscar is certainly not what people think he is.'

The comment would generate keen interest later, but at the time it passed largely unnoticed. Pistorius was still South Africa's untouchable hero and the public had taken a liking to the suddenly much-photographed Reeva. They were South Africa's closest thing to a Hollywood dream couple and Samantha came across as a peevish young woman scorned. As for Pistorius, he was far too besotted with Reeva to pay much attention to the whinings of an old flame.

But come January, the month before the shooting, he was already falling into the patterns of volatile behavior that had caused so much grief in his relationship with Samantha, and some of his other girlfriends before her. One moment they were crazy about each other – Reeva liked telling him how 'amazing' they were together – but then she would complain that he was all over her, not allowing her to be herself. On January 27 she sent him a message seething with recrimination. The catalyst was his behavior at an engagement party for a common friend of theirs, Darren Fresco, who would turn state witness against him, along with Samantha Taylor, in the trial.

The message, unusually long for WhatsApp, was full of the classic laments and recriminations of a woman saddled with a jealous, self-centered and unreasonably possessive mate.

'I'm not 100% sure why I'm sitting down to type you a message first,' she wrote, 'but perhaps it says a lot about what's going on here. Today was one of my best friends' engagements and I wanted to stay longer. I was enjoying myself but it's over now. You have picked on me incessantly since you got back from CT [Cape Town] and I understand that you are sick but it's nasty. Yesterday wasn't nice for either of us but we managed to pull thro and communicate well enough to show our care for each other is greater than the drama that attacked us.

'I was not flirting with anyone today. I feel sick that u suggested that and that u made a scene at the table and made us leave early. I'm terribly disappointed in how the day ended and how you left me. We are living in a double standard relationship where u can be mad about how I deal with stuff when u are very quick to act cold and offish when you're unhappy. Every 5 seconds I hear how u dated another chick you really have dated a lot of people yet you get upset if I mention ONE funny story with a long term boyfriend. I do everything to make u happy and to not say anything to rock the boat with u. You do everything to throw tantrums in front of people. I have been upset by you for 2 days now. I'm so upset I left Darren's party early. SO upset. I can't get that day back.

'I'm scared of u sometimes,' Reeva continued, 'and how u snap at me and of how u will react to me. You make me happy 90% of the time and I think we are amazing together but I am not some other bitch you may know trying to kill your vibe. I am the girl who let go with u even when I was scared out of my mind to, I'm the girl who fell in love with u and wanted to tell u this weekend.

'But I'm also the girl that gets side stepped when you are in a shit mood. When I feel you think u have me so why try anymore. I get snapped at and told my accents and voices are annoying. I touch your neck to show u I care you tell me to stop. Stop chewing gum. Do this don't do that. You don't want to hear stuff. You cut me off. Your endorsements your reputation your impression of something innocent blown out of proportion and fucked up a special day to me. I'm sorry if you truly felt I was hitting on my friend Sam's husband and I'm sorry that u think that little of me. From the outside it looks like we are a struggle and maybe that's what we are. I just want to love and be loved. Be happy and make someone SO happy. Maybe we can't do that for each other. Cos right now I know u aren't happy and I am certainly very unhappy and sad.'

This was another level of dissatisfaction from the kind he had experienced with the young Samantha Taylor. Reeva's grievances were commonplace, but behind them lay the experience of a worldy woman who had endured her share of difficult loves and who used to tell friends that she had been in an 'abusive relation-ship' before leaving Port Elizabeth for Johannesburg. She had thought through what she did and did not want in a man. He felt somewhat out of his depth. Although he had matured as an athlete and as a public figure, and had built up the Pistorius brand to be as powerful as it was convincing, his emotional development seemed to have been arrested; he remained stuck in the weak, whimpering phase of puppy love. He had twin person-alities and the women he fell for brought out the weaker of the two. There was subjugation in his love for Reeva, to whose scoldings he replied in the only register he knew: simultaneously defensive and abjectly apologetic.

'I want to talk to you,' he began, also via WhatsApp. 'I want to sort this out. I don't want to have anything less than amazing for you and I . . . I'm sorry for the things I say without thinking and for taking offence to some of your actions. The fact that I'm tired and sick isn't an excuse . . . I'm sorry I wanted to go but I was hungry and upset and although you knew it it wasn't like you came to chat to me when I left the table. I was upset when I left you cause I thought you were coming to me. I'm sorry I asked you to stop touching my neck yesterday, I know you were just trying to show me love . . . I had a mad headache and should've just spoken to you softly. I'm sorry.'

Reeva, as if aware this was territory where even the Blade Runner could not compete, held her ground. She responded by pressing home the advantage, defining the kind of relationship she wanted to have. She was who she was and he would have to accept her as such – not as an extension of himself, nor as some idealized image of perfection to which she could never hope to aspire.

'I like to believe that I make u proud when I attend these kinds of functions with u. I present myself well and can converse with others whilst u are off busy chatting to fans/friends. I also knew people there tonight and whilst u were having one or 2 pics taken i was saying goodbye to people in my industry and Fix wanted a photo with me. I was just being cordial by saying good-bye whilst you were busy. I completely understood your desperation to leave and thought I would be help-ing u by getting to the exit before u because I can't rush in the heels I was wearing. I thought it would make a difference in us getting out without u being harassed anymore. I didn't think you would criticize me for doing that especially not so loudly so that others could hear. I might joke around and be all Tom boyish at times but I regard myself as a lady and I didn't feel like one tonight after the way u treated me when we left. I'm a person too and I appreciate that you invited me out tonight and I realize that u get harassed but I am trying my best to make u happy and I feel as tho u sometimes never are no matter the effort I put in. I can't be attacked by outsiders for dating u AND be attacked by you, the one person I deserve protection from.'

Her use of that final 'from' allowed for two interpretations. What she meant, it appeared, was that he of all people should protect her against the attacks of 'outsiders'. What the prosecution could construe the phrase as meaning was that she felt she needed protection from his attacks. They might also try to make something of that passage where she said 'I'm scared of u sometimes and how u snap at me'. But Reeva had immediately followed that up by saying he made her happy '90 % of the time'. And the truth, later to be confirmed in court, was that more than 90 per cent of the messages they exchanged had expressed loving affection. Pistorius wanted to believe that, when the time came, his lawyers could demolish any prosecution attempt to divine a motive for his having wished to kill her from the contents of the iPhone messages.

Nevertheless, to have to endure the embarrassment of hearing those intimate exchanges read out in court when they were only ever intended to be read by two people, to see them blazed across the pages of the world's press, was yet another of the humiliations that awaited him when the murder trial began. Once more, he would be pilloried and laughed at. Reeva's words in that one fraught exchange would be analyzed at length. She was the one who would come across as the grown-up in the relationship, he as the petulant child.

But what his detractors were likely to ignore was how fleeting and atypical, as he chose to see it, that row had been; a day or two later they'd made up and had started planning trips abroad together. Whether the relationship would have withstood extended exposure to her need for independence and his insecurities was another matter. But to preserve what was left of his mental health as he waited for the murder trial he needed to believe that they had been heading for marriage; he needed to nurture his faith in their love as much as he did his faith in God. It had not been just about her beauty, he had convinced himself – nor that by having her as an appendage he was able to embellish the image he sought to present to the world of himself as a manly conqueror. It had not been a mere exercise in shoring up his frail vanity. She was more than a trophy. They had a lot in common. They were both quick-minded and curious about what happened in their country, politically and socially. She had a law degree and he had never finished university, but that did not intimidate him. When she negotiated her modeling contracts she sought his advice and found it helpful, for he was a more shrewd and experienced bargainer than she was.

But at least as important as all that, in terms of his future with Reeva, was their shared religious practice and belief in God. They were both church-going Christians who loved listening to Hillsong Church music on the car radio. Neither of them saw a contradiction between seeking earthly pleasures and prostrating themselves humbly before the Lord. They were bonded by mutual affection and the pursuit of glamor, money, luxury cars, sex and – simultaneously – Christ's redemptive love. Pistorius convinced himself he would find no other woman who combined the worldly attributes he sought with a habit of Sunday church-going and praying together, heads bowed and hands entwined, before each meal. Who else would pray for him every night before going to bed, as Reeva said she did? He loved her because she was beautiful and because she was devout. Just like his mother.

# 10

*This is the sublime and refined point of felicity, called*
*the possession of being well deceived.*

JONATHAN SWIFT, *TALE OF A TUB*

If winning the heart of Reeva Steenkamp proved Pistorius's worth to himself as a man, competing against the best able-bodied runners was the challenge he sought to prove himself as a runner. Long before meeting her, barely three years into his running career, he had already conquered the double-amputee world records at 100, 200 and 400 meters. Guided in all things by his mother's admonition that the real loser was the one who was too afraid to compete, he resolved to demonstrate that he could go stride for stride against the world's fastest men and fulfill his greatest dream – to run in the Olympic Games.

In July 2007 he made an audacious move in that direction. He decided to take part in a 400 meters race in Sheffield, England, against a top-class field which included the reigning Olympic champion. Having recently come second at that distance in the South African national championships, Pistorius did not harbor any expectation of winning, but he did hope he would acquit himself well enough to be invited to participate in able-bodied races on a consistent basis.

The event in Sheffield was part of the Grand Prix circuit endorsed by the sport's controlling world body, the International Association of Athletics Federations (IAAF). The stadium would be packed and all eyes would be on the Blade Runner. From the moment he got up in the morning, his eyes were on the sky. It was a midsummer day, but it was pouring with rain. Officials at the IAAF had been asking in previous months whether running with his Cheetah prosthetic blades would give him an unfair advantage, with some debating whether he should be banned from participating in able-bodied competition altogether. What Pistorius knew, though, was that wearing blades in wet, slippery conditions was indisputably a disadvantage. The irony of his predicament was that, in the event of him beating most of the competition, the arguments of those against him being allowed to continue to compete in IAAF races would be reinforced. Performing poorly might not do him any harm in the long run. But his competitive pride would not allow him to consider that possibility. He was 'a fearsome competitor', as one of his admiring rivals said before the race, and for that very reason the blow to his pride were he to disgrace himself would hurt all the more.

Fearing the worst, Pistorius spent the hours prior to the race looking out of the window of his hotel bedroom, hoping for a break in the clouds. But the rain continued to bucket down. Receiving the biggest cheer of the day when he took his place on the starting blocks did little to raise his spirits. The track was sodden but the stakes were high – it was entirely probable that he was going to make a fool of himself. He did, coming last by a good distance. More bad news followed. Pistorius learned just after the race was over that he had been disqualified for straying out of his lane. He was miserable, and he showed it during a tetchy exchange with journalists who, in what he took to be a maliciously mocking spirit, insisted on asking him whether to run with Cheetahs was cheating. His answer, delivered gruffly, was, 'I am innocent until proven guilty, not the other way round.'

A month later he had a chance to redeem himself at the Olympic Stadium in Rome in another 400 meters IAAF race against elite competition. This time the sun shone and the grip of his blades on the track was good. He was last coming into the final 70 meters, but then he powered through the field to finish second. Sheffield had been a fiasco, but Rome was his most satisfying triumph to date. The bad news was that he had done too well, causing alarm bells to ring at the IAAF. The fact that he had recorded a faster time in the second half of the race than the first, which happens rarely in a 400 meter race, served to intensify suspicions among those who ran the sport that there was something not quite right here. Was he a 'bionic' man running against ordinary men? Did his mechanical appendages violate the spirit of fair play? They decided to investigate.

After studying a videotape of his race in Rome, the IAAF's scientific advisers recommended that Pistorius undergo tests at the German Sport University in Cologne. Over two days, infra-red sensors, oxygen masks and all manner of sophisticated video equipment were used to measure his lung capacity, study his blades, and compare the return energy generated by the artificial legs when they hit the track with that from a runner with ordinary human legs. The scientist supervising the tests, Dr Peter Brüggemann, concluded that Pistorius used 25 per cent less energy and consumed fewer calories than able-bodied athletes running at similar speeds over the same distance.

Invoking a rule that prohibited the use of 'any technical device that incorporates springs, wheels or any other element that provides a user with an advantage over another athlete not using such a device', the IAAF declared that the Cheetah blades fell into this category and formally banned him from participating in able-bodied competitions. The announcement was made on January 14, 2008.

Pistorius, now twenty-one, should not have been surprised, but he was. People close to him reported that he was in shock. Not only was the ban the biggest setback of his career so far, killing his dream of competing in the Olympics, it drew a clear dividing line between him and runners with intact limbs, denying him the possibility of showing the world what he had always sought to show the people around him: that his disability was a misnomer, that there was no obstacle to him leading as full a life as anybody else. But he refused to be dispirited. He had overcome every obstacle in the way of his running career and he would overcome this one, too. He would appeal against the ban and win. Yet he had little idea how to go about it. Luckily for him, someone he had never heard of, a Milanese lawyer called Marco Consonni, took an interest in his case.

Consonni worked for the Italian branch of a New York legal firm called Dewey and Leboeuf. In the second half of January 2008, he and his American colleagues had a discussion about how to expand the firm's business globally. He proposed that they get involved with the case of an athlete called Oscar Pistorius, whom he had read about and who, Consonni supposed, would need legal assistance to overturn the IAAF ruling against him. His colleagues wanted a case that would be suitably transnational and agreed it would be perfect for them. Figuring that the media exposure would be worth millions of dollars, they decided they would represent the athlete pro bono. 'It was a win-win,' Consonni recalled. 'Everybody was happy.'

Consonni contacted Össur, who put him in touch with Peet van Zyl, Pistorius's agent. Van Zyl, a South African, said that he and Pistorius would be in Italy at the end of January and they should meet. Consonni studied the case before the visit and discovered that his potential new client had only thirty days to make a legal challenge against the decision. When he met Pistorius and Van Zyl, he was surprised at how relaxed they both were. They told Consonni they were considering litigation, but only as a last resort, imagining that a few calls to the athletics federation would resolve the matter. They would 'make a plan', they said. Consonni thought they were being naive. He asked if they would authorize him, without any prior commitment, to phone the general counsel of the IAAF, to see where things stood. They agreed.

'I called the IAAF lawyer, who was a Swiss guy,' Consonni said, 'and the minute I mentioned Oscar's name he began to shout and rant. "I have no time for this!" he said. He was incredibly rude. He would not allow me to talk. He said there was no room for arbitration, no possibility of reconsidering the decision. I did not understand why, but he was completely hysterical. I just said, "Okay, fine. We'll go for litigation."'

First, though, Consonni had to convince the athlete that his firm should represent him. A bigger law firm had also offered to act on Pistorius's behalf, but it turned out to be a much easier sell than Consonni had expected.

'Both said they liked the look of me. They said I reminded them of the guy in a film called *The Hitman*.'

Head shaven, six-foot tall, lean in a dark, pencil-sharp suit and stylish black-framed glasses, Consonni recalled the exchange with a cool smile over lunch at an elegant Milan restaurant. Speaking practically perfect English, he said that the moment he received the green light from his new clients he lodged a formal appeal against the ban and began preparing his strategy for when the case would be heard at the Court of Arbitration for Sport (CAS) in Lausanne in May. The CAS, set up by the International Olympic Committee in 1984, typically dealt with doping allegations. Never before had it come across a case in which the purported artificial stimulant was not a secretly consumed drug, but a pair of engineered artifacts that were there for all to see.

It was Pistorius's first trial. It felt like life and death at the time – but was a stroll in the park compared with the one he would face in his home country six years later. There was one thing the two cases had in common, however: they caused a wide division of opinion. The difference was here the general public had little input. This was a matter for specialists, a reduced group of individuals who would claim science as their guide, and some of whom would pen papers on the subject in magazines like *Scientific American* and the *Journal of Applied Psychology.* Yet, empirical as the experts wanted to believe their thought processes were, some were more motivated by their passions – just as the opposing camps following the murder trial would be – than they would have cared to admit.

**The first** expert with whom Consonni sought to join forces was Hugh Herr, a professor at MIT, head of the biomechatronics research group at the MIT Media Lab, entrepreneur, and designer of some of the most technologically advanced leg prostheses in the world.

Fortunately for Pistorius, the IAAF ban had caught Herr's eye. Like Össur Kristinsson and Van Phillips, the American who invented the Cheetahs, Herr had been initially impelled to invest his creative energy in the improvement of prosthetic devices by personal misfortune. A prodigiously talented mountain climber, he had suffered severe frostbite at the age of seventeen after being trapped in a blizzard. Both his legs had to be amputated below the knees. Mirroring Pistorius's spirit in the face of adversity, Herr promptly set about designing a type of prosthesis that would allow him to carry on climbing. Before long, he was ascending steep mountainsides better than before the accident, causing some of his rivals in competitive climbing to complain. Herr now had an unfair advantage, they said.

Naturally sympathetic to the plight of Pistorius, Herr did not hesitate to offer Consonni his services. The Italian was thrilled. 'Our task was to refute the arguments made by Dr Brüggeman,' he said. 'We needed someone capable of doing so convincingly, and in Herr we found the very best in the biomechanical engineering business.'

Herr's base of operations at the MIT Media Lab is a large, high-ceilinged room with giant video screens in each corner, where young scientists from all over the world huddle in circles, laptops at the ready, holding intense discussions. Herr, an intimidating figure to his students, had an android air about him that recalled *Star Trek*'s Mr Spock. Seen from the waist up, it would be impossible to tell from the naturalness of his walking gait that he lacked his lower limbs. But, as if he were a living advertisement for BIOM, the hi-tech prosthetics company he founded in 2007, he made no effort to disguise his condition. He was in the habit of wearing trousers cut off at the knees, exhibiting in all their futuristic wonder his bionically propelled prostheses. A tiny green light flashing on and off at the point where the ankle joint would be in a normal human leg signaled that the legs were electronically powered and needed charging, while at the same time drawing attention to the fact that the genius and innovation of Herr's creation resided in the joint's uncannily natural mobility.

'I want to get Oscar these,' Herr said, apparently not having considered the possibility that in the event of Pistorius going to prison, such artifacts would probably be prohibited, regarded as potentially lethal weapons. There was nothing the brilliant professor could do to help him now, but back in early 2008 his capacious scientific mind was exactly what the athlete had needed. The scientific challenge appealed to

Herr – as, perhaps, did the publicity that the association with Pistorius would give him. But there was also a personal motive behind his decision to enlist, free of charge, in the Pistorius cause. At first sight, Herr came across as dispassionate, but there was a moral principle at play here, one in which he had a fierce emotional stake.

'It was obvious as light that there was discrimination,' Herr said. 'It was the very same bias we've seen against women, gays, blacks.' To him, it became clear once he began to delve into the history of Pistorius's IAAF ban that prejudice was the starting point and scientific reasoning only came later. As with most prejudices – not least those that used to drive the apartheid system in South Africa – the underpinning, Herr believed, was fear. 'They said they wanted to preserve the purity of the sport, but the truth was,' he said, 'that they felt threatened.'

The threat was a vision of the future that thrilled Herr as much as it would appall the athletics federation.

'Before the end of the century we will have a bionic leg that is faster than a biological leg. No doubt,' Herr said. 'That means the Olympics will be a celebration of natural bodies while the Paralympics will be more a celebration of a human machine in action, like a driver and racing car at Daytona. This leg you see me wearing today will be obsolete in a few years. We won't use this piece of crap. Before the century is out, Paralympic athletes will far exceed the capacity of Olympic athletes and will draw far greater crowds. They will be jumping so much higher, running so much faster, that watching the natural bodies compete in the Olympics will seem boring by comparison.'

Warming to his theme, offering a glimpse of the pride he felt in his own story of redemption, Herr continued, 'I lost my legs, but now I climb better than people with biological legs and I am regarded as a threat, like Oscar. That was why they shunned him and tried to stop him participating. They see in him a frightening vision of obsolescence, and all the more so because people like me and him come out of our experiences stronger than hell, armed with far greater psychological reserves.'

Herr might not have made that point had he any notion of the tangles Pistorius would get himself into with women, or of the desperate fragility he had exhibited to the world. The Pistorius that Herr had met back in 2008 was as impressively steadfast in adversity as he was himself. Pistorius had also struck Herr as kind and gentle, he said. His reaction to the news that he had killed Reeva had been disbelief. 'I've been around him quite a bit and I never saw any aggression in him,' Herr said.

That would be another reason why he engaged energetically in the mission to overturn the Blade Runner's ban, but the chief one was that he genuinely believed there was no legitimate case against him running a fair race against anyone. The Cheetahs were crude implements – 'dumb, with no neural command', Herr said – compared with the internally powered bionic devices Herr was using, never mind the exponentially improved ones that the future would hold in store. Herr enlisted the expertise of professors from Colorado University and Rice University to see if they could help him prove it to the satisfaction of the CAS.

More tests followed for Pistorius, along the same lines as the blade-testing routines in Reykjavik and the tests he had undergone in Cologne, but this time in a Rice University laboratory in Houston, Texas. Herr and his fellow scientists convinced themselves they had come up with more than enough data to refute the arguments of Dr Brüggeman and they delivered their findings to Marco Consonni, who in turn handed them on to Jeffrey Kessler, a well-known Manhattan lawyer enlisted by Consonni's firm to present Pistorius's case. In May 2008, Pistorius and his legal team traveled to the CAS in Lausanne to fight the ruling.

'Professor Brüggemann's main argument,' Herr recalled, 'was that the Cheetahs store and release more energy than human legs and therefore use less energy, but we showed that contention to be deeply flawed. The point is that running fast has to do with force, not energy return. Force is about the guy who slaps ground harder over less time. What we were able to demonstrate to the court was that Oscar hits the ground with less force with his Cheetahs than a runner with biological legs. It's like running on a mattress instead of running on cement. There is no advantage.'

Herr's team had conducted a study on what he called 'unilaterals', single-amputee runners, and established that the biological leg actually applied greater force than the Cheetah, which meant it produced a more powerful return spring. These findings impacted critically on the key IAAF argument that running with the blades required 25 per cent less energy consumption. 'We measured how much energy was used in race conditions by Oscar and a biologically normal person and found no significant difference,' said Herr.

The reason he was fast, Herr continued, was the same reason all other top runners were fast: 'He cranked the frequency knob way up. His speed came from the incredible frequency of the movement of his legs.'

**Employing the** arguments provided by Herr and his peers, Jeffrey Kessler insisted before the CAS that his client's natural talent was hindered, not enhanced, by the Cheetahs. There were clear disadvantages to using them. One was the speed out of the starting blocks, significantly slower than it was for able-bodied runners, because they pushed with their calf muscles, whereas with a two-leg amputee the impetus could only come from the hips. Another was running around bends, where keeping one's balance was also measurably more difficult on prostheses than on natural legs.

These two arguments were accepted as common cause by the tribunal's arbitrators, who then invited the athlete himself to deliver a final address. Marco Consonni recalled the five-minute speech.

'Oscar was brilliant. He said he wished to take part in the Olympics because he did not wish to be set apart because of his disability. He said he wished to belong to the world, not be hidden away in a corner. He said he never saw himself as a disabled person and never felt disabled and did not want to be relegated forever to the ranks of disabled competition. He said he wanted to compete with normal people, because there he had real competition and a chance to improve his capabilities. He spoke intelligently, maturely, quietly and naturally. Kessler wept. I think everybody in the chamber was impressed and moved. I saw that day that Oscar touches people.'

The CAS tribunal informed Pistorius of their judgment by means of a fax sent to Consonni's offices in Milan on May 16, two weeks after the hearing.

'Quite by accident, Oscar was there with me at the precise moment a secretary called to tell me the verdict was coming through, and so was Peet van Zyl,' Consonni recalled. 'The suspense was terrible as I read the pages coming through, eighteen in all, and we waited for the last page with the final ruling. Then I shouted, "We won!" And Oscar and Peet went crazy, also shouting, "We won! We won! We won!" And we all hugged and jumped and screamed and cried like little kids. The way was clear at last for Oscar to run in the Olympic Games.'

The unanimous ruling of the three CAS arbitrators was that the ban should be overturned with immediate effect, the IAAF having failed to come up with the burden of proof necessary to demonstrate that Pistorius derived 'an overall net advantage' from using the Cheetah blades. It criticized the IAAF for failing to take into account the disadvantage in his inability to burst from the starting blocks as fast as his able-bodied competitors. It noted that the evidence assembled by Hugh Herr's team showed that Pistorius used the same amount of oxygen as other runners and, far from expending less energy than his able-bodied rivals, 'fatigued normally'.

Particularly satisfying to the jubilant threesome in Consonni's office was a paragraph that read: 'The Panel is reinforced in reaching this conclusion by the fact that the Flex-Foot Cheetah prosthesis has been in use for a decade, and yet no other runner using them – either a single amputee or a double amputee – has run times fast enough to compete effectively against able-bodied runners until Mr Pistorius has done so. In effect, these prior performances by other runners using the prosthesis act as a control for study of the benefits of the prosthesis and demonstrate that even if the prosthesis provided an advantage, and as noted none has been proven, it may be quite limited.'

That paragraph gave Pistorius special joy because it vindicated an argument he had repeatedly made when answering questions from the media, namely, 'If the blades give so much of an advantage, then why aren't other athletes who have them running as fast as me?'

Pistorius had got his way. He had taken on the highest authority in athletics, he had brushed aside the opinion of one of the greatest runners in history, and he had won his case. Never had he felt a more satisfying sense of vindication. He had proved his point. The phrase 'I can't' did not exist in his lexicon. He himself might have been aware of the limits of his condition in his bed at night, with his prostheses off, but as far as the world at large was concerned he had no boundaries. That public persona was the one he cherished, the one he longed to believe represented his authentic self. The more ready the world was to recognize his all-conquering image, the more cemented became his idealized notion of who he was. In Lausanne in May 2008, when he obtained the endorsement of sport's highest court, his public and private personas merged into one. He had gained confidence in the belief that he was who he said he was, a man defined not by his unusual disability but by his extraordinary talent.

He kept on believing it, success after success burying any notion of disability ever deeper in his, and the public's, mind – until shortly after three in the morning of February 14, 2013, when Reeva's death and his own life's great catastrophe laid bare the deceit. Everyone has weaknesses and fears, everyone tries to disguise or repress them. Pistorius's weaknesses and fears were extreme and he had disguised and repressed them by extreme means. He had pulled off a brilliant trick both on himself and on public opinion, but now, on the global stage where he had played out his life's drama, he was exposed for all to see. Frantic and fragile, stumbling gun in hand on his little stumps in the dead of night, in killing Reeva he had killed his own myth.

Now he faced trial for the second time. A court in Pretoria would have to judge whether the prosecution was right beyond reasonable doubt in its contention that he had known that the unseen individual at whom he had fired the four bullets was Reeva Steenkamp. Yet, for all the anguish and ignominy he endured, he retained just enough of his old self-belief to have faith that he could win this battle, too. He had got his way with the mighty IAAF. He could get his way again. After all, a year after that crowning moment at Lausanne, he had cheated death itself.

# 11

*The great advantage of a hotel*
*is that it is a refuge from home life.*
GEORGE BERNARD SHAW,
*YOU NEVER CAN TELL*

A week after Valentine's Day 2009, South Africans woke up to the news that Oscar Pistorius was in a coma after a boat crash, apparently hovering between life and death. Four years later, some would stretch a point and recall the incident as one more piece of evidence pointing to crazed intent in the death of Reeva Steenkamp. But at the time, most responded with shock, distress and prayers for his recovery.

He and a male friend were on a speedboat on the Vaal River, fifty miles south of Johannesburg. Evening was falling and Pistorius was at the wheel. He never saw the jetty into which the prow slammed. The impact pushed his face hard into the wheel and launched the propeller high into the air. His friend, who was unharmed, stared at him aghast. Blood poured from one eye, tissue seeped from his mouth, a flap of skin had peeled off his nose. The hull had been breached and the boat was sinking fast. Pistorius jumped into the water and somehow swam to the river bank where he and his friend were dragged onto another boat. It was his good fortune that a cousin of his who was at medical school, one of Arnold Pistorius's four daughters, had gone out with him that day and happened to be on the other boat. He was in shock and she calmed him down as best she could, but he remained alert enough to be in fear of his life. The boat moored at the nearest landing, an ambulance arrived, paramedics attended to him and he was airlifted to hospital in Johannesburg. He prayed the whole way. On arrival, doctors discovered that his jaw was broken, the bones of one eye socket were in smithereens, and he had broken several ribs and lost three liters of blood. He was given morphine and other sedatives to induce a coma, and then submitted to reconstructive surgery on his face. Three days later he awoke naturally from the coma in the intensive care unit to discover that he had 180 stitches on his face and his jaw had been wired shut. The doctors said they expected him to make a full recovery, but noted how extraordinarily fortunate he had been. It was a miracle he had not suffered permanent brain damage.

Chastened, he underwent two months of physical therapy and resumed light training seven weeks after the accident, in early April, armed with a new determination to socialize less and become more serious about his running. In Paralympics he reigned supreme, having won gold in the 100, 200 and 400 meters in Beijing the year before, but he had failed to run fast enough to qualify for the able-bodied Olympics, a big disappointment after the elation of winning the legal contest in Lausanne. Bringing his times down to compete in the Olympics in London in 2012 became his number one objective.

Speaking to the press in May, by which time he had fully recovered, he said he had lost thirteen pounds in weight since the accident and had a lot of muscle tone and physical endurance to rebuild. 'In my mind, there have never been any barriers for me in sport,' he said. 'I don't perceive myself as having a disability. I see only my ability.'

He did become more able, spending longer hours training, cutting out milk and red meat from his diet, limiting himself to a steady regime of fish, chicken and vegetables. Before the accident he had been drinking and eating like a normal person, now his body became leaner and more sculpted, his face – twelve months after the accident all signs of his injuries had disappeared – less chubby. Sobered by how close he had come to death, maturely aware that big potential sponsors were keeping a close eye on him and that there was a large monetary incentive to being able to perform at his peak, he made the shift, as his agent Peet van Zyl would note later, from amateur to professional.

**Part of** his new seriousness of purpose was displayed in his decision to train during the European summer, when most of his serious athletics competitions were held, at a European base. The place he chose in Italy served not only to tone his body but to calm his mind. He came to call it his home away from home.

He first visited Gemona del Friuli, a small town in the foothills of the Alps seventy miles north of Venice, in 2010. The mayor made him an offer he chose not to refuse. In exchange for becoming Gemona's 'ambassador', which meant publicly associating his name with the town's, he would be paid a nominal sum of 10,000 euros per year and have unrestricted use of the town's new running track and sports facilities, plus free accommodation. It suited him well. Flying back and forth from South Africa to athletics meetings in England, Germany, Holland and elsewhere on the European continent was not only tiring and time-consuming, it was bad for his health. With long-haul flights he ran the risk of developing blood clots in his legs due to the airlines' insistence that, for safety reasons, he keep his tight-fitting prostheses on from take-off to landing. The dryness of the air inside the plane also increased the chances of the skin at the end of his stumps becoming irritated. Gemona, an hour's drive from Venice airport, offered him relatively short trips to his European destinations, minimizing the possibility of him arriving for races tired or in pain.

He made Gemona his base camp from May to September in 2011 and 2012. It was a neat, quiet, picture postcard Italian town of 12,000 people. A sheer mountain dramatically overhung a 700-year-old cathedral, and a castle stood on a spot where ramparts were first built in the seventh century. Gemona's more recent, and unhappy, claim to fame was an earthquake in 1976 that had killed 400 people, left thousands homeless and devastated the town's ancient buildings. It took a decade for the cathedral to be restored; the castle was still being rebuilt when Pistorius installed himself thirty-five years later.

The people of Gemona saw in him a mirror of themselves. They were survivors. Not given to self-pity, they had overcome the consequences of natural disaster by dogged persistence. The town's motto could have been written for the man he tried to be when he stayed there: *'Senza lacrime a denti stretti'* – 'without tears, with gritted teeth'. Gemona was a place where sloth was despised and hard work was the highest virtue. The inhabitants' attitude to life had more in common with that of their Austrian neighbours, across the mountains to the east, than with the *dolce vita* associated with their southern compatriots.

The three-star family hotel where Pistorius stayed was the Hotel Wily, the name deriving from the nickname the original owner, Guillermo Goi, had acquired when he lived in Germany half a century earlier. His granddaughter, Luisella, ran it now, with her aging father and assorted relatives in perpetually busy attendance.

Luisella asked Pistorius when he arrived whether he wanted the one room of the fifty-four in the hotel that been adapted for people with disabilities, but he replied, much in the spirit of his mother when they had first met the headmaster of Pretoria Boys High, that there was no need to make any special allowances for him. He could get by as well as any man. She gave him room 201, the most spacious one she had – but, in keeping with the hotel's unassuming style, a world away from the plush suites he stayed in when he attended race meetings in London or Berlin. It was a spartan room with none of the period character one might have expected in a town ornamented with Renaissance architecture. The wood panelling was fake; the floor, linoleum. There was a double bed with a thin mattress and two rickety single beds, unremarkable framed pictures on the walls, the largest a stock portrait of the Virgin Mary, and a small television set. The window looked onto the hotel car park. But the bathroom was something else altogether. Strikingly at odds with the unpretentious functionality of the hotel, Pistorius had at his disposal an ample shower cubicle with two spouts facing each other across the two side walls and a third one at waist height. All manner of levers and buttons offered a confusing variety of watery possibilities, from gentle drizzle to stabbing squirts to thunderous cascades.

During his stay at the Hotel Wily he did not share the shower with anybody else. The person appointed by the municipality to interpret for him and attend to his everyday needs, a slim and attractive young English-speaking local called Anna Pittini, said that he remained celibate during his stays in Gemona, determined to spend his time there in professionally monkish solitude. (Peet van Zyl would describe his life in Gemona later as that of 'a running monk'.) Pittini was the one person in the town in whom he confided, chatting to her about his family, the loneliness of his world travels and the difficulty of being so far away from his girlfriend, Samantha Taylor – whom he missed, but who also stirred a jealousy in him that he tried to control, but could not. Rumours spread in Italian gossip magazines that he and Pittini were having an affair, but she said they were nonsense. More innocent of the wider world, but capable of seeing deeper into him than he into her, she became like a sister to him in Gemona, the trust that developed between them reaching such a point that once he allowed her into his hotel room when he had his artificial legs off. She was taken aback at how short he was, how odd-looking on his thin stumps, but she was grateful to him for having given her what she felt was the intimate gift of revealing his vulnerability.

Anna Pittini was, as she described it, his 'shadow' during the months he spent in Gemona, and his daily routines almost became hers.

'He would wake up at about 7.30,' she recalled. 'He would go down for breakfast to the hotel restaurant and have lots of eggs, but only egg whites. He would have a shake too, with nuts and berries. He had a shaker in his room where he made his own blends. After breakfast he would go back to his room to rest or contact friends back in South Africa on his computer and then he would head off to the track.'

Pittini offered to take him in her small car but he always insisted on walking. It took him fifteen minutes, always with a pack on his back in which he carried his protruding running blades. He made no attempt to hide his condition, as he did with most of his social set in South Africa. There was a childlike quality to the people of the town, and a kindness that suggested no one was trying to judge him or to take his measure in the way they did elsewhere.

Once at the sports complex he would sit on a bench and quietly change his walking prostheses for his blades. Some of the time his coach, Ampie Louw, would be there with him, but if he was not, Pistorius asked Pittini, whom he enjoyed calling his 'babysitter', to record his running times.

'Most days a small group of kids came along to watch and he was always nice to them,' Pittini said. 'He would smile and say *"Ciao, come stai?"* ("Hello, how are you?") and sign autographs and take pictures with them. But he was always far more focused than other athletes, including some from South Africa who also came to train here. He would say, "The track is my office. I am here to work." He did not allow pictures or videos to be taken and I remember once he got very angry with a woman who was standing by the track smoking a cigarette. It was surprising to see him explode like that, but then I thought it would have been strange if he did not from time to time. Always to be so sweet and polite would not have been natural.'

The training, so intense he often bled as Pittini recalled, lasted an hour and a half and then he returned to the hotel for lunch. The menu at the Hotel Wily was vast, as was the hotel's dining space, which could seat 580 people, but he always stuck to the same modest fare: salad with chicken breast. For dinner it would be more chicken breast, accompanied by vegetable soup. 'He did eat pasta and chocolate cake, but very, very rarely. Usually when he was a in a bad mood,' Pittini said.

In the afternoons he would train for an hour in the gym then go back to his room and Skype with friends, or play video games or watch movies using a video projector he had brought along with his luggage. 'He was a lone wolf,' Pittini said. 'Other foreign athletes would come out with me at night to a party or a bar but he almost always stayed in his room.'

The disciplined lone wolf was the man Pittini got to know, but she became aware that there was an entirely different side to his personality. From photographs he showed her and conversations they had she was able to paint a picture of the fast life he led back home in South Africa after the running season was over.

**In Gemona** he walked everywhere, in South Africa he drove flashy cars; in Gemona the people he mixed with were devoid of all pretensions, in South Africa his social set strove to ape the glamor of Hollywood or Cannes – men with gold chains and Mr Universe muscles, women in bandage dresses, stiletto heels and year-round orange tans. It was a world where everybody was on stage, perpetually on display, not so much conversing as performing, where the most valued social currency was to be seen in the company of the best-looking or most ostentatiously wealthy men and women, where leering males hunted for casual sex, where the chatter, the squealing and giggles were all about who was dating who, where intense whispered debates were held about who was wearing the tackiest dress in the room.

Afraid of crime as he was, Pistorius had the comfort of knowing that here the bad guys were on his side. Some of the men whose company he kept on his visits to Johannesburg nightclubs with names like The VIP Room or Taboo were either known or suspected gangsters. One of his pals, Kenny Kunene, had been jailed for six years for fraud. Another, a Johannesburg multi-millionaire called Craig Lipschitz, who always had four bodyguards around him, ran a tow-truck business – the South African press always referred to him as 'the tow-truck baron' – and had been involved in a savage brawl in 2008 in which, according to media reports, a nightclub bouncer was repeatedly stabbed. But there were more poseurs and parvenus than hardened criminals in the social scene Pistorius frequented, spoilt rich kids or small-time TV personalities who would enjoy the frisson of nudging each other and saying, 'Look, there's the guy they say ordered that gangland killing last week,' or, 'Is it true that so-and-so just bought his girlfriend a yellow Lamborghini?'

Pistorius also knew, to his secret delight, that there was no one they chattered about more than him, invariably in fawning terms. He was good-looking, he was a snappy dresser and, even if he was not as rich as some of the crooks or colorful characters he knew, he was rich enough. Above all, he had something money could not buy. He was a genuine superstar, in South Africa and abroad, in whose glow the beautiful girls and powerful men all wished to bathe. They did not register, as Pittini had, that at night when he went to bed he took off his legs and stood barely five foot on his knobbly stumps. They saw him as he wished to be seen. He was – like them, only more so – in an adolescent world where everybody strove to cover up their fragility by earning the approval of their peers through crassly obvious material display, where promiscuity was rampant, and being regarded as cool was the highest accolade.

Pittini described the women in the pictures that he showed her as 'Barbies'; many of the men, for all their efforts at sophistication, looked to her like cheap hustlers.

Pistorius succumbed to the allure of such individuals in Italy, too, when he was away from Gemona. Typical of the hangers-on who sought his company back in Johannesburg was an Italian called Federico Russo, from the Adriatic city of Trieste. Russo's mischievous self-confidence had procured him access to the masters of the nightclub scene in the fashion city of Milan, where his credibility was enhanced by describing himself as the celebrated Blade Runner's Italian agent. In the wide-eyed South African, eager to be welcomed into the hip Milanese elite, he saw an opportunity to make money. Steered along by Russo, Pistorius took part in a music video and received invitations to appear in low-brow, high-ratings Italian TV programs. In return for big sums of money, Pistorius appeared in a 'dance-with-the-stars' show where, before a live audience, on a vast stage bathed in blue, he performed a tango with a bleached blonde in a low-cut, black sequined dress. Another time he flew to a Pacific island to take part in a reality TV show called *L'Isola dei Famosi*, the island of the famous, where celebrities competed with each other to see which one of them could get by best in the tropical wild.

Anna Pittini found his participation in such shows silly, she said, and also disappointing because she felt they presented an image of her friend that did not do justice to what she regarded as the intrinsic nobility of his character. The frivolous side of him corresponded to the glimpses she had caught of his arrested emotional development, the teenage stews she saw him get into over Samatha Taylor five thousand miles away in South Africa. Pistorius phoned Samantha continually from Gemona, either jealously checking on her movements or complaining about how lonely he felt without her. The bad moods Pittini spoke of when he took solace in pasta and chocolate cake were the result not of a poor day's work on the running track, but of his long-distance squabbles with Samantha, whom he would describe earnestly to Pittini as 'the one' – which she was, until he met Reeva Steenkamp.

But for the most part he was at peace in Gemona, a sanctuary he so craved from the storm of his celebrity life that once he drove four hours through the night after a race meeting in Austria, arriving at the Hotel Wily at three in the morning. In Gemona there was no pressure on him to disguise his insecurities behind elaborate masquerades. Pittini interpreted his stays in her town as an opportunity for him to escape the disruption and play-acting that defined so much of his life. In contrast with nouveau riche Johannesburg or the Milanese beau monde, Gemona was a town whose inhabitants were not impressed by appearances. They had lived through a devastating earthquake, they carried in them the hard-won wisdom of a nation that had seen the rise and fall of mighty empires, they had no time for fops or idlers. Decency, respect and hard work were the yardsticks by which people were measured there. Pistorius could play that part, too.

'The Oscar I got to know was the opposite of a prima donna,' Pittini said. 'Once he bumped his artificial leg on a door and tore his trousers. After joking, "Imagine how painful this would have been if I had had a real leg," he asked me if I would get him a needle and thread. He mended the tear himself. The same thing when it came to washing his clothes. He went to the laundry, put his things in the washing machine, waited there for an hour along with other ordinary people from the town and then he folded the clothes neatly himself. He never ironed his clothes, he just hung them up. I never saw him complain about small stuff. He was never demanding with me and always expressed his gratitude for the things I did to help him.'

**The people** of Gemona saw those qualities in him and loved him for them. They also felt proud to be associated with him, in testimony to which they painted a colorful mural of him in Lycra running uniform and blades on a prominent street corner. At the entrance to the Hotel stood a large poster of him on which he had written a message of thanks.

'Here he was like another member of the family,' Luisella Goi, the Hotel Wily's manager, said, 'always smiling and gentle and polite, but also very playful. He would hug me and my children. One day in the garden he picked me up and I was dangling in his arms with my feet in the air. He loved being with my one-year-old daughter, loved playing with her and sitting down and spoon-feeding her.'

The Goi family gave him the run of the hotel. He was in and out of the kitchen at all hours, had the contents of the fridge at his disposal, as if he were in his own home. When the kitchen was busy preparing the industrial quantities of meals the restaurant served, he would sometimes join in, taking special pleasure in the patient task of making the little potato and pasta balls known as *gnocchi*. 'He said he was so glad we taught him to make *gnocchi* because doing so brought him peace,' Luisella said.

He had his meals in the big hotel dining room, almost always sitting alone. 'He was quiet and you could see he did not want to be disturbed,' said Luisella. 'Everywhere else he went he was probably bothered all the time, but here people let him be. Maybe it is because we are too busy working all the time or maybe it is because of our ignorance, but we did not treat him in this town as if he were a big celebrity.' Except for one memorable evening when he arrived back in Gemona after winning a big race and the people in the restaurant stood up and applauded, to which he responded by going from table to table to shake everybody's hands.

Town residents who spent time with Pistorius spoke warmly of him. A middle-aged single mother called Marisa once gave him a ride in her small car from Venice airport to Gemona. They chatted non-stop during the hour-long journey. 'When we were approaching Gemona he said, "Look, your sweet town," and I melted,' Marisa recalled in halting English. 'For me he was not a *campione*, he was just a nice young man. *Una persona stupenda.* He liked us here because we treated him like a normal person and he could be himself.

I think for a person like him who is accustomed to people trying to use him in different ways it was very calming to be here.'

The fact was, though, that the town did use him. It was the idea of the mayor, Paulo Urbani, to recruit him to promote Gemona's image. And yet, talking to Urbani, the sense was that while the head drove him in his initial calculations, the relationship between the two men ended up being heartfelt.

In the foyer of the town hall, built in the Venetian manner in 1502, there was a photograph on the wall of Mayor Urbani with the president of Italy, and another one next to it, the same size, with the mayor and Pistorius. In the mayor's office, on his desk, stood a framed picture of the two of them smiling. This was ten months after he had been charged with the murder of Reeva Steenkamp.

'It was easy to love him,' said Urbani, a bearish, handsome man in his forties. 'He was a simple person who became perfectly adapted to our community. He never complained about anything and he was *molto cortese*. He always jumped to open the door for my wife. It was easy to talk to him and he was curious about everything here, the food, the culture, the football. He spoke of the many places he had been and I was surprised that he traveled alone in the world, with his disability. I found him old in his behavior and was surprised he was so mature for his age.'

Nothing had prepared Urbani or the rest of Pistorius's friends in Gemona for what happened on the morning of February 14, 2013.

Pittini was the first person in town to hear the news. 'Peet van Zyl phoned. It was 6.30 in the morning. I asked him why he was calling me so early,' Pittini said. 'He told me, "Something's happened to Oscar." I thought, a car accident. He died in a crash. "No," Peet said. "No car accident. He shot Reeva. She's dead." I nearly fainted.'

Urbani nearly fainted, too. 'It was a terrible shock to me and a terrible shock to our community. Some people's first reaction was that it was a bad joke. We had adopted him as one of us and we could not believe it. It was impossible. That was not the person we knew.'

Urbani followed the bail proceedings closely the next week and on the morning of the day the verdict was delivered he went to the cathedral to pray that Pistorius would be set free. 'It was painful to see Oscar in court. He was the image of desolation. It made me think of people who lost family members in the earthquake here. But it was all made worse by the false news, the steroids, and the claims that he had bought a house in Gemona that he had not told the tax authorities about. All lies.'

Urbani stuck by his friend, but some people of his acquaintance, and many more far and wide, did not. For Gemona's mayor this offered a sad reflection on human nature. 'The greater the rise, the bigger the idol, and when he makes an error and falls, the greater the monster he has to become. When things go well, everyone cheers and you are a hero; when things go wrong, the *invidiosi*, the envious ones, emerge and now they have the strong voice and they celebrate his failure. I even had some political rivals using him to attack me. How low can you get?'

Urbani had no regrets about having invited him into the Gemona fold. Not politically – he was re-elected with 78 per cent of the vote in May 2014 – and not personally either. He made no apologies for keeping the photographs of Pistorius on display in the town hall.

'Oscar is a friend and I will support him. I cannot deny the friendship. If the judge says he did it on purpose I cannot deny that either, but there is a principle of loyalty and of gratitude here. We will follow the trial with passion in Gemona. If the judge says he is guilty, I will take down the pictures. We must show respect for the law. But if he is found innocent, it will be a day of joy for him and for our community.'

Pittini said that the mayor's sentiments expressed the majority view in the town. 'Many people asked me to send Oscar messages of support after the shooting. They said no one is perfect, everyone can mess up badly in life, we must be forgiving. One woman said to me, "I am a mother and a mother can really understand a mistake," and she started crying. She had not even met him.'

One person who had met him was Flavio Frigè, a fifty-year-old man with a beard and a ponytail who had lost an arm and a leg in an industrial accident when he was seventeen and wore prostheses on both amputated limbs.

'Being disabled myself, it was very important for me that people around the world should see him do those incredible things,' said Flavio, a lively minded man who showed no sign of resentment or even self-consciouness about his condition. 'I felt validated by him. For thirty-three years I have battled to make a life for myself, and I think I have done well, but he gave me something more. Oscar made disability visible. He made me proud.'

Flavio met his hero and found him to be, as he had hoped, *un bravo regazzo*, a great guy. He was '*una persona molto buona, un ragazzo molto disponibile, gentilissimo*,' Flavio said.

His first reaction to the news of the shooting was incredulity, he said. 'I could not believe it. I did not want to. And then, when it sank in, I felt a huge sadness for the *ragazza*, that girl, Reeva. Huge! Then I felt his sorrow and I wanted to see him again and hug him. I still do. The Oscar I knew, it is impossible he would do such a thing. But I will not judge. Only he knows what happened. I only hope he will be found innocent of murder, though for him the punishment is permanent.'

However great the battle had been for Pistorius to conquer his disability and triumph, Flavio said, it was nothing compared to the test he would face now. 'Losing an arm, a leg, is one thing,' Flavio said. 'Losing the woman you love and losing her in such a way . . . so hard. And on top of that, being a famous public figure obliged to take the scorn and the shame of the world . . . No, no. The challenge of the body can be overcome. You fight. You battle. I know it. It can be done. But far, far deeper and more painful is the suffering of the soul. What do you do with that? Nothing. You can never make amends and the sorrow will never go away.'

# 12

*Not one, but all Mankind's epitome.*
JOHN DRYDEN, *ABSALOM AND ACHITOPHEL*

The gentleness of Gemona magnified Pistorius's sense of South Africa's dangers. Sometimes, strolling from the Hotel Wily to the running track, he caught himself worrying about the safety of his relatives back home, in particular his sister Aimée. When they walked the city streets of South Africa, they did so warily, alert to the possibility of criminal assault. In that they were no different from the majority of white people, or the better-off black citizens, who signposted their economic ascent in the years after Mandela came to power by adopting the previously whites-only habit of traveling in the relative safety of their cars distances that in New York, Paris or London people would cover on foot.

The high crime rate in South Africa was a function of its economy and demographics. The large black and white middle class lived surrounded by an ocean of poverty. Twelve million people out of a total population of fifty million provided inviting targets for the malevolent or the desperate among the impoverished majority, generating a pool of willing recruits to the country's large web of criminal networks.

In Gemona, where incomes are evenly spread and nobody goes hungry, Pistorius could breathe more easily. The sense of a load being lifted was the common experience of South Africans who traveled to Europe or the US; on returning home they would feel a tightening of the stomach muscles as they braced themselves once again to be on their guard. Alertness was the natural condition of people who lived in South Africa – a country in which the private security industry employed more than 400,000 people, twice the number of police officers; where traffic bulletins on the radio would routinely include news of street crossings where 'smash-and-grabbers' were reported to be operating; where youths begging on street corners would carry boards that read 'I will die of hunger before I steal', signaling their own respect for the law but reminding potential benefactors of the constant threat of crime. Being away from this mayhem for a prolonged stretch in a place where crime was less prevalent only heightened the anxiety on one's return.

Pistorius always carried a gun for protection when he was in South Africa, and if he drove fast it was in part because he was obsessed with speed, but also to improve his chances of escape in the event of an attempted carjacking. On the road he often suspected he was being followed by another vehicle. At night, he would park his car only in a well-lit area. In a restaurant, he would check the exits and entrances on arrival and choose to sit with his back to the wall, in a position where he could scan the room should he need to respond quickly to a hold-up. When he stayed in a hotel and there was a knock at his room door, he would always first ask who it was and then keep the latch on as he opened the door. Peet van Zyl, his agent, said that when Pistorius heard an unexpected bang, such as a car backfiring, he would grab his arm in fright.

All South Africans are vigilant, few more vigilant than Pistorius. The measures people took to protect their homes would rise in proportion to their incomes. His uncle Arnold had twenty-four-hour sentries at the gate of his fortified castle of a home, as well as a sophisticated alarm system and a corrugated metal screen between the gym and the rest of the house, which he could lower or raise electronically at the press of a button. After apartheid, when people of all races were allowed to move at will in previously all-white residential areas, those with money increasingly took to living in gated communities. In the suburbs of East Pretoria, where Pistorius lived, most people sheltered themselves within compounds surrounded by high walls and razor wire, and patrolled by armed guards in quasi-military vehicles. Built on what had once been bare, dry veldt, they had names like Faerie Glen, or Forest Manor, or Nature's Valley, as if devised by the marketing departments of real-estate companies specifically to counter the impression of prospective buyers that they would be living inside an army garrison or behind the walls of a prison. But it was a price people thought worth paying, to keep the barbarians outside the gates.

And not just white people, as would have been the case in the early years of democracy. Silver Woods, where Pistorius lived between 2008 and Valentine's Day of 2013, offered an idealized picture of racial harmony in the New South Africa, unimaginable during the apartheid years. The 170 homes in Silver Woods were cheerfully inclusive of all races and, for that matter, sexual inclinations. Pistorius's two closest neighbors, with whom he had always got on cordially, were black, and a gay female couple lived four doors down from him. The residents here were either professionals (one of his next-door neighbors was a doctor) or senior civil servants or, in some cases, foreign diplomats.

New homes were being built every day in Silver Woods, but there were no rules enforcing a uniform architectural style. Some were designed in a grand, wedding-cake Tuscan style; others had the pastel feel of Spanish Mediterranean villas. In a few cases the owners had opted for large, brutishly imposing red-brick bunkers, somewhat at odds with the palm trees that lined the roads. But 286 Bushwillow Street, where Pistorius lived, was a cubic, streamlined, self-consciously modern construction, a fittingly sleek abode for a young man who in full Blade Runner dress could transform himself into a futuristic science-fiction superhero. The angles were sharp, the lines straight, the stone walls a uniform silvery-grey. Two big wooden doors guarded the garage where he kept his automobiles and, adorning the space in front of the main door, were a couple of cacti, shrubs, short trees and a small, impeccably tended, lawn.

He had an alarm system in the house – which to anyone who did not know South Africa would have seemed like an extreme precaution, given that the estate felt as secure as the Bank of England. In addition to the electrified twelve-foot perimeter walls that were standard in the area, CCTV and underground sensors ringed the complex, setting off alarms that would summon an armed response team if anybody thought to approach them. The security procedure for entering the Silver Woods fortress was exhaustive. A fingerprint coding device for residents automatically lifted the two sets of barriers that guarded the single entrance, but visitors not only had to supply official identity documents and have their vehicle license numbers noted down by a guard, but also had to identify exactly who they were visiting and then have the guard phone ahead to confirm before they could be let in. Sometimes the security measures became too much even for the people living there. One resident told how her seventy-year-old mother had arrived at the entrance one day and supplied all the information that was needed, except for her daughter's phone number, which she had misplaced, and as a consequence, despite her indignant protestations, was not allowed in.

On another occasion, a truck-load of laborers arrived from Johannesburg to work on the construction of a new home. Four of the them only had photocopies of their ID. The entire truck was denied entry. Laborers who did make it through the gates were obliged to leave the complex by 5 p.m. each day. If anyone overstayed that limit, his company would be fined and the laborer would not be allowed to go home; he would effectively be held hostage until the full amount was paid.

Once inside, visitors would notice that the bucolic atmosphere was tempered by the spectacle of uniformed guards on constant patrol, on foot with dogs or on bicycles. There were electronic devices at strategic locations around the complex where the guards were obliged to register their presence at predetermined times, by checking in with an individually allotted plastic card. This went on day and night.

But while other residents who admitted to being generally nervous about crime said that they had discovered at Silver Woods a peace they had not known before, Pistorius not only had his own home alarm system, he had also kept a gun by his bedside and a cricket bat and baseball bat behind his bedroom door for defense in case of attack. Others slept easily at Silver Woods, but Pistorius, often beset by insomnia, did not. Asked by a British journalist in 2012, before the start of the London Olympic Games, whether he ever felt vulnerable, he dropped his guard and replied that yes, he did, when he was lying in bed without his prostheses on and heard a noise in the middle of the night.

On one occasion, hearing just such a noise, Pistorius rushed out of bed to confront the suspected intruder with his gun in his hand. It was a friend who was sleeping over and had got up to fetch a glass of water.

Yet Pistorius felt vulnerable inside his home even when he did have his artificial legs on, such as the time when he arrived home after dark and heard a noise in the kitchen. He drew a gun he was carrying and advanced stealthily towards the suspected intruder in what he would later describe to friends, self-mockingly, as 'full combat mode'. On entering the kitchen, he discovered that the sound he had heard was the churning of a tumble dryer.

On another occasion, he was watching a film on TV at the home of a friend in Johannesburg when he dozed off. The noise of gunshots awoke him with a start. The sound was entirely fictional, part of the action in the film, but he jumped up and ran out of the room in a panic.

One incident in 2012, two months before the London Olympic Games, revealed to two startled onlookers the degree of not just panic, but hysteria, with which he was capable of reacting when he felt his safety was under threat.

A TV crew for an American network, comprising a cameraman and a sound-man, both South Africans, came to his home in Silver Woods to prepare for an interview. When they arrived an hour early to set up their equipment, Pistorius was not there. His live-in Malawian domestic worker, Frankie Chiziweni, whom he usually addressed in African style as 'my brother', let them in. Theirs was an unusual arrangement in a country where well-off people, both black and white, typically kept female domestic workers in their homes.

Chiziweni would be part of the small group who would see Pistorius coming down the stairs on February 14 the following year, with Reeva Steenkamp's bleeding body in his arms. He would tell police he had not heard anything, even though he had been in his room on the ground floor when the shooting happened. The police were baffled, believing him either to be either extraordinarily loyal or an extraordinarily deep sleeper. The question would not be resolved either then or in the subsequent murder trial, for he never appeared as a witness in court.

Chiziweni was a small, sweet-natured and obliging man in his thirties, who welcomed the TV crew into Pistorius's home and assented to their request to be allowed to bring in their unwieldy equipment not by the front entrance but through the big garage doors. Half an hour later, his boss, who had been training at a nearby athletics track, arrived.

On seeing the garage doors open, leaving the whole house vulnerable, Pistorius stormed into the kitchen and confronted Frankie in a thundering rage. He was not his 'brother' any more. He was 'a fucking arsehole'. With the cameraman and sound-man looking on, he screamed, 'What the fuck are you doing? Have I not told you a thousand fucking times to close that garage door? Are you fucking mad? Don't you hear what I fucking tell you?' On he continued in that vein, frightening and humiliating his employee, shocking the two TV men. They had regarded him as a national hero and had only ever seen him the way he projected himself in public, as mild, courteous and self-effacing. Now they were seeing him in a hot rage and were staggered by the violence of his language. They sought to intervene and explain that it was all their fault, that they should take the blame, for it had been they who had proposed entering through the garage doors. But he would not hear them and continued heaping the vilest recriminations on the terrified Chiziweni. Then, abruptly, he turned round and went up the stairs to take a shower.

He reappeared refreshed and in a change of clothes, the picture of aplomb, with a broad smile of welcome on his face, as if the incident with his housekeeper had never happened, as if he were a different man. All the rage of a few minutes earlier had gone and he sat down before the camera composed, reciting the old prefabricated phrases, drawing the usual distinctions between his disability and his ability, proclaiming his pride at being able to represent his nation in London. The feature that was later broadcast made no mention of his outburst and portrayed him in a glowing and heroic light.

**Everywhere Pistorius** went in London in the summer of 2012, he saw posters of himself advertising either one of the products he endorsed or the Olympics themselves. He struggled to believe it at times, but he was vying with Usain Bolt, the Jamaican who was the fastest sprinter in history, for the title of King of the Games. He had failed to qualify for the Beijing Olympics in 2008, but after two months of preparation in Gemona he had smashed his own personal 400 meters record at a race in July 2011 in Lignano, on Italy's Adriatic coast, which he won with a time of 45.07 seconds. On his return to Gemona, an hour's drive north, he was met with scenes of wild delight. It was in the same spirit that he was greeted now in London whenever he made a public appearance.

No South African visitor to the city had received a more fawning reception from the media since Nelson Mandela, who four years earlier had chosen London to celebrate his ninetieth birthday. Photographers, journalists and members of the public turned up to gawp at a training session at the end of July, a week before Pistorius's first race. He greeted everyone present with a handshake. Should he have happened to miss someone, he would go back, reach out a hand and say, 'I think I forgot to greet you.' He paid special attention to his younger fans, children who regarded him as a sort of cartoon action superhero. Some would ask him, 'How can I get legs like yours?' To the more inquisitive ones who wanted to know how he had lost his lower legs, he would reply with the old joke his mother had taught him to tell at school: a shark had eaten them.

Charmed and in awe of him, sports journalists produced one article after another celebrating him as the very incarnation of the Olympic spirit, stretching back to the Games' beginnings in ancient Greece. In tribute to his virtues they would quote Lucian, the author who wrote in the second century AD about the Olympic athletes' 'unstoppable passion for victory'. In his hotel room, Pistorius would read the purple prose with delight, pausing at passages such as this one, from London's *Daily Telegraph*: 'That he has confounded all logic is evidence not of something mechanical but very human: the triumphant power of will . . . Pistorius's very presence in London should be lauded to the murky skies as the epitome of the Olympic purpose.'

But as the clock ticked down for his Olympic debut on August 4, Pistorius was secretly consumed with anxiety. What if he made a laughing-stock of himself? What if he repeated the fiasco of Sheffield in 2007, when he had competed against able-bodied runners and not only came last, but way last, and was disqualified for straying out of his lane? Pistorius the hero would be reduced to Pistorius the plucky disabled athlete who should have known better than to pit himself against the world's best. Those who had argued that he should never have been allowed to take part in the Olympics, that a disabled runner should not compete against able-bodied competitors, would be vindicated. He would have to endure the fate he most dreaded, of finding himself provoking more pity than admiration.

No one, not even Pistorius, expected that he'd win a medal. Rarely, if ever, had an athlete with no hope of winning ever played such a starring role at any sports event, let alone the Olympic Games. Pistorius just wanted to do well in the preliminary heats of the 400 meters competition, maybe beating at least some of his rivals in the field of eight. To run a time fast enough to make it to the next round, the semi-finals, would be a dream. Reaching the final, the last eight, was almost out of the question, given the times already recorded by the world's fastest competitors. That first race was the moment he had been preparing for since winning the CAS ruling in Lausanne in 2008 and which would put the stamp of victory on the battle he had waged all his life to deny the limitations of his disability.

On the day of his race, all other Olympic events and competitors were overshadowed by the excitement, trumpeted in newspapers the world over, at the realization that history was about to be made. It would be the first time a runner with amputated legs would compete in the Games – one of the unlikeliest sports stories ever told. It felt Homeric, the stuff of myth. Or thus, at any rate, did the TV commentators and sports journalists rhapsodize, echoing the public mood. Tickets for the Olympic Stadium were sold out. Eighty thousand people would be there to roar him on, among them his uncle Arnold and his wife Lois, his sister Aimée, his brother Carl, and their grandmother Gerti. Glory beckoned, but all that morning he could not keep out of his mind the alternative possibility, that it could all fall embarrassingly flat for him. Would people say when the race was over that he had earned his right to be there, or would they regard his presence in the competition as clownish, as many had done with the Jamaican bobsled team in the Winter Olympics? Would they end up dismissing him, after all, as a freakish sideshow?

In these moments of self-doubt, Pistorius summoned up the memory of his mother. He recalled, for the umpteenth time, the note she had written him when he was a small child that said, 'The real loser is never the person who crosses the finishing line last. The real loser is the person who sits on the side, the person who does not even try to compete.' He recited those old words to himself in the locker room; he imagined how unutterably proud she would have been of him, or how unutterably proud she was as she looked down on him from heaven – and all doubts flew away, replaced by a resolve to do justice to the limitless faith she had shown in him.

His mother remained in his mind as he stepped out into the vast arena of London's Olympic Stadium. It was only a preliminary heat, but the roar of the crowd suggested that it was the biggest, most eagerly awaited event in the entire Games. It might have been a soccer World Cup final or a heavyweight boxing championship in which he was the crowd's undisputed favorite. Pistorius saw a few South African flags, but they gave no sense of the unanimous support he had in a foreign arena where they were all South Africans now. No one wanted him to run the race of his life more, or knew how much it meant to him or what the humiliation of failure would mean, than his family members seated low down alongside the starting blocks, studying his eyes. They could see that he was fighting to control his nerves, all the more so when a TV cameraman, ignoring the rest of the field, headed straight for him and pointed the camera in his face. The image was being watched live by millions worldwide, among them his father and Dr Gerry Versfeld in a Johannesburg bar, but Pistorius rose theatrically to the occasion, as he had done many times before, giving a thumbs up first, then raising his right hand to his temple and making a military officer's salute. The stadium announcer ran through the names of the eight runners. In lane number five, he bellowed, 'Oscar . . . Pisto-o-o-ri-us . . . the Blade Runner!'

Giant screens flashed images of two other runners who had left an indelible mark on the Olympic Games: Jesse Owens, the black American runner who confounded Hitler's notions of Aryan racial superiority with his four gold medals in Berlin in 1936; and Cathy Freeman, the Aborigine who won gold for Australia in the 400 meters in Sydney in 2000. Each had triumphed after overcoming poverty and prejudice.

Pistorius had no feet, no ankles, no calves, but in their place his charcoal-colored Cheetah blades. Wearing aerodynamic wraparound sunglasses, his one-piece Lycra uniform in South African green and

gold, he went down on one knee to take up his position for the start of the race in lane five. The stadium
fell silent, save for one man who shouted out to him so
loudly that he heard it, bringing the glimmer of a smile
to his face. 'You sexy beauty!' the man cried. Then his
grandmother piped up with a word of encouragement
in Afrikaans, and his uncle whistled in a special way
he had – and hearing them both gave him, as he would
gratefully acknowledge later, a much-needed sense of
calm. The gun went off and he sprang out of the blocks,
but less explosively than the other runners, as invariably happened when he raced against men with legs.
All eyes in the stadium were on him, but what they saw
over the first 50 meters was a runner who looked slug-
gish, as if his body's machinery were rusty and needed
greasing. He was losing ground fast and the dismay in
the stadium was palpable. But within 100 meters he
had gained his stride. Viewed head-on, he had a sham-
bling action, ungainly in contrast to the feline mobility
of the other seven runners. But viewed in profile he
was smooth and powerful, and by the halfway mark he
had eaten up almost all the lost ground, surging past
athletes to his right and left, as he had done on that
occasion nine years earlier at the schools' athletics competition when he was sixteen, to the astonishment of his
teacher, Paul Anthony, and all those present. Pistorius

did not win the race, but he came a comfortable second, even giving the impression he had eased up over the final few meters.

He had qualified for the next heat, the semi-finals, and the crowd's roar was for him. In place of the embarrassment he had feared, Pistorius savored the euphoria of his life's supreme triumph. All the blood and pain, the relentless work on the track and in the gym, the self-denying discipline, the disappointments and insecurities he had battled with to arrive at this point, were both justified and forgotten in the adrenaline rush of the moment. As he reminded one journalist after another during an hour of interviews after the race, he was not disabled by an accident of fortune, he was enabled by his God-given talent.

His uncle and aunt, his brother and sister, his grandmother, were hoarse with shouting by the side of the track, but it was his mother he remembered when he talked to the press. 'I thought of her a lot all day today,' he said. 'She was a bit of a hard-core person. She didn't take no for an answer. It's definitely her sprit that has helped me to be here today. She always said the loser isn't the person that gets involved and comes last, it's the person that doesn't get involved in the first place.'

He had been involved and he had achieved the dream he had set for himself. That in the next race he was not fast enough to make it to the final eight did not diminish his elation. Never had failure in the Olympic Games received such acclaim. He left with no medals, but he carried the South African flag at the closing ceremony. Pistorius had proved the point he had sought to prove and, what was more, his fellow able-bodied runners agreed as much. Endorsing his right to take part alongside them, the Dominican runner who had beaten him to first place in the first race said, 'We've got guys out here doing drugs; any advantage that Oscar might have is the least of my concerns. He's amazing. He's inspiring.' Kirani James of Grenada, who would end up winning the 400 meters gold, said of him, 'I just see him as another competitor, another athlete. I really respect him. It is what it is.'

**Except that** it was not quite what it was, or seemed to be. It was never quite that straightforward. He had wanted to imagine himself as the public and his fellow competitors did, but there came a point, sooner or later, when he looked in the mirror and was reminded of his inborn vulnerability. He had wanted his life to be perfect and whole, yet even back then in London, where he had climbed the summit, a voice inside told him that it would never quite be. Then, six months after London, he had shot Reeva, and since then he had felt vulnerable every hour of the day. The memories of his athletic triumphs served more to mock than to inspire him now. When he lay in bed at night in his bare stumps at his uncle Arnold's cottage, unable to sleep, there was no respite from the struggle with that fragile individual beset by anxieties of all kinds who was now awaiting trial for murder.

He had said once in a newspaper interview that what he most wished for was to live and die without regrets. But he had been deceiving himself, because even in the glorious year before disaster struck it had been impossible for him entirely to deny the limitations of his condition, the insecurities in love, the exaggerated fears, the bursts of irrational temper and the regret that accompanied it. He thought he had more or less learned to live with it. But not anymore – not now that Reeva was dead and the trial date was drawing near.

# 13

*We are all full of weakness and errors; let us mutually pardon each other our follies – it is the first law of nature.*

VOLTAIRE, *A PLEA FOR TOLERANCE AND REASON*

In August 2013 the date of the murder trial was set. It would begin on March 3 of the following year – one year and seventeen days after the shooting. On November 20, 2013 the indictment was served. There was a surprise. In addition to murder, the Director of Public Prosecutions for North Gauteng, Pretoria, had issued three more charges on which he would stand trial, all of them relating to contraventions of the Firearms Control Act that had passed into law in 2000.

These were trifles in comparison with the primary charge, and in the context of the general gun violence prevalent in South Africa. One held that he had fired a shot from his 9mm pistol into the air through the open sunroof of a car in which he was traveling with two friends, one of them his then-girlfriend, Samantha Taylor, 'on or about' September 30, 2012. The second was that in January 2013 he had negligently fired a shot from a Glock pistol in a crowded restaurant, Tasha's in Johannesburg, causing damage to the floor and endangering the safety of patrons. The third was that in February 2013, after the shooting, he had in his possession several rounds of ammunition for which he had no license.

Why, Pistorius wanted to know, had Gerrie Nel, the prosecutor at the bail hearing, who would now be the prosecutor at the trial, chosen to bring these three matters to court? The answer his defense team gave him was fourfold. First, that Nel could do so, even though the police had overlooked them before. Second, that in presenting the evidence Nel would endeavor to portray him as a reckless gun fanatic capable of carrying out murder. Third, that it presented Nel with the opportunity to bring Samantha Taylor to the witness stand, in the expectation that she would paint an image of him consistent with a volatile, angry, jealous lover who might plausibly have shot his girlfriend in a rage. Fourth, that if he pleaded not guilty, Nel might think he would be able to expand the possibility of catching him out in contradictions or outright lies during cross-examination, thereby casting a shadow over the veracity of his testimony on the main charge of murder.

Barry Roux, Pistorius's chief defense lawyer, saw a value in pleading guilty to at least one of the firearms charges, maybe even to all three. In the event that Pistorius expressed due remorse in court, there was a good possibility that, on these charges at least, he would get away with a suspended sentence, or maybe just a fine. More important, he would come across as truthful, which would lend more weight to his version of the events of Valentine's Day. Also, it would keep Samantha Taylor, who was apparently in vengeful mode after being dropped by him in favor of Reeva, away from the witness stand. South African trial rules in a murder case did not allow the prosecution to present character witnesses unconnected to the specific incident under scrutiny. Samantha Taylor could only be called to testify about a particular incident of which she had personal knowledge. Such was the case, or so the prosecution held, in the charge that he had fired a gun from a moving car. Yet, as Nel understood very well, her appearance on the witness stand might allow him to reveal explosive aspects of Pistorius's personality that might reinforce the prosecution's case on the murder charge, in one important respect. Nel intended to demonstrate in court that Pistorius had killed Reeva Steenkamp after a violent argument. Taylor's testimony might reinforce the notion that this was an entirely plausible scenario.

Looking coldly at the impending trial and the dangers the three minor firearms charges posed, it would have suited Roux for Pistorius to confess to them – but Pistorius had no intention of doing so. He told Roux and the rest of his defense team that he did not consider himself guilty of any of the charges: that the story of the shot in the air from a moving car was an invention; that while it was true that he had been holding the gun that went off under a table at Tasha's restaurant, it had been an inexplicable accident, for which he had no wish to admit criminal liability; and that the bullets in his house belonged to his father, who did have a license for them, and that he had simply been keeping them for him in his safe.

Pistorius would not budge. He would not tell what, he insisted, would be strategic lies just in order to appear truthful. Nor did Roux put any further pressure on him to do so. Defending the murder charge would be more complicated, but his client insisted he was not guilty of any of the firearms charges, so that would be the end of the matter.

**The question** that remained to be decided was the identity of the judge. In South Africa the jury system had been abolished in 1969, the apartheid government at the time having displayed a rare enlightenment in acknowledging that an all-white jury could not be depended upon to dispense fair justice to a black defendant. The cultural and linguistic differences between the forcibly separated races were just too great.

On the other hand, placing all the responsibility for matters that sometimes concerned life and death in the hands of a solitary white judge during the apartheid years was not much of an improvement. The system produced some scandalous aberrations. In the late eighties, a white farmer who beat one of his laborers to death was given a suspended sentence, while fourteen black people judged to have shared common purpose in the death of one policeman were sent to death row.

Yet there had been no call for the jury system to be reinstated after the coming of democracy, when capital punishment was abolished. In a country with eleven official languages and what Archbishop Desmond Tutu, the 1984 Nobel Peace Prize winner, called a 'rainbow' mix of races, religions and cultures, the consensus was that it would be wise to leave the final word in the hands of one eminently qualified judicial expert. The difference after 1994 was that judges of all races began to be appointed to the bench.

The inevitable flaw in the system was that some judicial experts were more able and experienced than others, and that all of them were human beings whose private experiences, views and political inclinations would diminish the possibility of their exercising their authority with absolute impartiality. In high profile cases, it was hard to believe they would be able to insulate themselves entirely from the biases of public opinion and the media. Judges do not live in a vacuum. Yet, on the premise that there was no such thing as perfect justice, and that juries merely dispersed more widely their individual fallibilities, South Africa stuck to what it knew.

Before the name of the judge in this particular case was announced, both the defense and the prosecution were anxious to know whether the person chosen would be experienced in murder trials and would have a reputation for severity or leniency, for strong-mindedness or lack of resolution. The decision was made in December 2013 by Dunstan Mlambo, the Judge President of the High Court of Gauteng, the South African province that comprised both Pretoria and Johannesburg. Judge Thokozile Matilda Masipa, a black woman, was chosen.

A High Court judge in South Africa since December 1998, at that time only the second black woman to be appointed to that position, Masipa stood out among her peers for her industriousness. One senior lawyer who worked closely with her said she struck him as someone who would have been the hardest-working student in her class at law school. He also described her as a good person, happily free of the wordy pomposity that sometimes afflicted the robed members of the South African bench.

Born in 1947, a year before the apartheid laws were written into the South African constitution, Masipa grew up in Soweto, the vast segregated black township south-west of Johannesburg where Mandela spent sixteen years of his life before his arrest in 1962. She lived with her parents and siblings in a small, red-brick, two-bedroom house identical to the one in which Mandela lived. When she grew up and married she moved to a home with one room which, as she would say later, served as 'bedroom, sitting room, bathroom . . . everything'. Hers was the typical experience of an urban black person under apartheid.

That meant that, among other indignities, she had received a state education deliberately inferior to that provided for white people. The clear but unstated purpose was to ensure that black South Africans would lack the abilities necessary to challenge whites for the better jobs. But Masipa was part of a stubborn and

talented minority of the black population who con-
trived to overcome the educational obstacles placed
in their path. She learned to write excellent English
(her first language was Zulu) and obtained a degree
in social work in 1974, finding the time along the way
to marry and raise two children. On finishing university, she opted for journalism, a career in tune with her
developing political consciousness, which grew more
militant in 1976 when student riots in Soweto sparked
a black resistance movement that had lain largely dor-
mant after Mandela and other black leaders had been
jailed in 1964. As Masipa reported on clashes between
demonstrators and police, who were detaining black
activists in their thousands, she became ever more
politically engaged herself. One day, she joined a march
in downtown Johannesburg, along with several female
colleagues, in protest against the arrest of black male
reporters from her white-owned newspaper, *The Post*.
Five of them, including Masipa, were detained, locked
up in a jail cell and taken to court, where they refused
to enter a plea, declaring that they did not recognize
the authority of the apartheid state.

The five were released after their newspaper agreed
to pay a fine. Recognizing Masipa's talents, the paper's
bosses promoted her to a position previously held only
by white journalists, as women's page editor of *The*

*Post.* From there, she moved to *The Sowetan*, then black South Africa's leading newspaper, where she was appointed court reporter, an experience that persuaded her to broaden her horizons and study law.

Often studying at night while continuing to work as a journalist and raising her children, she graduated in 1990, the year Mandela was released. Pistorius was then four years old. Masipa, then forty-three, had fought to do away with the racial privilege that the extended Pistorius family symbolized. While she was growing up in a tiny home in Soweto, Gerti Pistorius and her husband were building up the family dynasty, living in a mansion in Pretoria, the citadel of white power.

Now the fates of Masipa and Pistorius were about to meet. On the face of it, this was not good news for the dynasty's most celebrated son. His defense team's scrutiny of her record revealed that her judgments in recent trials indicated a harsh disposition towards men whose victims were women. She had handed down a 252-year sentence in May 2013 to a man found guilty on eleven counts of housebreaking and robbery, three of rape and one of attempted murder. In sentencing him to fifteen years for each of the eleven robberies, twelve years for the attempted murder and a life sentence for the three rape charges, she said she was particularly concerned that he had 'attacked and molested the victims in the sanctity of their own homes, where they thought they were safe'.

In 2009 she gave a life sentence to a police officer who had shot and killed his wife during an argument. 'No one is above the law,' Masipa declared. 'You deserve to go to jail for life because you are not a protector, you are a killer.'

Might it be, some in his family wondered, that Masipa shared the sentiments of those women from the ANC Women's League, and beyond, who yearned to see an example made of Pistorius? Would she succumb to the pressure of those who believed that gender violence was the key issue here, and that the opportunity should not be missed to send a message to the nation that attacks on women would be punished with extreme severity?

Masipa would no doubt strive to separate her own views from her interpretation of the evidence in the case, but experience indicated that, in the event of a close call, she would be as likely as any judge to be swayed by her personal susceptibilities. As to the color of her skin, would the fact that she was black, and had a history of political activism, be a factor at the moment of reckoning? Pistorius's defense team feared initially that it would be. They were mistaken.

Masipa had been a beneficiary of her country's revolutionary changes and her thinking had moved with the spirit of the times. Politically, as legal colleagues testified, she was a moderate. Following the example of Mandela, she, along with the vast majority of black South Africans, had opted to forgive, if not necessarily forget, the sins of apartheid. Reconciliation, rather than revenge, had been Mandela's prescription for successful democratic change, and the majority of black South Africans had shown a disposition to embrace it.

Such a willingness to reject retribution not just for forty-six years of apartheid but for more than three centuries of systematic racial exploitation was hard to understand for many white South Africans. The explanation, however, lay in a mixture of pragmatism and generous-heartedness among black South Africans, qualities that Mandela did not possess in isolation, but that he embodied.

**The pragmatism** was a function of poverty. All black South Africans craved the dignity of political freedom, but most were also slaves to the daily urgency of putting food on the table. They wanted the vote, but even more pressing was the need to get by from day to day. In that light, most had the clear-sightedness to understand the reality that white South Africans had a monopoly on the skills required to keep the water and electricity systems running, and that it was they who ran the businesses that provided them with work. Driving the whites into exile – or 'throwing the whites into the sea', as the Pan-Africanist Congress and some other radical black minorities proposed – might afford a pleasing short-term satisfaction, but were such a course to be taken, before long the economic consequences would be catastrophic.

When Alan Dershowitz, a celebrated American lawyer who served on the defense team in the O. J. Simpson case, said on CNN on the eve of the trial over which Judge Masipa would preside that South Africa was 'a failed state' and 'a lawless country', he was only displaying his ignorance. It was true that the ruling party that Mandela once headed had not been immune to the corrupting effects of twenty years of uninterrupted power, and the administration of the state was often incompetent and lax. Crime rates were high and burglaries were on the rise, yet police statistics showed that between 1994 and 2010 the annual number of homicides had dropped from 26,000 to 16,000. The economy grew year in year out and the poor, who now had far greater access to water and electricity than during the apartheid era, were getting less poor. The average increase in the income of black households between 2001 and 2011 was 169 per cent, compared with 88 per cent for white ones; and though whites still commanded a disproportionately high share of the national wealth, the richest person in the country was a black man. It was possible, by a careful selection of the facts and by setting the bar at Western European or American standards of prosperity, to make the case that the new South Africa had been a disappointment. But the truth was muddled and ambiguous. Things could have gone better but, as examples in the Middle East and elsewhere in Africa showed, they could have gone an awful lot worse.

Don Gips, US ambassador in South Africa between 2009 and 2013, observed that one's view of South Africa depended on what side of the bed one got out of in the morning. Vestiges of racism remained, especially among older white people, and gross incidents of discrimination sometimes surfaced in the press, but Gips, who was appointed by Barack Obama, noted that 'the everyday racial atmosphere between black and white is more relaxed in South Africa than in the US'. Afrikaner society was, in the main, more free-thinking than it had been when Mandela came to power and, in the big urban areas at least, black and white people mixed in bars and nightclubs with an ease that startled foreign visitors primed to think of the country in apartheid terms.

Baffling to outsiders who studied international politics was the fact that all the usual reasons for countries to fall apart abounded in South Africa. In addition to the racial and cultural fault lines, there were religious ones, too, with Christians, Jews, Hindus and Muslims living side by side. Inequality in terms of income and standards of education remained among the widest in the world. Yet South Africa was a stable, politically vociferous country, where there were no limits on freedom of speech, elections were free and fair, institutions such as parliament and the press were solid and, in terms of almost every democratic box worth ticking, ahead of most nations – not least another country that had abandoned tyranny about two decades earlier, Russia.

As to the generous-heartedness that provided the emotional fuel for the peaceful transition, that also derived from the poverty and the day-to-day disorder in which most black South Africans had always lived. They were more accustomed to tragedy, less expectant of tidy or happy endings than their relatively pampered white compatriots. But there was a cultural element to it, too, a disposition to empathize and to forgive, which black parents had been passing on to their children from generation to generation. A mystery, though not unique to South Africa, was how a country with so many people who had the milk of human kindness flowing through their veins could yield such a high incidence of rape and, despite the drop in the murder rate, so many horrific crimes, not just against women but often against children. The conundrum was as hard to decipher as the character of Oscar Pistorius himself.

South Africa was a country of extremes, of rich and poor, and good and evil, living side by side. Pistorius, a kind and considerate individual given to hair-trigger explosions of anger, exemplified the national schizo-phrenia. He mirrored South Africa in that he contained much of the best and the worst of the country within him. And he served to illustrate the bigger truth that individuals, like nations, are unfathomably varied and complex, eluding easy definition.

One thing that was certain, however, was that black South Africans displayed a capacity rarely found else-where for understanding and forgiving their enemies – helping to explain not only why they had made peace with the whites but also why the ANC had only turned to armed resistance as a last resort, fifty years after its foundation, and why even then the number of civilian victims over three decades was a tiny fraction of the toll exacted in parallel liberation struggles in Africa, the Middle East, Asia and Latin America.

This magnanimous disposition of black South Africans had a name, 'Ubuntu', described by one of its most enthusiastic advocates, Archbishop Tutu, as the custom of seeing that 'a person is a person through other persons', and that if you seek to diminish others, you diminish yourself. 'Ubuntu' was the reigning spirit of the Truth and Reconciliation Commission which Mandela appointed and over which Tutu presided from 1996 to 1998. It was a way to exercise justice that was in keeping with the political circumstances of South Africa at that time and the values that Mandela and Tutu embodied. Rather than pursue retribution, as in the Nuremberg Trials that followed the Second World War, a pact was sought whereby in return for the confession of crimes committed in the apartheid era – confessions made in the presence of the victims or their surviving relatives – the perpetrators would receive state-sanctioned amnesties from prosecution. Over the two years the commission ran Tutu chaired innumerable anguished encounters and ceremonies of forgiveness, as members of secret apartheid-era police units, but also individuals who had killed on behalf of the black liberation struggle, came forward and made their confessions.

In one especially memorable instance, a notorious assassin in the security police called Eugene de Kock appeared before the commission. De Kock, who had served as a colonel at the head of a state-sanctioned clandestine death squad, had already been convicted of eighty-nine charges, including six counts of murder, and sentenced by a regular law court to 212 years in a maximum-security prison in Pretoria. More killings had been carried out under his leadership that the court had failed to register. He chose to confess to them before the truth commission, even though he had no realistic hope of obtaining a reprieve from jail. His reputation had been such that his own security police colleagues used to call him 'Prime Evil'. What he confessed to at the commission was his participation in the murders of four other activists, with which he had not been charged. In the presence of a horrified Archbishop Tutu, De Kock gave honest, vivid and gruesome accounts of how he had shot his victims and then incinerated their bodies. He also expressed remorse for his crimes and begged forgiveness of their relatives. They granted it.

De Kock duly went back to his cell to continue serving the sentence imposed by the law that Judge Masipa served, though Tutu might have wished for more leniency. In early 2014, around the time when Masipa was preparing for what was likely to be the biggest trial of her life, Tutu gave an interview in which he spelled out his views on what he regarded as the spiritual limitations of the state's criminal justice system. 'There is nothing that cannot be forgiven, and there is no one undeserving of forgiveness,' Tutu said, adding, 'We cannot ever say a person is a monster. We can say what they did is monstrous. But once you say someone is a monster you are actually letting them off because a monster does not have moral responsibility. You are also saying they do not have the capacity to become different. You are saying they are totally and completely lost and you cannot say that of a human being, ever.'

Those principles were harder to implement within the professional world that Judge Masipa inhabited, but as she herself would have noted prior to the Pistorius trial, there existed two significant and possibly relevant legal precedents for dispensing mercy, even when the identity of the killer was beyond dispute.

In one instance, in May 2004 a man called Rudi Visagie saw his car being driven out of the driveway of his home at five in the morning. He fired one shot at the car, killing the driver instantly. The driver was his nineteen-year-old daughter. When the case came to be heard, the judge deemed that Visagie had suffered enough and set him free. Approached for comment by the press ten years later, after the shooting of Reeva Steenkamp, Visagie, who had once been a professional rugby player, sided with his country's greatest sporting idol. 'I can tell him, I feel for you,' Visagie said. 'You can't take it back . . . you can't take that bullet back.'

There was also the case of 'Bees' Roux, the rugby player who beat a black policeman to death but received a suspended sentence for culpable homicide, with the approval of the victim's wife and brother, who hugged him in the prosecutor's office after the deal was agreed.

It is possible that had the victim been a white South African his relatives would have displayed a similar willingness to understand and to forgive. The response to the killing of Reeva Steenkamp was similarly divided among those who had 'Ubuntu' in their ancestral culture and those who did not. And also between those who habitually used social media – who were disproportionately white, because whites had a disproportionately greater access to technology – and those who didn't.

Random samples of opinion among South Africans in the year between the shooting incident and the trial indicated that the attitude of white people towards Pistorius was more vindictive than that of their black compatriots. 'Pistorius intended to kill her. Let him rot in jail,' was the majority white view. The ANC Women's League, a predominantly black organization, had taken the same position after deciding to use the case in its campaign against gender violence. The Women's League had a credibility problem, though. They had kept quiet when the country's ANC deputy president

Jacob Zuma was tried for rape in 2006 and then, after he was controversially acquitted, openly backed him in his successful bid for the presidency three years later, overlooking the fact that he was a polygynist with four wives.

But among ordinary black people of both sexes and all ages who were not professionally involved in politics, the prevailing response to Pistorius was more sympathetic than it was among whites, regardless of whether or not they were inclined to believe the prosecution charge that he knew who was behind the bathroom door when he fired the fatal shots.

Time and again in conversation with older black women one heard them saying, 'I think of him and it breaks my heart,' or, 'He lost his mother when he was fifteen. I feel I am his mother now.' Young black men would say, 'Look how he is suffering. He must not go to jail,' or, 'Anyone can do something terrible in a moment when they lose control. It could happen to anybody. We must forgive him.' Over and over, from Johannesburg to Pretoria to Cape Town, random encounters with black people revealed sentiments along these lines. It was 'Ubuntu', as Archbishop Tutu would have been quick to point out, but it also derived from the long history of poverty and curtailed freedom that black people in South Africa had endured. Before, but also after, the end of apartheid, white people entertained the illusion enjoyed by well-off people everywhere that they had control over their lives. Black people, even those whose lives had improved after apartheid, were more likely to carry with them a deeper knowledge, rooted in a keener experience of misfortune, that all individuals were subject to random forces over which they had little control. From this came a greater predisposition to put themselves in the shoes of others, even their enemies. Had blacks done to whites what whites did to blacks for centuries, whites would in all likelihood have shown far less mercy when the day of reckoning came.

Mandela said many times during the four-year transition between his release and 1994 when the terms of the handover of power were negotiated that he understood white fears of black rule. He understood that had he been born white in South Africa he would probably have assumed white racial prejudices. Having been born black, he shared most of his black compatriots' readiness to judge people on their individual merits rather than on the color of their skin. Not all white South Africans understood that. A number chose to see Mandela as unique in his racial generosity. White South Africans came to venerate him as much as black South Africans did. When he died, three months before the start of the Pistorius trial, on December 5, 2013, his life was celebrated and his death mourned equally by South Africans of all races. But the truth was, as Mandela once said, that the 'non-racial' philosophy that had been the driving impulse of the organization he served for seventy years, the African National Congress, came from the people. It had not been imposed from the top down, but from the bottom up.

Judge Masipa was no exception to the general rule. She would be as fair-minded as any white judge in dealing with the white accused, and possibly more capable of imagining herself in his predicament. There was a particular reason to believe so. She, too, was, in practical terms, disabled. A diminutive woman, barely five-foot tall, she was now sixty-six years of age and her bones were riddled with severe arthritis. She walked slowly and haltingly, swaying so precariously that she needed to hold onto someone's hand to keep her balance when she tried to cover anything but the shortest distances. Pistorius could move more nimbly on his stumps than she could on her feet. In a country where everybody was afraid of crime she would know first-hand that to have limited physical movement increased one's feeling of vulnerability. The defense's hope was that in listening to the evidence she might detect a ring of truth in Pistorius's explanation of what happened that might have eluded a physically more robust, ordinarily able judge.

# 14

*He was a man of a strange temperament,*
*Of mild demeanour though of savage mood.*
BYRON, *DON JUAN*

Pistorius had always dreaded the notion that people might be sniggering at him behind his back. Now it felt as if the whole world were laughing in his face. In theaters and on TV South African stand-up comics were milking his shame with relish. Nik Rabinowitz, a merciless mimic, who captured his voice perfectly, portrayed him as a moany, trigger-happy psychopath.

During the first three months after the shooting packed houses guffawed at Rabinowitz's jokes, but one day he was presented with an unexpected dilemma. He ran into the very man he was so profitably ridiculing at a lunch party in Johannesburg, finding himself alone in a room with only Pistorius and one other person present. Rabinowitz had a choice to make. Greet Pistorius or flee the room. For half a minute Rabinowitz froze, pondering what to do. 'I thought, What if I introduce myself and he says he enjoys my shows? What if I like him? What if I feel sorry for him?' Rabinowitz said, recalling the absurdity of his predicament with self-mocking delight. 'The possibilities were frightening. I wouldn't have the heart to make any more jokes about his legs, about shooting people in toilets. It would ruin my act.' Rabinowitz raced out of the room without saying hello.

Rabinowitz did not regret his choice. To portray Pistorius as a criminal buffoon, it helped not to know him. Rabinowitz traded on the fact that most of his audiences had only ever regarded Pistorius in caricature terms, as hero or villain. It would not have served his purposes to know that, in person, the famous Blade Runner could not just be likable, but he inspired loyalty. From Gemona, to Boston, to Reykjavik, to London, to Texas, to Pretoria, to Johannesburg, his friends stood by him, for the most part, and lamented his predicament.

It would not have been helpful to Rabinowitz to meet some of those friends, least of all one who was the exact opposite of Pistorius in almost every imaginable way.

Samkelo Radebe was black, Pistorius was white. Samkelo came from a poor background, Pistoris from an affluent one. Samkelo had been raised in a stable family and his mother remained ever present in his life, Pistorius came from a disrupted family and had been effectively orphaned at the age of fifteen. Samkelo had a law degree, Pistorius never completed his university studies. Samkelo had both arms cut off below the elbows, Pistorius had both legs cut off below the knees.

They first met at an athletics track when Samkelo was sixteen and Pistorius, already famous, nineteen. The one thing they had in common was that they were both fast runners.

'I went up to Oscar, nervous, thinking he might be arrogant or aloof and, most probably, not interested in talking to a guy he'd never seen or heard of, like me,' Samkelo recalled, drinking from a straw in a Johannesburg restaurant shortly before the beginning of the murder trial. 'But I plucked up my courage and I said to him, "You've done us very proud." And he shook my arm and said, "Thank you, that means a lot to me," and then he said, "I've seen you on the track. You're really fast. Keep running. Work hard, and you'll get far." And I said to myself, "What the fuck? He's seen me – me – and he says I must keep running?" It was crazy, unbelievable. I mean, he was so big. That made a huge impression on me. It changed my whole attitude. I did as he said. I worked hard, stopped playing and made it my aim to make the Paralympics team in 2008. After that meeting with Oscar I was on fire. On fire!'

Samkelo was a man who had every reason to have a complex, but betrayed no suggestion of one. He was short and wiry, chirpy in his manner, but walked with an athlete's princely strut. He wore no prosthetics in public, went about in short sleeves, saw no need to hide his mutilated limbs from himself or other people. Betraying no self-consciousness on a first introduction, he would reach out his right stump, inviting one, with an impish smile and a wink, to wrap one's fingers around it and give it a shake. He was good-humored, funny and clever, exuberantly determined to accept life on the terms he had received it. Hugh Herr, the MIT professor who had lost his legs in a climbing accident, had said that amputees like himself and Pistorius came out of their experiences 'stronger than hell'. This seemed to be especially true of Samkelo, who had endured a loss far more punishingly restrictive than either Herr or Pistorius, and whose easy, impish nature disguised a big reservoir of moral courage.

How he had lost his arms was not a taboo subject. He would, quite matter of factly, tell anyone who asked that it had happened when he was nine years old when he grabbed a pair of live electrical cables while playing with friends in the Johannesburg township where he grew up. He was laid up in hospital for nine months and every day his mother came to sit by his side, looking cheerful and optimistic. It was only very recently, fifteen years after the accident, he said, that his mother had confessed to him that she had cried every time on the way to hospital and cried all the way back home. 'It shocked me when she told me because she was always smiling when I saw her,' Samkelo said, 'but it made me love my mother even more. It made me realize how fortunate I am to have the family I have.'

His other stroke of fortune was to have met his favorite sportsman at a point in his life when he was not sure what his own priorities should be. From one day to the next, he threw himself into disabled athletic competition, from 100 to 800 meters, to long jump, to high jump, to cycling. He set new records, won gold medals. 'And all in the very year I met Oscar! It was absolutely no coincidence that I made it into the South African national team. Hard, hard, hard work was the key, and Oscar was the spark that got me going.'

Samkelo gesticulated exuberantly with his stunted arms as he spoke, excited to talk about his athletics career and the role the champion who would become his friend had played in it. Five years after they met, in 2011, the two were competing side by side at the world disabled games in New Zealand. 'Me and some of the other younger athletes hung out with Oscar and he completely confirmed that first impression he'd made on me. He was just a regular guy. He was a superstar, but he never made you feel that he thought he was superior. He showed us pictures of the cars he'd driven, places he had been, of his home. But it wasn't showing off. We really wanted to know all about him. But he also helped us with practical stuff, telling us what we should do and not do to avoid getting injured and be in peak condition when we needed to be.'

The highlight of Christchurch for Samkelo was when he represented South Africa in the 4×100 meters relay alongside his boyhood hero. Samkelo ran the first leg. 'Oscar said to me before the race, "If you false start I'm gonna run all the way around the track and smack you." I said, "You won't catch me." He said, "Trust me, I will!" We were smiling and laughing but then he turned serious and said, "Okay, let's have fun, enjoy it, do what we have to do." It was captain talk and we accepted it as such. He said enjoy it and we did. And we won the race. For me Oscar was a big brother.'

But Samkelo also saw something in his big brother during that visit to New Zealand that took him aback.

He discovered that the man he had put on a pedestal was much more emotionally fragile than he let on. For the first time in his seven years as a disabled runner, Pistorius lost a race. It was in the 100 meters, against a one-legged American runner called Jerome Singleton. Samkelo was there watching.

'Oscar cried after the race and on the team bus on the way home it was really awkward for the rest of us. He was so upset, fighting back tears until he just let go and wept inconsolably. I remember thinking, Wow! This really is his life, his whole life.'

Samkelo, then at law school, reflected that he had done well to spread his options more widely. Running fast gave him joy and made him proud, but studying for a degree consumed his energies as much, giving his life a balance, a perspective, and a contact with the real world of everyday work that his friend lacked. Samkelo did not receive sponsorships or the free use of fast cars but he had a future beyond sports. Seeing Pistorous break down on that bus in New Zealand gave Samkelo a glimpse of the vulnerability behind the superhero facade. Yet, he said, it made him value his friend's virtues all the more.

Just as vivid for Samkelo was the recollection of Pistorius's generosity on a night out in Christchurch after the games were over. 'We wanted to go out and see the town but we were a bit nervous. We didn't know our way around and we also had very little money. So he said, "No, guys. I'll pay. I'll look after you. Let's go." And he paid for the taxi and took us to a bar and he bought the drinks and made us all feel so special. He'd say, "You guys still okay? You ready to go home? If you want to, just tell me." He was so considerate. He knew this was his world, but not ours. He really was like a big brother, herding the kids around, introducing us to this grown-up, foreign world.'

Samkelo never socialized with Pistorius outside of athletics, but they formed what would become a lasting bond a year after New Zealand when they ran together in the 2012 Paralympic Games in London. The Olympic Stadium was as full every day as it had been a month earlier for the Olympics themselves. At previous Paralympic competitions, in Beijing, Sydney and elsewhere, there had always been plenty of empty seats, but for several of the events in London there was standing room only. Scalpers sold tickets at inflated prices outside the venues. There was wall-to-wall coverage on British TV and the broadcasts were transmitted live around the world. Big banners in London read 'Paralympics, we are the superhumans'. The more sober message the event's organizers strove to convey was that the games were 'about ability, not disability – about what people can do, not what they cannot do'.

There was more than an echo there of one of Pistorius's favorite catchphrases. The MIT professor Hugh Herr, who followed his performances in London keenly, picked it up. 'It was Oscar, fresh from making history in the Olympics, who drove the whole thing,' Herr said. 'The image projected with brilliant orchestration by the Brit marketing people was that their stories here were not about cripples but about gladiators, and Oscar was the big brand around which the marketing strategy was built. His story was THE story. Everyone knew it. He was at the top of that wave, the king of the Games.'

Through the ages, disabled people had endured a kind of apartheid. Discriminated against, they felt they lived in a separate world. The London Paralympics helped bridge the gap as never before. Opinion polls conducted in Britain before the closing ceremony showed that 81 per cent of respondents believed that the London Games had made a positive impact on the way people with physical impairments were viewed. Disabled men and women who were not involved in the games began appearing before the media to say they were experiencing a degree of recognition and social acceptance they had never known before.

As for the disabled athletes, mostly left alone in the cities where previous Paralympics Games had been held, in London they would find themselves mobbed when they wandered out of the residential compound, besieged for photographs by members of the public – all the more so in Samkelo's case when it was discovered that he was the Blade Runner's team mate.

**Tadhg Slattery,** another member of the South African Paralympic team, had been with Pistorius at the Games in Athens and Beijing in 2004 and 2008. Tadhg was old enough to be Pistorius's father and had been winning medals in Paralympic swimming since the Barcelona games of 1992 – two years after Mandela's release from prison, when the ban on South Africa competing in international sports was lifted. Tadhg was deaf and had cerebral palsy. Through sign language and with the help of his brother and swimming coach, Cormac, he spoke of the esteem he felt for his celebrated team mate, recalling one moment in Beijing in 2008 when Cormac and his mother had come across Pistorius in the athletes' village. Pistorius detected a family resemblance, asked them if they were Tadgh's mother and brother, and told them he was immensely grateful they had flown all that way to support them all. 'He was the nicest man you could ever hope to meet,' said Cormac, with Tadhg nodding vigorously alongside.

On Pistorius's triumphant return to Johannesburg after Beijing, having won gold in three races, he gave a press conference at the airport, making a point of calling Tadhg over to the camera and putting an arm over his shoulder. But it was an encounter in London that sealed the Slattery family's love affair with him. It happened in the large dining room where the athletes always ate, just two days after his angry outburst following defeat in the 200 meters against Alan Oliveira, the Brazilian runner he had accused of cheating. 'He wasn't in a good place,' Cormac recalled, 'and I would have forgiven him if he had been less considerate than he was.'

There was no need. Tadhg had recently announced his decision to marry a woman who had a twenty-two-year-old son. The son, who was called Calvin, and had some misgivings about his future step-father, was in the athletes' dining room with Cormac when they saw Pistorius sitting at a nearby table. Calvin could hardly repress his excitement, but when Cormac suggested they go and say hello he turned shy. Cormac persuaded him to come along with him, and duly made the introduction. Tadhg learned what happened next from his brother.

'Oscar saw us approaching and he immediately got to his feet,' Cormac recalled. 'He didn't just shake Calvin's hand, he gave him a big man-hug, shoulder to shoulder, and said, "Great to meet you!" But then he went further, as if immediately understanding what the situation was. "You should know," he told Calvin, "that your future stepfather is one of the greatest guys I've met." Tadhg, who was devastated when he heard of the shooting of Reeva Steenkamp six months later, would never forget his kindness.

Nor would Arnu Fourie, another disabled South African athlete, forget how much he owed Pistorius. A sprinter and, like Samkelo, a member of the South African 4×100 meters relay team, Arnu Fourie had suffered a terrible misfortune when he was eighteen years old. An Afrikaner and a rugby fanatic – two characteristics that tended to go hand in hand – Arnu had what seemed like a glorious career ahead of him as one of rugby's top players when he lost a leg in a boating accident. He was in the water and the propeller of the boat caught him twice, severing first his foot, then his leg, just below the calf. That was in 2003. It took him four years to begin to make peace with his disability. He wore jeans, never shorts. Bitter and depressed, he struggled to confront his loss. 'I went once to take part in a golf tournament for disabled people and I'd hear some of them make jokes about their missing limbs,' he said. 'I had no sense of humor about what had happened to me.'

In 2006 he decided to try running, but the experiment might have been short-lived. He took part in a 100 meters race against able-bodied runners, with calamitous results. He ran using his regular, walking prosthetic leg and came last, thirty meters behind the rest of the field, in 13.9 seconds. Embarrassed and forlorn, he had a choice to make – never to try this again, or to ensure that, if he did, there would be no repeat of his humiliation. He decided to try again, but in order to have any chance of success that meant acquiring a Cheetah running blade, and Cheetahs were expensive. He could not afford it. As with Samkelo, the turning point came when he met Pistorius.

'I got in touch with Oscar and asked him if I could come along to one of his training sessions. He said, "Sure," so I went to Pretoria and stayed with my mom, who lives there. Oscar was open and friendly and took an interest in me. I also remember that he went out of his way to greet my mom. He was very polite to her. To me, he said he would do anything he could to help.'

Pistorius was as good as his word, giving Arnu one of his old blades and putting him in touch with his childhood prosthetics specialist, Trevor Brauckmann, for the all-important business of fixing him up with a socket that would fit snugly. 'The first time it felt very weird,' Arnu said. 'The brain does not realize the blade's there, so you have to make a sort of leap of the imagination. But I got running and in two months my time was down to 12.1 seconds. I realized that even against able-bodied runners I did not have to be last. I was suddenly incredibly motivated.'

So much so, that he brought his time for the 100 meters down to 11.9 seconds and made it into the Paralympic team in Beijing in 2008, and again in London four years later, both times sharing a room and becoming close friends with Pistorius. Arnu got to learn that Pistorius was a more complex person than he had imagined when he first met him. One day at the Beijing Games, Pistorius had flown into a fury with South Africa's Paralympic management team for what he saw as their failure to provide him with adequate training equipment. It was not the only time he became enraged with team officials who, he believed, fell short of the total dedication that he himself invested in his sport. His obsession with sticking to the strict requirements of his diet also produced some ugly incidents; people who had been in restaurants with him reported that sometimes he would explode with rage when a waiter did not bring him exactly what he believed he had asked for.

What few were as aware of as Arnu Fourie was the wild, tortured state he got into over his girlfriends – in particular Samantha Taylor, and specifically in the middle of 2012, when the relationship was going through a difficult patch.

Pistorius found out during the London Games that she had gone on a trip to Dubai with Quinton van der Burgh. Samantha, who had accused him of having an affair in New York with a Russian model, understood that they had broken up – but this did not stop him from succumbing to fits of raging jealousy. With his mind half on the races ahead and half on his aching heart, continually beset by requests from the media, sponsors and fans, he spent his time away from the track in the athletes' village making frantic phone calls, checking his text messages and WhatsApps, veering from hysteria one moment to measured, professional calm the next.

Arnu, a level-headed and happily married man, sympathized with his friend, but asked to be allowed to move to a room on his own. 'Oscar is a guy who loses his temper easily, sure,' Arnu said. 'He's always lived with stress and I think he feeds off it, but sometimes it gets too much for him. The stress on him in London was enormous. London was the center of the world in the summer of 2012 and after Usain Bolt, or maybe right alongside him, he was the biggest thing there. Never mind the public, all the other athletes wanted pictures taken with him, and autographs, and he always went along with it, to keep that worship thing going, to live up to it. But you saw him at night when he was off the stage and the lights went out and he was just a normal guy and you could feel how it all weighed him down, that pressure to remain unbeatable, untouchable, perfect . . . But on the other hand, he couldn't live without it. He loved being the center of attention.'

Arnu did not begrudge him that. 'He earned it. His whole life he's had to fight – losing his mum, losing his dad – and he has always shown this huge drive. I love his attitude. All his life he's been like this. He just cannot believe he cannot do things.'

That helped explain Pistorius's fury when he lost to Oliveira, the Brazilian, in the 200 meters in London. He had won the 400 meters Paralympic gold – his third in successive games – with his accustomed ease, but coming second in the 200 had shattered his sense of invincibility, and it rankled. A chance to avenge that defeat came in the 4×100 meters relay, where Samkelo and Arnu, who had won bronze in the individual 100 meters, would be his team-mates.

The race took place on September 5, 2012, and Pistorius assumed the unofficial role of relay team captain. When he and the three other runners went to limber up on the practice track alongside the Olympic Stadium before the race, it was he who gathered them round, gave the team talk, reminded them that the danger came from the Brazilians but also from the Americans, who had won this race in Beijing.

There was an odd symmetry about the South African four. Samkelo, who would run first, was missing both arms; Zivan Smith, who would run second, was missing one arm; Arnu, third, was missing one leg; Pistorius, running last, was missing both legs. As Samkelo would joke later, 'We were the perfect team. A double-leg amputee, a double-arm amputee, a single-leg ampu-tee, a single-arm amputee. How perfect is that? God looked at the four of us and said, "Okay, I'll make this one perfect, just because I can." God, man, has a great sense of humor!'

So did Samkelo, yet, for all his attempts at light-heartedness, he was the team's biggest worry as they gathered on the practice track. He had torn a ham-string the week before. 'It was the London weather's fault,' Samkelo smiled. 'Cold, hot, rain, hot, cold – you get four seasons in one hour over here.' But he was des-perate to run. He had prepared ten years for this, the greatest moment of his life; he was determined to take part even if it meant the end of his career. Wanting

Pistorius's blessing, Samkelo approached him the day before the race and said, 'Running with you, Oscar, and running for my country is my dream. I will not let you down.' Pistorius took him at his word and the South African team decided to take the risk and let Samkelo run.

But now, as they went through their preparations on the practice track, with only minutes to go before the big race, Samkelo was giving Pistorius, his other two team-mates and the coaches new grounds for worry. He was overexcited, or excessively nervous – 'or something', as Samkelo said – and when all four lined up for a rehearsal he messed up. Samkelo was the team's starter, the one who would run the first 100 meter leg, and he bolted from the blocks too soon. The worst thing that could possibly happen would be for him to make a false start when the real race began, for if he did he would be disqualified, along with the rest of the team.

Pistorius saw that Samkelo was distraught. He heard the coaches groan, noticed them shaking their heads. If the little guy was messing up now on a practice run, how would he cope when the real race began in front of 80,000 people? All seemed lost.

Pistorius took charge. He went up to Samkelo, took him to one side, looked him in the eye and said, 'Okay, Sam, listen to me. Relax. Think. Do not move a muscle when you hear "Get set!". Wait until you hear the gun. Wait! And then, and then you must run faster than your shadow. Chase your shadow! Chase it! And, I promise you, you will catch it.'

The pep talk worked. As Samkelo confessed later, 'Had Oscar not come over and given me that confidence, I'd have crapped myself I was so nervous.'

Samkelo tried again in practice, and again one more time, and both times he got the start right. Then all four gathered in a huddle, prayed in English and in Afrikaans, and stepped out into the amphitheater, greeted by a roar that sounded to Samkelo like a hundred jumbo jets at take-off. When his name was called out, he raised his arms in the air and blew kisses to the crowd, pressing his stumps to his lips.

Pistorius saw Samkelo's reaction on the big stadium screen. He looked not just happy, but ecstatic. He would be just fine, Pistorius realized. But would the others be? Would he? He wasn't smiling. His face was grim-set, imagining the race ahead. Would Samkelo, Ziva and Arnu give him the lead he felt he needed for the final stretch, where he would be running against the feared Oliveira?

A lesser consideration, but one that mattered to him all the same, was how the crowd would react to him after his behavior a few days earlier when he had lost to the Brazilian. He need not have worried. When his name was called out, he received the loudest cheer of the Games. It felt as if they had forgiven him – a huge relief. Now he had to show that he merited their faith.

At the cry 'On your marks!', the stadium fell silent, as if someone had turned off a switch. It was so silent that, as he stood there, watching Samkelo on the other side of the field, he could hear his own pulse. Then it was 'Get set!', and the gun went off. Another roar blasted from the stadium, only to subside a second later when the runners slowed down, ordered back to the blocks. There had been a false start. 'Not Samkelo, please!' he thought. It had not been Samkelo. Pistorius thanked God for that.

Again, 'On your marks!', 'Get set!' – and again, a false start. Not Samkelo this time either. And then, at the third attempt, the race began. Batons were not an option when there were runners in the field, like Samkelo, with no hands. At the changeovers, the runners only had to tap the team-mate ahead.

Samkelo finished his 100 meter leg neck and neck with his far bigger and more muscular American rival, but the South African changeover was smoother and Ziva led the field by a whisker around the first bend. Pistorius clenched his fists with satisfaction and glanced at Arnu, who would be next up. He had never seen his friend so pumped up. The changeover between Ziva and Arnu was flawless and now Arnu was charging towards him like a mad bull, extending the South African lead. Pistorius would have no excuse if they didn't win, and he knew it. His heart beat faster and faster as Arnu drew closer and closer, the muscles on his neck almost bursting, his face twisted, almost terrifying, as he reached out to touch him and then bellowed to him, as if in a wild rage, to run, run for his life. Pistorius did. He felt Oliveira breathing down his neck. The Brazilian was gaining ground, but he was not going to let him win a second time. Not today. Pistorius dipped his head, broke the tape, made it across the line first. He had won. South Africa had won. Pistorius covered his face in his hands, he grinned, then he covered his face in his hands again, as if not knowing whether to feel relief or joy. The stadium exploded. Samkelo, Ziva and Arnu ran towards him, screaming, as Samkelo would remember later, 'like girls'. Samkelo wrapped his stumps around his neck and jumped into his arms. Then they saw the time: 41.75 seconds. A new world record. They screamed again. Samkelo was going nuts, shouting, 'We won gold, man! And we broke the world record! We broke the world record! Fuck, man! Fuck, man! Fuck!'

And then the lap of honor; but before that, at Pistorius's bidding, a team huddle and a prayer of thanks; and after that, the medal ceremony and the South African anthem – a blend of two songs, first the old anthem of white South Africa, 'Die Stem', 'The Call', and then the old anthem of black protest, 'Nkosi Sikelel' iAfrika', 'God Bless Africa'. Samkelo sang and smiled and laughed. Pistorius struggled to get the words out. The stadium's giant screens showed that his eyes were filled with tears.

**Five months** later, on February 7, 2013, Pistorius had a meeting with his agent, Peet van Zyl, to discuss the commercial opportunities that had come his way since London. 'You're going to make stupid money. Stupid money!' Van Zyl had told him. Contracts that needed to be signed or to be examined lay on a big table before them. There was the sportswear brand Nike; there was the sunglasses manufacturer Oakley; there was Össur, the company that made his running blades – all of which were extending arrangements they had had in place for several years. Among the new deals on offer, there was one he was about to sign with a big US company that would net him, according to Van Zyl (who refused to name the company), three times what even Nike paid him, as well as a deal with

France's Thierry Mugler to promote a new men's cologne called Pure Shot.

Initially, the idea had been for Pistorius to retire after the Rio de Janeiro Olympics and Paralympics in 2016, but Van Zyl had persuaded him to continue for one more year, until he was nearly thirty-one. His financial future – and Van Zyl's – seemed assured. The stupid money he would earn would allow him to buy himself a large new house in Johannesburg, as well as a fabulously expensive state-of-the-art McLaren car, which he had already ordered and which was due to arrive in South Africa from the factory in England in March. He'd be able to add to a collection of racehorses, a recent passion, in which he already had shares, and would be free, most of all, to enjoy his life with Reeva.

He told Van Zyl at that meeting about plans he had made to travel with Reeva to Italy, his favorite country, later in the year. He was going to show her Milan and Venice, Gemona too, and they were both so excited at the prospect. They had also planned a trip to Rio de Janeiro, where she, who had never had the money for expensive foreign trips, had always dreamed of going. And they'd visit lots of other places, too. But there was more to it all than fun, he told Van Zyl. He was serious about Reeva, and he planned to do something with her in the European summer that he had never done with a girlfriend before: take her to an athletics meeting in which he would be competing – specifically, to one in Manchester. He wanted her to get to know him in his work environment, to give her a chance to see him when he was distant, obsessive and self-engrossed, so she could see all the facets of his personality and judge whether she would be able to put up with his grumpiness and outright bad temper when he was focused, to the exclusion of all else, on a big race. He would be honest with her, but he hoped he would pass the test, laying the basis for the possibility of a future life together, of marriage and maybe children. The two of them had been spending time on the internet poring over options for the furniture for his new Johannesburg home.

A week after the meeting with his agent, Pistorius had shot Reeva, killing her, as well as his dreams, his career, his reputation, his peace of mind – and condemning himself, when he was obliged to sell everything he owned to cover his legal costs, to bankruptcy.

**His Paralympic** team-mates, who had won so much with him, had a sharper sense of his loss than most. On the morning of February 14, 2013, they reacted to the news with horror and incomprehension. Tadhg Slattery saw a headline on his smartphone that read

'Pistorius' and 'murder' and asked himself, 'How can this possibly be true?'

Samkelo woke up to learn what had happened from his girlfriend. 'I was in a state of utter disbelief,' he said. 'First, I thought she must have surprised him and he thought it was an intruder sneaking up on him, but as the story unfolded I saw it wasn't that. It wasn't the kind of accident I initially had in mind. I didn't know what to think.'

The Pistorius that Samkelo had known bore little relation to the man he read about in the newspapers over the following days and weeks. Samkelo had no knowledge of the people Pistorius mixed with, or the fast life he led outside athletics; neither did he know that he was mad about guns. Now he was coming across stories of Pistorius being drunk and angry and abusive to people. Some were exaggerated, in keeping with the South African media's need to give the public the portrait of a villainous Pistorius that they seemed to want. But much was true. Pistorius's own lawyers would seek to come up with support for Pistorius's explanation at the murder trial, offering evidence of scientific research to demonstrate that it was not unusual for individuals with physical disabilities to harbor a deep existential frustration at their condition, inclining some of them to respond to a perceived threat in a shockingly disproportionate manner.

'I never saw any of that in Oscar myself,' said Samkelo, who appeared to contradict the research, offering an example of a disabled man serenely reconciled to his limitations. To him, what had happened at his friend's home on Valentine's Day was a mystery.

'Only God and that poor girl and Oscar know what happened,' Samkelo said. 'He wasn't thinking, he went crazy, with no mind for the repercussions. If it was an intruder, he was so scared, so out of his mind to protect himself and his girlfriend. Whatever the case, the time in which it happened was nothing, the time that divides a win and second place in a 100 meters race. Often we act on instinct, THEN we reason. That instinct was let loose in a split second, a split second that will decide how his life will be defined.'

Discussing the looming murder trial, Samkelo abandoned his good cheer, turned solemn and became more legally precise in his use of language, as if assuming the role of articled clerk that he was soon to take up at a top Johannesburg law firm. For all the affection and gratitude he professed towards his friend, he would not play God, as millions of people who did not know Pistorius had done, and state unequivocally whether or not he had intentionally killed Reeva Steenkamp. Yet Samkelo said that on one point his mind was clear: it was not fair to define Pistorius's entire life by what had happened that night, even if he understood why people might wish to think that way.

'It's a human nature thing. Everyone who does not know Oscar personally is influenced by the media. It happens to all of us. I do it with cases of murder I hear about involving people I do not know, especially if the ones who did it were once regarded as heroes. But that's not how I think about Oscar. For many people he's a monster now. Not for me. Never.'

Samkelo had suffered as a man born into a black family in South Africa during apartheid's last days, and he had suffered a great deal personally. He could imagine himself in Pistorius's mind now, and he felt that whatever he had done that night, it had been less a conscious criminal act than a cruel blow of fortune. His life should be measured in the round, not on the events of a few seconds, Samkelo believed.

'Yes, of course, we must accept the gravity of what he did, but we seem to have forgotten what he has achieved and done for the world. It's something I don't think any athlete has ever done. He's ruined his whole life now, sure. But it's wrong to define him only by that incident. Even if he is convicted on all charges, it's wrong!

'Some of my friends say he showed his true colors that night and I say, no, that night his true colors lapsed.

Yes, he may have been reckless, but he's young and we all do crazy things when we are young. If I drive a car and kill someone, it's not all me, Samkelo. It's a different me. A stupid, dumb, idiot version of me, maybe, but not the real me. And the man who fired that gun that night is not the true Oscar. If Mandela suddenly woke up and killed someone now, would that erase the fact that he changed the lives of millions for the better? No, it would not. We are too quick to judge.

'Everyone wanted a piece of his story before and now they don't want it any more. They shun him. But he is the biggest South African hero since Mandela. I don't care what happens in the trial. It will make no difference to what I feel about him. Whether he is convicted or acquitted, the man's work from 2004 to 2012 changed my life and, be it accident or intentional, what he did, it's not going to change the impact he's had on me, nor the impact he's had on millions and millions of lives out there. What happened that night cannot obliterate that, as the media are trying to do in South Africa. They build you up, they destroy you. People gloat at his fall, but I am not one of those people. I am on the subjective side. It was my dream for years and years to run with him in front of a big crowd and win gold, and finally it came true. Nothing he's done will ever erase the person he's been to me and what he did for me, out of the goodness of his heart. One night does not turn you into a monster.'

Arnu Fourie would not commit himself any more than Samkelo would, refusing to make a blanket pronouncement on what had happened that night. But he agreed with Samkelo that nothing should erase the past, 'the good stuff'.

'He did kill someone, it is a fact,' Arnu said, 'and a family is bereaved and that is terribly tragic and sad, but nothing can ever take away what he has achieved. It's horrible how people seem to wish to forget that. The media are seizing on the bad stuff now to confirm the monster image, just as before they looked to confirm the superhero image. All the time now I get stupid phone calls from the very same journalists who a year earlier wanted good stuff, to feed the superhero image. I used to tell them before that the team he led in that relay race in London, we were a brotherhood; that he helped me achieve what I have achieved, opening all the doors for me. Now they don't want to hear that. They want bad news so they can confirm that he did it. It makes me angry and it makes me sad.'

Arnu knew him more intimately than Samkelo did, but never went out with him on his nights in Johannesburg. He knew him as a fellow athlete and as a friend who would talk to him about the problems he had with his girlfriends. But he never revealed all, and it was there, in the personal side of life, away from the running track, that Arnu felt he had lacked guidance. 'He was on stage all the time and it was difficult for him to step off it. What he needed was someone to talk to about normal stuff, love and girlfriends, where the joys and satisfactions in life really are.'

Arnu said he came to see Pistorius as 'an ordinary guy' and, as such, a flawed guy. 'No one's perfect. When he's off the spotlight he is like the rest of us, his dad, his family, you, me – like every other human being. The absurd idea is for people to think that he is perfect. I'd be very disappointed with myself if I were ever to worship another human being.'

Samkelo harbored no such reservations. Pistorius would remain his hero, irrespective of what came out in court. 'Even if he is in prison,' Samkelo said, 'I shall tell my kids that this was my friend and my role model and he inspired me and the world. He blazed that trail. There is only one Oscar, and that is our Oscar. For me, he is immortal.'

# 15

*The terrible thing is that everybody in South Africa has a gun . . . You shouldn't have those things around because when people get irrational and emotional and drunk, terrible things can happen.*

CHARLIZE THERON, SOUTH AFRICAN ACTRESS

'I am a black man in a white man's court,' Nelson Mandela famously declared at the start of a trial he faced in Pretoria in 1962. More than half a century later, and three months after Mandela's death, things in South Africa had changed utterly. The country's most celebrated white man was on trial in a black woman's court.

'The Matter between the State and Oscar Leonard Carl Pistorius' began, as scheduled, in the High Court of North Gauteng on the morning of March 3, 2014, on the ground floor of a drab, red brick, nine-story building a short walk from the Old Synagogue courthouse where Mandela was tried. The Old Synagogue faced Church Square, the geographical heart of Pretoria, at the center of which there still stood a statue of Paul Kruger, South Africa's first Afrikaner president, the face of his people's resistance against the British during the Boer War at the turn of the nineteenth and twentieth centuries. The new High Court building stood on the recently renamed Madiba Street – 'Madiba' being the ancestral tribal title by which Mandela was affectionately known to South Africans after he became their country's first black president.

Pistorius arrived at the entrance to the court building at nine in the morning. A mob scene greeted him. TV cameramen and photographers battled to get clear shots of him, grunting and cursing as members of the general public – so many of them that they spilled from the sidewalk onto the busy road, blocking the rush-hour traffic – jostled with them for a glimpse of the Blade Runner. Drawn and thinner than in his athletic days, he had chosen to wear a dark suit, white shirt and black tie. Whether it was a coincidence or not, it was the very same outfit he had worn on the first night he had gone out on a date with Reeva, to the South African Sports Awards event. Pistorius ran the media gauntlet, escorted by three of Arnold's sons-in-law, strong, silent men, with whom he lifted weights in the gym and who had made the half-hour trip from Arnold's home with him in a van. Trauma was written all over Pistorius's face, but his mind was clearer than when he had appeared before Magistrate Desmond Nair at the bail application hearing five days after the shooting, when the media crush had been just as bad. He had lain not on the floor of a cell the night before but in his own soft bed at the cottage that had been his home since Nair let him out on bail. But he had barely slept. His body's adrenaline would have to carry him through.

The judge made her entrance later than expected, at 11.32 in the morning. 'All rise in court!' a uniformed policeman cried, a door opened at the back left-hand corner of the chamber, and Thokozile Masipa revealed herself for the first time to the man whose destiny she held in her hands.

Pistorius was taken aback by how frail she was, startled to see that she walked with far greater difficulty than he did. No taller than he was on his stumps, she limped slightly, her body swaying unsteadily inside a long red robe as she negotiated the three steps up to the raised platform from where she would preside over proceedings. Behind her came two assessors, legal officials she had selected who would sit either side of her throughout the trial ready to dispense advice when she needed it. One was a middle-aged Afrikaans woman called Janet Henzen-du Toit, who had considerable experience as a defense lawyer in criminal cases; the other was Themba Mazibuko, a young, sharp-suited, black legal academic freshly out of university, about whom little was known to either the defense or the prosecution.

Judge Masipa bowed reverently before the court and Pistorius bowed back, as did his lawyer, Barry Roux, the prosecutor, Gerrie Nel, and everyone else in the packed courtroom. Then she took her seat on a black orthopedic chair, while the assessors settled down either side of her, in burgundy leather chairs of the type on which judges normally sat.

Pistorius sat alone, facing the judge, on the extreme left of a wooden bench long enough to have accommodated thirty defendants. In front of Pistorius, between him and the judge, sat his defense team: his attorney and old friend Brian Webber, two junior defense clerks, Barry Roux, and Roux's number two, Kenny Oldwadge. Roux and Oldwadge, in black gowns, had the title of advocates. They were the trial lawyers, their job to speak on Pistorius's behalf. Roux, the more senior of the two, would do the lion's share of the interrogation of witnesses and presentation of the defense case;

Oldwadge, a junior counsel, would be his occasional backup.

Oldwadge had handled some high-profile cases before. He had successfully defended the driver of a car that had crashed four years earlier, killing Mandela's thirteen-year-old great-granddaughter, Zenani, the night before the start of the 2010 soccer World Cup in South Africa. The driver was charged with culpable homicide, driving under the influence of alcohol, and reckless and negligent driving. It was a difficult and politically delicate case, but Oldwadge won it, securing the defendant's aquittal on all charges. Olwadge persuaded the magistrate that there had been no evidence of alcohol consumption or of negligence on the part of his client, and came up with two expert witnesses who convincingly testified that it had been a freak accident.

Oldwadge had a bigger personal stake in the current trial's outcome. He had not known Pistorius since childhood, as Brian Webber had, but they had struck up a friendship after Oldwadge represented him in 2009 following the incident at a birthday party at his home when he was arrested, and spent a night in police custody, for having allegedly assaulted a young woman. She claimed that he had slammed a door on her, injuring her leg. Oldwadge's swift intervention ensured that no charges were ever pressed.

Oldwadge, like Webber, was almost family, and while it was comforting for Pistorius to hear his lawyer rage indignantly in private at the iniquitous way in which the news media had turned against him, it would not have been wise to place his fate entirely in Oldwadge's hands. Oldwadge was a big man, with a blustery nature, and there was a risk that if he played too central a role in the case Gerrie Nel might rattle him. His judgment might be swayed by his emotions.

Roux, on the other hand, approached his task as a surgeon would an operation. A cold-blooded professional in the courtroom, away from it he was a mild-mannered man, light-hearted and affable, a wine lover who was never happier than in the company of his many friends. Silver-haired and stockily built, he was regarded by his peers as one of the top two criminal defense lawyers in South Africa. Roux had been in legal practice since 1982, often taking on cases without regard for his personal belief as to whether the defendant was innocent or guilty – sometimes, not unusually for a defense lawyer, even when he suspected his client was lying to him. In such instances he would recommend a guilty plea, but if his advice was turned down the ethics of his profession required him to go ahead and conduct the defense to the very best of his ability. In this case, the biggest of his life, he had sincerely convinced himself of his client's innocence. At least in the sense that Pistorius had not shot his victim knowingly, that Reeva's death had been a terrible mistake. Roux's considered judgment in this matter was that it had all been, as he would tell friends over a bottle of red, 'a fuck-up, the epitome of a fuck-up'.

Pistorius trusted Roux. It was going to cost him a fortune to pay for his services, draining him of his savings and, in due course, of his house. But Oldwadge and Webber had told him that he was the best advocate money could buy and Pistorius was grateful to have him on his side. Roux was at least the equal of his adversary, the short, ginger-haired prosecutor sitting parallel to him, over on the far right of the court.

Nel was an Afrikaner, as was Roux. Doggedness came with the culture and the two shared a reputation for nitpicking persistence in their interrogation of witnesses. But where Roux saw himself as a hard-eyed lawyer trying to make an honest living, Nel had a touch of the moral crusader about him. As an employee of the state, he earned less than private practitioners like Roux, but he found sufficient compensation in the belief that he was contributing to the consolidation of his country's new democracy by upholding the law without fear. A prosecutor since 1984, he had played an Eliot Ness role as the chief in Gauteng province of South Africa's

'Untouchables', a supra-police organization called the Directorate of Special Operations (known popularly as 'the Scorpions') that specialized in combatting organized crime and corruption in government. Nel, whose hobby was wrestling, was known by his peers as 'pit-bull' for the aggressiveness of his cross-examinations, though colleagues who knew him outside court described him as self-effacing and likable. He had leapt to national fame in 2008 when he led an investigation into the national commissioner of police and former head of Interpol, Jackie Selebi, who was accused of receiving bribes from a convicted Johannesburg drug-smuggler and mafia chief. As Nel prepared to arrest Selebi, he himself was arrested – twenty armed policemen loyal to Selebi had detained him at his home, in front of his wife and children. He was released on bail and absolved of what were revealed to have been baseless fraud and per-jury charges, but, far from being intimidated, he pur-sued the police commissioner with still greater animus, eventually putting him in the dock and subjecting him to a brutally relentless cross-examination. 'You know what this means, Mr Selebi?' Nel said at one point. 'It means that you are arrogant and that you lie.' Nel won the case and Selebi went to jail.

Roux, familiar with Nel's reputation, had a grudg-ing professional regard for him, but detected a measure

of vanity behind his image as a man with a mission. Sensing that Nel might be unable to resist playing up his pit-bull persona on the big stage, Roux's greatest fear in this case was that his emotionally fragile, manifestly traumatized client would fall apart when the two came face to face in court.

Sitting alongside Gerrie Nel from the first to the last day of Pistorius's murder trial was Mike van Aardt, the policeman who had been put in charge of the investigation after the first detective at the scene of the crime, Hilton Botha, had been taken off it. Tall, heavy-set, jowly, with bulbous, melancholy eyes, Van Aardt was divorced with two teenage children, wished to give up smoking but could not, wished also that he was paid more, but contemplated nothing other than persisting at a job that he found endlessly compelling and, he wanted to believe, socially useful. Liked and admired by his colleagues, black and white, he had been a homicide detective for twenty-two years, witnessing unutterable horrors but striving always to keep a clinical distance from the cases he took on, finding solace in his children, watching rugby and reading books.

The Pistorius case had demanded a great deal of his time, day and night, over the previous year because of the four different charges against the accused and the large number of witnesses he had needed to interview, but it

had presented far fewer difficulties than other crime. he had been tasked to solve, and keeping himself emotionally disengaged had not been difficult. The cases he usually took on tended to be gruesome, along the lines of ones that had come to light just the previous month, such as the murder and rape of two little girls, two and three years old, whose bodies had been found, coincidentally, in a toilet cubicle; or the serial killing and burning of three girls aged six, nine and eleven; or the seventeen-year-old boy who had raped and murdered a girl of fourteen, then killed both her parents.

The particular crime he was engaged with now was itself quite routine in a country where murders of women by men were a dime a dozen. The case would have generated no public interest whatsoever had it not been for the identity of the accused. Unusually for a South African, Van Aardt had not paid much attention to the exploits of the celebrated Blade Runner, and he undertook the case with no strong feelings either way. His chief concern was to ensure that he left no loose ends in the investigation, in the manner of the hapless Hilton Botha. His superiors would be watching carefully and any publicized lapses would do his prospects for promotion or a salary increase little good. Otherwise, it was one more case in his busy life in a country where the grisly rate of forty-five murders a day had not

diminished over the past year. On the other hand, Van Aardt did take some satisfaction from the notion that his work might serve as a deterrent, for the fact was that, in spite of public perceptions, during the time he had worked in the homicide department the number of murders nationally had dropped almost by half. He also noted with satisfaction that thefts were being accompanied by less violence, the message having got through to criminals that they would be pursued with more vigor in the event of murder than for just theft.

Van Aardt was satisfied too that he had supplied Gerrie Nel with the raw material, chiefly in terms of witnesses, to present a solid enough case. He would sit in court alongside Nel for the duration of the trial and, warmed by the belief that he had done an honest and thorough job, and redressed the damage done to the police force by his chaotic predecessor, he was content for the law to run its course and for the judge to draw her own conclusions. Van Aardt had no dog in the fight.

Pistorius understood the nature of the detective's job and had no quarrel with him. It was not on him but on Nel that Pistorius concentrated his loathing, never forgetting how at the bail hearing a year earlier the prosecutor had sought to portray him as a man whose regret at shooting Reeva did not extend beyond the damage he had done to his own life.

---

**Pistorius had** never felt this way towards an adversary before, not even towards the Brazilian, Alan Oliveira, who, he would always believe, had cheated him of a gold medal. Yet he understood that the one thing he must not do when the critical moment of the trial came, when he came face to face with Nel, was to allow his anger to explode the way it had in London. To remind him of this, and to provide him with the love and support he needed, Pistorius had a dozen members of his family sitting on the bench immediately behind him. Arnold Pistorius, in dark grey suit and tie, and his ever-elegant wife, Lois, were there; Aimée, in a black jacket and skirt, her dark hair coiled up in a severe bun, and Carl, wearing a suit but no tie. His mother's sister, Diana, and other uncles, aunts and cousins on his father's side were there, too. He was particularly glad to see his cousin, Maria, there, the one who lived next door to her father, Arnold. Six months after he shot Reeva, Maria had given birth to her first child, a boy, and as a gesture that both moved him and would give him more relief from his black moods than anything else, she and her husband had named him as the child's godfather. The vote of confidence from the family gave a boost to his morale; the connection between him and his godson would endure whether or not the court deemed him a murderer, whether he went to prison or not. During the months before the trial he had spent long periods cradling the baby, gazing at eyes that held no knowledge of misfortune, pity or reproach. Of all the human beings he knew, only this one was innocent of the horror of what he had done, and in the connection with him he found a refuge and some measure of peace.

Not so with his father. Henke Pistorius was not there on the first day of trial, nor would he be until near the very end. Pistorius had no desire to see him there. He had had practically no contact with his father for six years, a period during which he had refused to take his calls. Now the suffering he had endured had brought home to him more clearly than ever how negligent a father Henke had been, how dismally he had failed to fill the parental vacuum left by his mother's death. Henke's presence now would have brought him scant comfort.

On the same long wooden bench as Pistorius's family members, separated by a small gap imposed by tacit mutual consent, sat family and friends of the woman he had loved. Barry Steenkamp, Reeva's father, was not there. He feared that the shock of exposure to the details of what had happened to his daughter the night she died would be dangerous to his fragile health. But June, Reeva's blonde mother, was in the courtroom and the eyes in the public gallery were on her almost as much as on Pistorius. His feelings towards Mrs Steenkamp combined guilt and shame, made only worse by his failure to express his sorrow to her in words, not even in a letter, in the year since the shooting happened. He had summoned up the courage to say, 'Good morning, Mrs Steenkamp,' but she had responded only with a curt nod. The blank, bitter look he saw on her face as he slid in front of her to take his place in court only encouraged the suspicion that she would not have responded well to him telling her how much he had loved her daughter, and treasured her memory her still. Sitting alongside June Steenkamp were her daughter Simone, older than Reeva and born to a different father, and friends of Reeva's whom Pistorius had barely known but who, he sensed, shared the prosecution view that he had killed her deliberately, following an argument. So did two black ladies sitting next to Mrs Steenkamp, both in the green and black uniform of the ANC Women's League, an organization that had never ceased to proclaim that the shooting of Reeva fell into the category of gender violence.

Behind them, on four more rows of wooden benches stretching to the back of the room, sat members of the public who had managed to get in to watch the most eagerly anticipated event in town, among them his two Icelandic friends, Ebba Guðmundsdóttir and her mother Sigga Hanna Jóhannesdóttir, who had flown to South Africa to reciprocate the kindness he had shown them. Sitting close by them were eighty journalists from South Africa and elsewhere in the world. Such was the global interest that a similar number of journalists had also been accommodated in an overflow court room, where they were able to follow the case on CCTV screens.

The case, as Mike van Aardt knew better than anyone, was not in itself especially complex, save for the identity of the celebrity at its center. This was not a classic whodunnit like the O. J. Simpson case. The who was beyond dispute. The only question the judge would have to rule on was why. If she found that he had acted with conscious premeditation, even if it were only for a matter of seconds before he pulled the trigger, she would have the option to pass a life sentence, which meant a statutory minimum of twenty-five years in prison. She might also determine that it was not murder but culpable homicide, known elsewhere as manslaughter, following which she would have to make a judgment on the degree of criminal negligence he had shown. The highest jail term in such an event would be fifteen years but – following the precedents of the man who had shot his daughter in what he thought was his stolen car, or the rugby player who had unintentionally beaten a policeman to death – she could also spare him jail altogether, settling for a suspended sentence, or even community service. Given that Pistorius's sole responsibility for Reeva's death could not be denied, that would be the best outcome he could hope for, the one Barry Roux would endeavor to obtain.

But there was also a third possibility, and it was the one that a number of South African lawyers who were not involved with the case anticipated. They said that, even by his own version of events, and even if the judge found that he had not known that the person behind the toilet door was Reeva Steenkamp, he had known that there was a human being in there, and he was therefore still likely to be found guilty of murder – a lesser charge than premeditated murder, in terms of the sentence he would receive, but murder nonetheless. Barry Roux understood this as well as anyone. There was a name for this category of murder in South African law, *dolus eventualis*, or legal intention – present, as the statutes put it, when the perpetrator subjectively foresees the possibility of his act causing death, but persists regardless of the consequences. Were it to come to that, the question would boil down to whether or not Pistorius had murder in his heart when he fired the shots.

Roux's first challenge was to defeat the premeditated murder charge by undermining the state's contention that Pistorius knew at whom he was shooting and that he did so as a result of an argument. The judge, were she to prove as tough-minded as her sentences in previous cases indicated, would need some persuading that he had fired four shots not in a fit of rage but out of a mistaken fear of an invisible intruder. She would also ask herself why he did not check that his girlfriend was in bed next to him before advancing down the passage that led to the bathroom, gun at the ready. The question would also be raised in her mind – as it had been in that of the magistrate at the bail hearing a year earlier – whether Reeva would have screamed out in terror or pain before he opened fire or in between the shots, alerting him to the fact it was her he was firing at. In short, Judge Masipa might struggle to understand why he had shot first and asked questions later.

Yet the prosecution would not have it easy, for, in the absence of any eyewitnesses, they would have to prove beyond reasonable doubt that Pistorius had knowingly killed Reeva Steenkamp. The defense team had had access to the core points of the state's case before the trial started, as required by law, and they led them to believe that, in terms of challenging the charge of premeditated murder, they had the upper hand.

So, while the question that agitated the millions of people who were following the case worldwide – did he or did he not know at whom he was shooting? – was critical in terms of the public opprobrium he would encounter and the length of the sentence he might receive, it would not be decisive in relation to whether or not he would end up behind bars. Under South African law, killing a person, unless that person was found to have posed an unequivocal danger to one's life, was still classified as an intentional act of murder. By way of example, a lawyer who was not engaged in the case told the story of a situation he had recently faced at his own home which could have landed him in jail.

The lawyer and his wife were in bed at night when they heard a noise coming from a window downstairs. He looked out and saw two men trying to get in, whereupon he grabbed a gun he had by his bedside, moved towards to his bedroom window and prepared to fire. His terrified wife cried, 'Shoot them! Shoot them!' For a moment he debated whether to act on her words, but then, he said, his legal mind kicked in. He realized that if he killed one of the intruders he might well be charged with murder and, quite possibly unable to prove that he had acted out of a legitimate fear for their lives, be found guilty. Wisely, he limited himself to firing a shot in the air, which was enough to persuade the two men to run away.

'Pistorius's problem,' the lawyer said, 'is that even if his victim had been a burglar and not Reeva Steenkamp, even if the victim had been carrying an axe and had run into the bathroom and locked himself in, under South African law, unless it could be proven that he faced an imminent threat to his life, he would still be facing trial, he would still be looking at a possible guilty verdict for murder.' As the law saw it, he explained, 'a reasonable person – this is the key – would not have reacted to the perceived threat in such a gross and lethally disproportionate manner'.

Some white media commentators suggested that another possible difficulty for Pistorius could be that the judge might regard the accused as racist. The reason for this was subtle, but, at first sight, not unconvincing. His version of what happened at his home that night did fit into a familiar South African crime narrative, where the aggressor was always black. As the judge would not have failed to register, if his story were true – and even if it were not – the faceless intruder of his imagination had to have had a black face, because the fact was that for white people crime mostly did have a black face. The point she might have understood just as well, however, was that this did not necessarily have to reflect a racist perspective. The face of crime in South Africa was overwhelmingly black for black people, too. Jesse

Jackson, the black American civil-rights leader, had once said, 'There is nothing more painful to me at this stage in my life than to walk down the street and hear footsteps . . . then turn around and see somebody white and feel relieved.' It took courage for Jackson to say that. The average black South African, less squeamish about race matters than most Americans, would have volunteered that observation more readily. Judge Masipa would have been no exception. Contrary to what some might have imagined, race was highly unlikely to be a factor in her calculations.

The nub of the matter for Roux, rather, was how to persuade the judge that his client's state of mind at the time of the shooting was such that he might reasonably have been expected to respond the way he said he did. In the likely absence, as he chose to see it, of compelling evidence either way, he believed that much rested on 'softening the judge's heart', as he would put it to his colleagues, by persuading her to redefine her notion of what constituted the legal figment known as 'a reasonable person'.

Barry Roux saw an opportunity in seeking to persuade her to determine that as a disabled person his client should be granted more leeway than an able-bodied person, in terms of what constituted a reasonable response to the threat he said he had perceived.

The way Roux would have to do this would be by presenting the famous Blade Runner as a far more vulnerable, stressed and fear-ridden individual than the public had been allowed to see. In other words, the defense case rested on exposing as a lie, or at least as a giant act of self-delusion, the entire premise on which Pistorius had constructed his public persona.

Roux would seek to persuade the court that Pistorius's private endeavour to deny his disability had shaped his public persona. Shunning compassion, detesting the idea that people might feel sorry for him, Pistorius had portrayed himself as a man with no limits to his physical achievements, succeeding to spectacular effect by qualifying to compete against the world's fastest runners in the Olympic Games. In order now to win the toughest contest of his life, he had to reveal himself as a weak, twitchy, nervous wreck, a man psychologically burdened and physically constricted by the absence of his legs. He had to obliterate the wall of pride that had preserved his fragile self-esteem since childhood, turn his entire personality inside out, and persuade the court to take pity on him.

The worst of it was that he would have to do so before a worldwide audience of millions. Against his objections, and those of his defense team, the Judge President of the Gauteng High Court, Dunstan

Mlambo, the man who had appointed Judge Masipa to the case, ruled that for the first time in South African history the entirety of the trial could be televised live. Barry Roux believed that having cameras in court would undermine his client's right to a fair trial, but Mlambo overruled him. Mlambo's reason for doing so had its origins in the apparently scant regard he had for journalists' ability to report on the case adequately. He wrote that journalists' 'summarized versions' were 'liable to be inaccurate', and that it would be better to let the public follow the proceedings as they happened without the dubious filter of the news media. The Judge President's one provision was that while the testimony of witnesses would be carried on audio, each would have the right to choose whether he or she appeared on camera, except the state experts and police witnesses who had no choice.

The prosecution's support for the motion helped carry the day, encouraging the suspicion harbored by the defence lawyers that Gerrie Nel's zeal was fueled in part by vanity. It would also lead to the creation of a new South African pay-TV channel whose sole mission would be to provide live coverage of the trial, broadcasting repetitions and expert opinion twenty-four hours a day. ESPN in the United States and Sky Television in the United Kingdom ran live feeds from the courtroom throughout. Reporters for the BBC, the big American news networks and the world's biggest newspapers flocked to South Africa, drawn by the knowledge that there was only one thing the public found more appealing than the story of the hero, and that was the story of the fallen hero.

The upshot was that as many spectators would witness Pistorius's shame in Pretoria as had celebrated his glory in London – but one thing would not change: they would be following the courtroom drama as if it were a sports contest.

Most viewers had made up their minds beforehand which side they wanted to win; once the game got under way, one camp would cheer and the other grimace when Gerrie Nel landed a blow for the prosecution, then do the opposite when Barry Roux struck back for the defense. On the 'Oscar Channel', as it became known, experts would provide blow-by-blow commentary, complete with edited reruns of the liveliest court action. Foreign channels would do much the same, inviting guests to be interviewed during breaks in the trial in one of a number of tented studios erected by the big American and British networks specially for the event, on a terrace overlooking the court building on Madiba Street. Newspaper and broadcast journalists inside the courtroom would provide up-to-the-minute commentary for their employers' internet blogs or on social media, providing subscribers to both Twitter and pay-TV with the opportunity continually to switch between screens as the drama unfolded. The chatter, the indignation, the jokes, the spoofs, the wise and witty pronouncements would then migrate to other virtual meeting venues and thence to bars, restaurants and living rooms where individuals would debate the case face to face in New York, London, Paris, Barcelona, Rome, Sydney, Buenos Aires, Berlin, Amsterdam and, with varying degrees of fascination, all corners of the globe.

In South Africa there was a general election coming up two months after the start of the trial and all parties were furiously campaigning, but it was a measure both of the country's political stability, with the ANC certain to win, and the pull of celebrity, that there was only one subject people wanted to talk about. On the morning the trial began the deputy editor of *The Sowetan*, the newspaper for which Judge Masipa had once worked, went on the radio to say that, never mind the election, for her overwhelmingly black audience the Pistorius trial was the story of the year.

Pistorius was among those who used to believe that there was only one thing worse than being talked about, and that was not being talked about. He had changed his mind. He looked on with helplessness and dismay as he found that he would be facing trial not only before a legally appointed judge, but in the court of public opinion. Inside the courtroom he would be subject to the solemn rituals of the criminal justice system; out in the internet ether, mob justice would rule.

Aware of the sound and fury he was generating, he fought the temptation to enter the conversation. A busy Twitter participant until the shooting, he had remained silent since then, on the advice of his legal team. Except once, two and a half weeks before the trial, on the anniversary of the day he shot Reeva, when he had issued a statement to the media that read: 'No words can adequately capture my feelings about the devastating accident that has caused such heartache for everyone who truly loved – and continues to love – Reeva. The pain and sadness – especially for Reeva's parents, family and friends consumes me with sorrow. The loss of Reeva and the complete trauma of that day, I will carry with me for the rest of my life.'

He could no longer restrain restrain himself from telling the world how much he had loved Reeva, nor could he resist the opportunity to make an appeal to public opinion – one that might reach the ears of the judge – to try and believe him when he said that he had killed Reeva by accident.

Alert as he had been since childhood to the impression that he made, he knew full well that the prevailing view of him in the South African media was unsympathetic. Pistorius was aware, too, that in order to amplify the horrendousness of the crime and to embroider his newly minted image as a monster, Reeva had not only to be a beauty to his beast, but to be portrayed as a woman who embodied all the virtues and had had a triumphant career cruelly cut short. Not only in South Africa but far beyond, newspapers and broadcasters gathered testimony from friends and loved ones variously describing her as 'angelic', 'intelligent', 'diligent', 'vivacious', 'classy', 'generous', 'kind', 'funny', 'witty', 'humble', 'self-deprecating', 'selfless', 'caring', 'gentle', 'loyal', 'strong-willed', 'consistent', 'amazing', 'socially engaged' and 'a child of God'. As was to be expected, no dissenting voices emerged during the year leading up to the start of the trial.

Pistorius himself would have been the last to dissent. He idealized Reeva in death more than any journalist could ever have done. What he had wanted to show in that statement he put out – as he would later, when he testified in the trial – was how much he had loved her and, despite the quarrels between them which the prosecution would inevitably bring to light, how much she had loved him.

She certainly regarded him as more than a passing flame, investing in the relationship. She would accompany him to training, taking tips from his coach, Ampie Louw, on how to keep her legs trim, and when Pistorius finished his sessions he would lie down exhausted on a bench with his head on her lap, while she stroked his hair. She prayed with him, knowing how important his Christianity was to him, and she went out of her way to take an interest in the things that interested him, to the point that on at least one occasion she accompanied him to a shooting range and fired a gun at a target under his fond and approving eye. Their appetite to preserve intimate photographic records of their relationship was not dulled by their continual exposure to the flash of cameras in public. It was those pictures of the two of them in affectionately unguarded poses that he would pore over at his uncle Arnold's cottage during the year before the trial, gazing with special wistfulness at the one where she lay cradled asleep in his arms.

She was loyal to him, too, her commitment having been put to the test soon after she told her mother of the seriousness of her intentions towards him. One night in December, Pistorius was assaulted in a Johannesburg nightclub and, though he had to go to hospital for stitches to the back of his head, he never revealed who the assailant was. The background to the attack preceded

Reeva's appearance in his life, lying in the last days of his relationship with Samantha Taylor. At the Kyalami race track, the very same place where he would meet Reeva, he had had a furious altercation with Quinton van der Burgh, the man who had taken Samantha on a trip to Dubai while he was away in London for the Olympic and Paralympic Games. The trip had been the reason for the heartache and all the frantic phone calls his room-mate, Arnu Fourie, had had no choice but to overhear. Van der Burgh, a wealthy businessman, saw nothing wrong in having taken Samantha to Dubai, as he had understood that her relationship with Pistorius was over. At that encounter in Kyalami he realized that Pistorius did not see things that way. He screamed at Van der Burgh and, as was amply reported later, called an acquaintance who intervened on Van der Burgh's behalf, a former professional soccer player called Marc Batchelor, who alleged that Pistorius threatened to break his legs if he did not back off.

Pistorius took the nightclub assault on him two months later to be a delayed reaction to that bust-up over Samantha. He had hoped to keep the incident quiet. Even though he was the victim, he did not want it to be spread about that he moved in the kind of social circles where such altercations took place. But a news reporter from the Johannesburg *Sunday Times* got wind of what had happened and phoned up Pistorius. 'It's the first time I have heard of this,' Pistorius said. 'I am not that type of person . . . Please don't write this. It could ruin me.'

Sensing that the reporter was not entirely convinced, Pistorius asked Reeva to back him up. When the reporter phoned her, she played a properly supportive role, explaining how worried her boyfriend was that the publication of such a story would undermine his public image. 'Please don't write this,' she said. 'Oscar is worried this will ruin his reputation.'

Pistorius's vanity was in play, but also, she understood, his sponsorship deals. Nike, for example, already damaged by their association with Tiger Woods and Lance Armstrong, might begin to ponder the wisdom of extending their association with him if the public began to see their brand icon as a quick-tempered brawler. As it was, the story was not published until a year after Pistorius had shot Reeva dead.

While she lived, the image the public saw of the couple was the one they themselves wanted to see, and that friends saw too. A couple they had dinner with in January 2013 would report after Reeva died that they had seemed 'extraordinarily happy' and 'awesome together'. By that third month into their relationship, even his jealous fits appeared to be under control.

Wayne Lahoud, Reeva's previous boyfriend, spent time with the two of them at social events and reported no discomfort in their presence, nor any visible ill feeling towards him.

At a party in a fashionable Johannesburg shopping mall on January 26, a few days after the tetchy WhatsApp exchanges in which Reeva had said he scared her sometimes, they were the center of attention. The party was held at Tasha's, a restaurant whose owners' delight at having him among their clients had not been tempered by the incident in which, only a few days earlier, he had accidentally fired a bullet under a table, and for which he would face a charge of criminal negligence. Everybody at the party was dressed in white – with dubious humor, the party was billed as a 'Whites Only' event – and the chatter among the guests was all along the lines of 'Oh, they look so in love' and 'What a great couple they make' and 'This looks like the real thing'. The editor of *Heat* spent the night badgering them to pose together for the cover of the magazine, but they told him, 'It's still new. Give us some time to enjoy each other's company before we jump into the celebrity circus.'

**Now, on** March 3, 2014 – one year, one month and one week after that happy event at Tasha's – the celebrity circus had reappeared with a vengeance.

Pistorius had spent weeks going over the case with his lawyers, applying the rational part of his mind to the task at hand, quieting his demons in a way the haunted wreck he had been a year earlier could not have done. He had come prepared. He knew more or less what to expect. Barry Roux and the rest of his legal team had explained to him, and he had understood, the possible outcomes of the case and the elements on which the judge's verdict would turn. They had also explained that he had always to address the judge as 'My lady', that he should bow deeply when she bowed, that he should adopt a serious and contrite demeanor, and that, while he should entertain no illusions as to how piti-less an adversary Gerrie Nel would be, he should retain a poker-face when the prosecutor spoke and reveal no glimmer of the animosity he felt towards him.

Now the day Pistorius had been dreading had arrived; the judge sat before him in her blood-red robes, ready to initiate proceedings. He tried to con-vince himself that he felt some relief that the ordeal was finally under way. If the public saw it as a sports con-test, it would serve him to try and see it that way, too. For them, it was an optional entertainment, in which they could invest or withdraw their passions at will; for him, it was a race for his life, and now that it was about to begin he experienced a familiar pang, the mix of high-strung tension, hope and fear that he used to feel when he took his place on the starting blocks in that earlier life he had destroyed. It was at this point on the running track that he had always bowed his head and said a prayer, and he repeated the ritual now. It really did have the feeling of a big race, because his family was there on the sidelines supporting him, as they had been at the London Games – and while his large, genial coach, Ampie Louw, was not present today, in his place he had Barry Roux, who looked in his element in his black advocate's robes, calm and smiling.

It was Gerrie Nel who spoke first, rising to his feet at a nod from the judge and starting the proceedings with a recital of the first of the four charges of which the state hoped to find Oscar Leonard Carl Pistorius guilty.

Pistorius stood up, too, facing the judge as protocol demanded, with his hands clasped before him at waist height, his shoulders hunched and his body bent slightly forward. The judge, her left elbow on the desktop in front of her, scrutinized Nel through a pair of round, grey-rimmed glasses. Count one, Nel read, was that on February 14, 2013 the accused 'did unlawfully and intentionally kill a person, to wit, Reeva Steenkamp, a twenty-nine-year-old female'. The judge turned to him. 'Do you understand the charge?' Her eyes did not seem unkind; her voice was soft and low-pitched. He noticed the tight corn-row plaits of her black hair. 'Yes, my lady', he replied. 'How do you plead?' 'Not guilty, my lady.'

He continued standing as Nel, bouncing briskly on the balls of his feet, a habit he would keep up throughout the trial, read out count two, which stated that in contravention of the Firearms Control Act the accused had discharged a firearm through the open sunroof of a car. The judge turned to Pistorius again. Did he understand the charge? 'Yes, my lady.' How did he plead. 'Not guilty, my lady.' Count three was another contravention of the firearms act, discharging a gun recklessly and unlawfully in a public place, namely a restaurant in Johannesburg called Tasha's. 'Not guilty, my lady.' Count four, again in contravention of the firearms act, the illegal possession of ammunition. 'Not guilty, my lady.'

Nel sat down. Pistorius remained standing up, holding his hands together as if in prayer. If he let them hang loose by his side, the judge might see he was trembling. But he had answered in a steady voice. He had not broken down.

It was not Barry Roux but Kenny Oldwadge, so taut he seemed in danger of bursting a blood vessel, who launched the defense case. Oldwadge stood up, a head taller than the bantamweight Nel, exchanged glances with the judge and began reading his client's 'explanation of plea', a sworn statement written in the first person in which he stood by the sequence of events he had given at the bail application hearing, rejecting the accusation of murder 'in the strongest possible terms'.

'In fact at the time of the tragic accident that led to Reeva's death we were in a strong loving relationship,' Oldwadge read on Pistorius's behalf. 'Whilst I admit that I inflicted the fatal gunshot wounds to Reeva, this occurrence was indeed an accident in that I had mistakenly believed that an intruder or intruders had entered my home and posed an imminent threat to Reeva and me.'

He had got out of bed, the plea continued, in the middle of the night to bring in two fans that stood outside on a terrace adjacent to his bedroom. Then came something new, not mentioned in the bail application.

'I had shortly before spoken to Reeva who was in bed beside me.'

This was an important detail, since it might answer a question many had asked: why had he not checked to see that she was in bed before advancing down the corridor to the bathroom and opening fire? The brief conversation had led him to assume she was still in bed, he maintained, and that the noise he heard in the bathroom was that of an intruder who had slipped in through a window.

'Unbeknownst to me,' the plea statement continued, 'Reeva must have gone to the toilet in the bathroom at the time when I brought in the fans . . . I approached the bathroom with my firearm so as to defend Reeva and me. At that time I still believed Reeva was in the bed. The discharging of my firearm was precipitated by a noise in the toilet that I, in my fearful state, knowing that I was on my stumps unable to run away or properly defend myself physically, believed to be the intruder or intruders coming out of the toilet to attack Reeva and me.

'I respectfully believe that the State has no basis whatsoever for alleging that I wanted to take Reeva's life.'

Oldwadge, still reading from his client's first-person plea statement, noted that two of the critical points on which the state's case rested, the details of which the defense team had already received, as required by South African law, would be shown in court to be wrong. A state witness who said she had heard screaming at his client's home prior to the shooting could not have done so; the state hypothesis that there had been an argument between his client and the victim prior to the shooting was groundless.

'I deny this allegation in the strongest possible terms because there was no argument.'

Finally, on the firearms charges, he flatly denied guilt on all three counts.

Oldwadge sat down and, upon receiving permission from the judge, wiping a tear from his eye, prompted by the painful recollections contained in his plea, so did Pistorius.

The terms of battle had been set and he was determined to see it through, clinging on to his innocence and to his version of what happened, whatever the prosecution might throw at him. He had steeled himself for the necessity of losing his dignity in this trial, and of the public image he had labored so long to build being annihilated, but even in his sorrow and fear he would not relinquish his life's driving force, the conviction that no challenge was beyond him. This challenge was of a different order from anything he had faced before. But he had his guardian angels, two people he had convinced himself he could count on to watch over and protect him, both of whom were dead. One was his mother, the other was the woman who, he had wanted to imagine, would come closer than any other to compensating for his mother's loss.

Alone in his cottage, seeing her gaze down on him from the framed photograph on the wall, and now in court, he sensed Reeva's ghostly energy. The night before the first day of the trial he had placed a candle under the photograph, and lit it. When he left for court the next morning, the last thing he did before stepping out to face his torment was to blow the candle out. He would light it again on returning home that night, and he would blow it out again the following morning. The ritual gave him a passing reassurance and calm. He would repeat it every night and every morning until the day came when the living woman who loomed largest in his life now, Judge Thokozile Masipa, would pronounce his fate.

# 16

*Even sound seemed to fail in this air, like the air was*
*worn out with carrying sounds so long.*
WILLIAM FAULKNER, *THE SOUND AND THE FURY*

Gerrie Nel, the state prosecutor, called his strongest witnesses first, the ones who said they had been awoken by the sounds of screams or shots, or both, in the early hours of February 14, 2013. They were Michelle Burger and her husband, Charl Johnson, who lived on the other side of a high wall on a neighboring estate, 177 meters (580 feet) away; Estelle van der Merwe, who lived 100 meters (330 feet) away, within the Silver Woods Estate; Johan Stipp and his wife, Anette, who lived directly behind the house where the shooting took place, across a stretch of open ground, 72 meters

(230 feet) away. All five of them were Afrikaners; all asked for their faces not to be shown on the live TV broadcast.

This first batch of state witnesses, the neighbors, were the only ones whose evidence might support the prosecution's core contention that Pistorius had shot Reeva Steenkamp intentionally, after an argument, and that accordingly he should be found guilty of premeditated murder. It was circumstantial evidence, as Nel himself conceded, based not on what people had seen but on what they had heard. It was the best he could come up with, given that there were only two eyewitnesses, one of whom was the accused, while the other was dead.

Nel led Michelle Burger, a trim and elegantly dressed university professor, through her testimony. She began by saying that she had woken up at about 3 a.m. on the night in question, to the sound of a woman's 'terrible screams'.

'It was the most helpless screaming I have ever heard in my life, my lady,' she said, observing the South African legal protocol whereby, irrespective of whether the prosecuting or defense lawyer is asking the questions, it is always the judge who is addressed.

'I knew something terrible was happening in that house,' she continued. 'You would only shout like that if your life was really threatened. It was blood-curdling.'

Burger said she thought it was a house invasion – the biggest fear of South Africans, across all racial lines, according to research by the University of Cape Town, though it is far from being the most common form of crime.

'I was convinced that a woman was being attacked, that she and her husband were being attacked in that house,' Burger said.

Barry Roux, reclining with one arm over the back of his chair, eyed Burger lazily over the top of his glasses. Nel, on his feet and leading her through her testimony, encouraged her.

'I heard a man crying for help, then more woman's screams. It was like a climax. I heard her anxiety. She was very scared.' Then Burger said she heard a gunshot, followed by a pause, then three more shots in succession. 'It was bang . . . bang, bang, bang.' In between the shots she heard a woman scream for the last time, then silence.

Burger sounded compelling, but Roux looked unflustered. He took off his glasses and slowly nibbled at the end of them, his eyes fixed on Burger, as if relishing the chance he would soon have to submit her testimony to scrutiny. Pistorius watched her with undisguised skepticism, shaking his head from time to time, pausing every now and then to look down and scribble comments on a white notepad he had brought in the briefcase that he carried into court every day. Every now and again he would lean over and, via his attorney, Brian Webber, pass a note across for Roux to read. It had been said that O. J. Simpson looked morosely absent during his famous trial two decades earlier. Pistorius was determined to take an active part.

'Her shouts, her screams were petrifying,' Burger continued. 'It is the most helpless feeling I have ever had in my life. It was something that leaves you chilled. You can't explain it, you just know that a woman's life was very threatened.'

Nel turned to the judge – 'No further questions, my lady' – and Roux stood up to begin the cross-examination. His tone, right from the start, expressed incredulity. His client had told him she was lying, he said, and he believed that, in the most charitable of interpretations, she was confused – and that, at worst, she was tailoring her testimony to fit the news reports she had been following during the year since the shooting.

The defense's contention, as Roux put it to Burger, was that Pistorius had fired the four shots, shouted in confusion as it dawned on him that he might have mistakenly shot his girlfriend, then shouted for help, then bashed down a panel of the bathroom door with three blows of a cricket bat, and then screamed hysterically on discovering her wounded body inside.

Roux tested this version against Burger's, his purpose being to find enough holes in her testimony to sow in the judge's mind a reasonable degree of doubt as to the credibility of what she said she recalled hearing.

'I put it to you that if Mr Pistorius is very anxious,' Roux said, 'his screams sound as if they come from a woman's voice. He was screaming higher and lower and that is why you would hear what you, at that time of the morning, would associate with a woman screaming.'

Burger remained adamant that she had heard a woman. Roux insisted, but Burger would not concede the possibility that it might have been a man she had heard.

'To me it's obvious, madam, you will not make this concession,' Roux said, 'because you think it will be good for Mr Pistorius.'

Roux turned to her contention that she had heard screams in between the shots, a critical point because the prosecution maintained that Pistorius had heard Reeva screaming behind the bathroom door and kept on firing regardless. Was Burger sure about this? She said she was. 'A moment after the shots I heard the woman's voice fading away, my lady.'

'You are not sure,' Roux replied, raising his voice. 'I put it to you that you are adapting, you are speculating, trying to close all the gaps . . . You have watched Sky News, you watched other news channels, you have a retrospective knowledge and you come to court with that.'

Burger denied it.

The clincher for Roux was that she could not possibly have heard the victim's cries after the shots were fired, even 'fading away', because, as he put it, 'She already had brain damage.' It was the first reference made in the trial to Reeva Steenkamp's injuries and the brutality of the statement caught Pistorius off guard. He clutched his head, as if for protection, and released a loud, sharp sob.

It was a shocking interruption to the silence of the court, but Roux, who had anticipated the possibility of his client breaking down, and expected it to happen again, pressed on as if he had heard nothing,

'You had the ability from 177 meters to hear emotion and fear and growing intensity?' Roux asked her, a note of exasperation in his voice.

'Our windows were open, we had no air conditioning on,' Burger replied.

Roux begged her to try and be objective. She had said in her testimony to Nel that she had heard a man crying for help before she heard the shots; if a man was about to shoot his girlfriend who was hiding in a bathroom, was it not inconsistent that he would shout for help before doing so?

'She shouted for help. He shouted for help. I don't know why, my lady,' Burger replied.

Roux paused, pointed a finger at her, and asked her point-blank: 'As you stand there, as you testify in chief, you do it from the perspective that Oscar Pistorius lied in the bail application and his defense is a lie?'

She replied, 'I could not understand how I could clearly hear a woman scream but Mr Pistorius could not hear that.'

'You decided, if he said the victim was not screaming, he was lying. In your view, he cannot be telling the truth. Do you believe Mr Pistorius is lying?' Again, she said she had heard a woman's terrified screams, and again Roux insisted, 'Do you believe Mr Pistorius is lying?' Burger insisted that she could not understand how she could have heard the cries while Pistorius did not.

Five times Roux repeated the question and five times she would not give him a yes or no answer. Nel stood up to object, but the judge, who never stopped taking notes during Burger's testimony, overruled him.

Roux turned to the cricket bat. The defense version was that Pistorius screamed between the time he fired the shots and the time he struck the cricket bat against the door to try and break it down. Burger maintained that the screaming came from Reeva.

Roux put it to her that if the second gunshots she had heard had in reality been the noise of the bat against the door, then the screams she had heard would have to have been Pistorius's, not Reeva's, because by that point Reeva was dead. Roux suggested that she did not know how to distinguish between the sound of a gunshot and of a cricket bat.

'I put it to you,' said Roux, 'that you made up your mind not to believe his version and interpreted cricket bat sounds as gunshots, his cries as her screams.'

It was another critical point.

'I'm sure the sound of a gunshot is louder than a cricket bat,' Burger retorted, matching Roux's sarcasm with her own.

Burger had held her ground, she would not be browbeaten; but when the cross-examination ended and Judge Masipa gave her permission to leave, thanking Burger for her assistance, the effort she had been making in standing up to Roux showed. He had done what good advocates were trained to do and boxed her into a tighter and tighter corner until she hardly had space to breathe, let alone think. When Burger stepped off the witness stand, she bent over in tears.

**For Nel,** there would be similar mismatches with later defense witnesses. Under Roux's experienced interrogation – thirty-two years' practice at it – many people might have struggled to recall what they had for breakfast that morning, let alone the details of what they had heard on waking up in drowsy confusion twelve and a half months before.

Roux was more gentle with the next witness, Estelle van der Merwe, however, partly because she was more visibly nervous on the stand than Burger and he did not wish to be seen by the judge as a bully, partly because her main piece of evidence was not backed up by any other witness, and partly, too, because in one important respect her evidence indirectly reinforced the defense case.

Van der Merwe, a middle-aged woman, was the sole state witness able to back up the prosecution's hypothesis that the shooting had been preceded by an argument. Speaking in Afrikaans, with a black interpreter alongside translating her words into English, she testified that she was woken up just before 2 a.m., more than an hour before the shooting, by a row in a neighboring house. 'It seemed people were involved in a fight.' She said people continued talking 'in loud voices' for an hour, giving an added ring of truth to her story by saying that she recalled being irritated because her son had a school exam the next day. At one point she said she put a pillow over her head to muffle the noise.

The problem for the prosecution, as Roux established when he questioned her, was that she did not hear what the voices were saying, nor in what language they were speaking, and neither was she clear where exactly in the estate the argument had taken place.

She did hear four gunshots at around three, she said, but not with a pause between them, as Michelle Burger had testified; rather, they had rung out 'one after the other'. Then, she said, there was total silence, followed by a commotion. Her husband woke up and looked out of the window but could not see anything. But then she heard someone crying out loudly. Roux asked her what those cries were. 'I asked my husband that and he said it was Oscar's voice. To me, it sounded like a woman's voice.'

Roux declared an end to the cross-examination. Unsurprisingly, the prosecution did not call Mrs van der Merwe's husband, Jacques, to the stand, even though his name was on the state's witness list. The list originally had 107 names on it, but most of them – some were paramedics who had arrived at Pistorius's home after the shooting, some were policemen there just to protect the crime scene – had been included by the prosecution as a precaution, in case some small or unexpected detail emerged in court that needed to be backed up with evidence. Nel would end up calling only twenty-one witnesses to testify.

A curious detail that Mrs van der Merwe mentioned in her testimony was that she said she had gone back to sleep after hearing the shots and the commotion that followed. She also testified that she did not discuss the previous night's events with her husband over breakfast the next morning. It said something about how routine a part of South African life it was to hear shots in the night, even within a residential compound heavily fortified against criminal intrusion. A night of mayhem was not considered anything out of the ordinary.

The next witness, Charl Johnson, Michelle Burger's husband, corroborated the basic elements of his wife's testimony by testifying that he had heard screams before and during the shots. The only significant discrepancy with his wife's story was that he said he was not as sure as she that he had heard four shots. It might have been three. Roux's main line of attack in the cross-examination was that his testimony bore a suspiciously uncanny resemblance to his wife's.

'She spoke about the scream fading after the last shot and you spoke about fading too. How is that, Mr Johnson?' Roux asked.

'If two people witness the same incident ten meters apart then they will have similar recollections of the event,' replied Johnson, a tall, lean, placid witness, determined not to be shaken by Roux the way his wife had been.

Picking up another phrase of Johnson's that was identical to one his wife had used, Roux shook his head, smiled wanly, and said, 'Mr Johnson, I must stop you. You don't know what you are doing to yourself. You discussed the evidence with your wife.'

'I can honestly tell you we did not discuss it,' Johnson insisted. To which Roux replied, 'When witnesses start to use "honestly" then I wonder about it. Your interpretation of events is designed to incriminate the accused and it's unfortunate. You and your wife could just as well have stood together in the witness box.'

Nel objected and this time Judge Masipa was on his side. In a calm, soft voice she said, 'Don't you go too far, Mr Roux?'

'That is for the court to decide, my lady,' Roux replied, by 'the court' meaning the judge. But he had made his point and did not continue this line of questioning, turning instead to what he considered to be a decisive piece of evidence indicating that Johnson and his wife did indeed mistake the cricket-bat sounds for gunshots.

The timing of a phone call Johnson made to his security company, just after he heard what he thought were shots, was at 3.16. Yet at 3.19.,the record showed that Pistorius had made his first phone call, to Johan Stander, his friend and manager of the estate. There was not enough time for him to have fired the shots, run to get his prosthetic legs, knocked down the door with the bat and made that call, Roux said. It must have been the cricket bat he had heard. Johnson, unruffled, repeated that what he had heard were gunshots.

'Sometimes people genuinely believe something has happened and then that is what they tell people. It is a different thing from it being correct,' Roux said, chiding Johnson for what he seemed to think was his frivolity by remarking, 'A man's life is at stake, Mr Johnson.'

The next state witness was Dr Johan Stipp. Of the five neighbors who testified for the state, Stipp, a doctor in private practice, was the most impressive in terms of the apparent clarity of his mind, his eloquence and the steadiness of his English-speaking voice. At 72 meters (230 feet), he and his wife, Anette, who would testify later but added little that her husband had not mentioned, lived closer to the scene of the crime than Burger and Johnson or Estelle van der Merwe.

Stipp appeared to be on all counts the best state witness, yet his testimony ended up backfiring for the prosecution case. It also delivered one of the most dramatic episodes of the entire trial.

What Stipp said in his evidence in chief to Nel was that, first, he was woken by three loud bangs, which, as he immediately told his wife who had also woken up, he believed to be gunshots. Second, he heard screaming. 'It sounded to me like the voice of a female,' he said. 'She sounded fearful. She sounded to be emotional, anguished, scared almost scared out of her mind, I would say.' Third, after noticing that the lights were on in the accused's home and seeing a person behind a window move from right to left, he called the estate's security guards, but the phone was busy and so he dialed the emergency number for the police. Fourth, while on the phone he heard 'two to three' louder, rapid bangs. Fifth, he went out onto the balcony of his home and heard a man shout, 'Help! Help! Help!'

Except for Stipp's belief that the screams he heard were a woman's, the sequence of events correlated more neatly with the defense's version of what had happened than the prosecution's – namely, that there had been shots, then Pistorius's screams, then the cricket bat striking the door. The prosecution agreed that after the four shots, one of which struck Steenkamp's head, she would not have been able to utter a sound ever again. Nel, it dawned on Roux, had made a mistake in calling Dr Stipp as a witness.

But Pistorius would have a price to pay for this unexpected gift. Dr Stipp, he well recalled, was one of the first people to show up at his home after the shooting. Stipp had identified himself as a doctor and Pistorius had hoped, for a despairing moment or two, that Reeva might be saved. But Stipp had not been able to do anything for her, and here he was now, come to destroy Pistorius's life too, a witness for the state, on the side of the detested Gerrie Nel. Pistorius feared that, sooner or later in his testimony, Stipp would sketch in words the horrors that assailed him in his nightmares and that he had struggled for more than a year to keep from invading his waking mind. He was right to be afraid. Nel had no intention of sparing him this torture.

Nel asked Stipp what had happened when he arrived at the accused's home.

'I was motioned inside,' Stipp replied. 'A lady was on the ground, a man next to her on his knees. His right hand was on her groin, the fingers of his left hand in her mouth, her teeth clenching. He said, "I shot her. I thought she was a burglar. I shot her."'

Pistorius, sitting on his wooden bench, bent over, his head almost down between his knees, his face in his hands, his shoulders shaking. But Stipp kept on regardless.

'I think the accused had his fingers in her mouth because he was trying to open her airway. I tried to assist her, check for signs of life, but there were none. There was no pulse. I opened her right eyelid but her cornea was already milky . . .'

Pistorius let out a sharp, wrenching sob. Peering through the gaps between his fingers, he saw that the judge's eyes were turned not towards him but towards the witness, to her left, and that she was listening carefully and taking notes. Pistorius had broken down and wept like this alone in his cottage, or with his sister by his side with her arms around him, and now here he was breaking down and weeping before a roomful of startled strangers.

Stipp carried on, clinically describing the scene he had found that night. Pistorius laced his fingers behind his neck and clamped the inside of his forearms over his ears, but he could still make out the words.

'Her teeth were clenching down hard on his fingers. It was obvious she was mortally wounded . . .'

'Yes, Dr Stipp, please continue,' said Nel.

'There were wounds to her right thigh and arm, brain tissue visible, the top of her skull open . . .'

Pistorius retched. The smell of her blood flooded his nostrils. The court sketch artist, sitting alongside, passed him a white plastic bag, but though his stomach was heaving he did not vomit. Not this time. He retched again and Aimée, sitting behind him, covered her face in her hands, weeping too. Brian Webber reached over and put a hand on his shoulder. Barry Roux stood up and, with arms outstretched in supplication, asked the judge for a recess. Instantly assenting, she stood up, bowed to the court and limped out of the chamber. Aimée rushed over to Pistorius, his brother Carl close behind, and the three siblings sat with their arms huddled around one another, heads bowed, like orphans in a storm.

It was March 6, the fourth day of the trial, the twelfth anniversary of their mother's death.

Floundering as he was in the cross-currents of the two most devastating episodes in his life, it seemed impossible that Pistorius would be able to regain his composure sufficiently to endure what remained of the day in court; yet, to the surprise of everyone present, he did. Half an hour later, when Judge Masipa re-entered the room, he had collected himself and soon after, when Roux began his cross-examination of Stipp, he was listening attentively again, taking notes, revealing himself to the court, not for the last time in the trial, to be a man of rapidly shifting moods.

Roux had been listening very closely and with growing surprise to Stipp's testimony for the prosecution, and when the time came for him to conduct his cross-examination he was courtesy itself, addressing the doctor as one esteemed professional to another, engaging him not so much in an argument as in scholarly debate. Roux sought not to undermine Stipp's evidence so much as to ratify it.

Finding himself in the rare circumstance of not wishing to sabotage a state witness's credibility, Roux informed Stipp that a medical specialist had told him the victim could not have screamed after the shots were fired. Did he agree? Stipp said he did. So, Roux continued, it could not have been the deceased who screamed after the shots, given that there was no other woman present in the house.

Nel stood up abruptly. 'I object my lady.' He seemed flustered. It was becoming apparent that he might have erred badly in calling Dr Stipp to the witness stand. Should Nel doubt it, Judge Masipa made the point for him. The witness appeared to be stating Mr Roux's case, not the state's, she said, sounding gently perplexed. But this was hardly a reason to stop Mr Roux from persisting in his line of questioning. She overruled Nel's objection and asked the defense lawyer to carry on.

Roux acknowledged the judge's intervention with a gentle nod and turned again to the witness. 'So, Dr Stipp,' he said, 'if we accept the screams could not have been the deceased's, who else could have screamed? Could it have been Mr Pistorius's voice?'

'I don't know. Could it?' Stipp, somewhat at a loss, replied.

Roux, satisfied this particular point had been made, moved on to the most surprising inconsistency in Stipp's testimony. He said he had heard two sets of shots, even though both prosecution and defense agreed there had been only one set.

'I'm going to put to you that the last two to three sounds, those sounds, were caused by a cricket bat breaking down a door, but it sounded to you again like gunshots,' said Roux.

'They sounded identical,' said Stipp.

'You had already heard the gunshots, so there must be another explanation for the next sounds,' replied Roux.

Stipp shrugged his shoulders. Nel looked tense. His chief police investigator, Mike van Aardt, usually as impassive as he was silent, sat bolt upright in his chair.

'If the state tells us there were shots first and then shots later, my lady,' Roux continued, 'then they must make statements available to us. Or has the state misled us all this time?'

Roux was mischief-making. Nel wriggled. Roux ended Stipp's cross-examination by asking him to confirm another piece of evidence he had offered earlier, under Nel's curiously self-destructive guidance, concerning the accused's state of mind when Stipp entered his home approximately fifteen minutes after the shooting. Stipp obliged. He said he found Pistorius to be 'very distraught and beside himself', begging God to save his girlfriend and crying out, 'Please let her live!'

'Did he seem sincere to you?' Roux asked.

'He seemed sincere to me. He was in tears,' Stipp replied.

Stipp left the witness stand, an adjournment was called, and Arnold Pistorius, who hitherto had sat listening to the proceedings straight-backed, alert and poker-faced, broke into a smile. He stepped forward and said something in his nephew's ear. For the first and last time in the trial that anyone in the courtroom would remember, Pistorius smiled. Then, as if emboldened by the unexpected triumph, and as if beginning to believe that his story might at last be believed, even by his most vociferous detractors, he strode across to where the three ANC Women's League ladies were sitting in their green and black uniforms, shook each one of them by the hand and said, 'Pleased to meet you.' They looked confused, but all took his hand.

Later, outside the courtroom, someone suggested to Arnold Pistorius that his nephew was getting good value from Barry Roux. Arnold nodded, grinned and said, 'From Gerrie Nel too!'

**He would** not feel that way a month later, once his nephew's cross-examination had got under way. Then he would snarl to family and friends that Nel was a vindictive little man, that he strove not to get to the truth but to feed his ego, that he was determined to win the case at any cost, that he was a traitor to the Afrikaner race. But until that moment came, Arnold Pistorius and his family, while never complacent, allowed themselves to think that things were going their way.

The days and weeks passed, interrupted by unscheduled adjournments, and the prosecution waded through the remainder of its case, some of which was so tediously repetitive and inconclusive that even the man whose future was at stake, who at times would retch so violently that a point came when a court official judged it wise to place a large green plastic bucket by his side, would sometimes stop making notes and start doodling on his notepad instead. More instructively, during breaks between sessions he sometimes withdrew from the briefcase he brought into court a Bible study guide, or a book written by Jim Cymbala, pastor of the Brooklyn Tabernacle Church, called *Breakthrough Prayer: The Power of Connecting with the Heart of God*. In it, he read stories of people who had turned to prayer at times of difficulty, among them relatives of individuals who had died in the attacks of September 11, 2001, in New York and Washington DC.

Nel had stated at the beginning of the trial that his case would rest principally on circumstantial evidence, meaning what the neighbors had heard, but also on ballistic and forensic evidence. None of this provided conclusive answers to the core question: why had the shots been fired? But what it might do, Nel hoped, was point to implausibility or outright lies in the accused's version of events. The ballistic and forensic evidence the prosecution produced concerned the manner in which the accused had attacked the locked toilet door with a cricket bat, the location of the phones and clothes found in the bathroom and bedroom, and the trajectory of the bullets and the order in which they were fired. Nel sought most of all to demonstrate that the first bullet did not strike the victim's brain, thereby indicating that she would have had a moment to scream in terror or pain during the shooting, alerting the accused to her identity.

To this end, the prosecution introduced into the courtroom a wooden door, off its hinges, that would remain on display, propped up with some rudimentary scaffolding, until the trial's end. It was the bathroom door through which the bullets had been fired that had ended Reeva Steenkamp's life.

The door, mute witness to what had happened that night, was studied by all parties in court, as if they were archeologists before a slab of ambiguously understood hieroglyphics. It stood as a symbol of the difficulties the prosecution would face in the attempt to prove beyond reasonable doubt that the man in the dock had pulled the trigger in a fit of murderous rage. The exact locations of the four bullet holes were clearly marked, rising and then falling in an arc just above or below the level of the door handle, roughly at waist height.

The prosecution produced an Afrikaner police colonel, who testified with the help of a black female interpreter, and a black police captain, who spoke in English. Wisely, the prosecution did not call Hilton Botha, the first police investigator on the scene. Botha had not only been a poor witness at Pistorius's bail hearing a year earlier, but soon afterwards he had been charged with attempted murder.

Colonel Johannes Vermeulen, the first of the two to testify and a forensics specialist, had had a year to analyze the bathroom door, but it turned out in court that he had failed to register, let alone scrutinize, a significant mark on the door frame. Roux contended that this was the point where his client had kicked the door with his prosthetic leg in an attempt to break it down after firing the lethal shots. Roux said forensic experts for the defense would prove as much. Colonel Vermeulen had no reply.

The prosecution also tried to prove that Pistorius had lied when he said he had stumbled to his bedroom to put on his prosthetic legs before attacking the locked door with a cricket bat. Roux, dripping scorn at times, had the hapless colonel get down on his knees in court, cricket bat in hand, in order to show that Pistorius could not possibly have been on his stumps when he struck the door. The marks were too high.

Colonel Vermeulen performed so ineptly under cross-examination by Roux that there was an outcry in the South African media at the bumbling inefficacy of the country's police investigators.

Nel's next witness, Christian Mangena, a police captain and gun expert, restored some confidence in the force. Scientifically precise in his manner, he argued that the first bullet would have hit the victim in the hip, shattering the bone, that the second missed, and that only the third or fourth shot would have struck her skull. The bullets in the accused's 9mm gun, said Mangena, were black metal-jacket Talon bullets, expanding missiles with folds like petals and jagged edges – dumdums intended to mushroom on entering the human body, causing maximum tissue damage.

As Mangena spoke, the attention of the court suddenly switched, alerted by a sharp cry, to Pistorius. Again he crouched in his seat, again he put his hands behind his head, again he let out a sob, then another sob, and again he retched, but this time, overpowered by the convulsion in his stomach, he vomited into the green bucket.

Aimée wept. So did Lois Pistorius. Her husband, Arnold, remained as unmoved as if he were posing for a portrait. Later, during the lunch break, on the street outside the courtroom, Arnold said, 'He knew this was coming. He just has to go through it, as we all have to.' Aimée, her eyes red, rushed out of the court building, past the photographers and TV cameras permanently camped at the entrance, and turned down a side street, as she would do every day of the trial, to fetch a sandwich for her brother from a nearby café owned by a Russian woman who asked no questions.

After lunch, Roux ploughed on with his questioning of Captain Mangena. The breakdowns Pistorius was experiencing two rows behind him were becoming ever more frequent, but Roux could not keep asking the judge to allow for further pauses in the proceedings. The court would have to get used to the background noise of Pistorius's sobs and whimpers, and keep going.

Captain Mangena was not making thing easy for Roux, outclassing him with his specialist knowledge of guns. The policeman had used laser beams to trace the trajectory of the bullets, which, he explained, traveled from this particular gun at a speed of 380 meters (1245 feet) per second. He had measured the probable distance from which they had been fired, and the position of the person firing. Roux sought to get Mangena to concede that the order of the impact of the bullets might have been different, but he made little headway. Later on in the case the defense would provide its own expert witness, a retired Afrikaner policeman, to refute Mangena's hypothesis. The defense's expert, more experienced but less articulate and convincing than Mangena, argued that it was not possible to establish the precise order of the bullets. But another possibility, raised by a further defense witness – namely, that the loud bang of the first bullet inside a bathroom with reverberating tiled walls would have deafened the accused, making it impossible for him to have heard any screams, even if there had been any – cast doubt on the overall value of the lengthily explored ballistic evidence.

Various days were expended, too, in analyzing the veracity of Pistorius's claim that Reeva did not get out of bed in the middle of the night. Experts in gastric digestion were called in by both sides and learned medical documents produced to try and prove from the study of the contents of her stomach how many hours before she died she had last eaten. The objective of the prosecution was to try and demonstrate that Pistorius had lied – that, contrary to his claim that she had never got out of bed after she fell asleep at around 10 p.m. on February 13, she had got up after midnight to eat something and, presumably, have an argument with him. Members of Pistorius's family and his defense team declared themselves baffled by the energy the prosecution case put into this ultimately unresolved question, not least because it had always been possible that Steenkamp had indeed slipped out of bed unnoticed in the middle of the night to grab something from the kitchen.

**Of all** the witnesses the state produced, none stirred more eager anticipation among the reporters in court than Pistorius's ex-girlfriend, Samantha Taylor, the woman scorned, who had a more intimate knowledge of him than anyone else who would testify in the trial. She had been called by the prosecution to support another of the four charges against Pistorius – namely, that he had violated the firearms act by firing a shot through the open sunroof of a car. But his defense lawyers believed Nel's parallel and deeper purpose was to elicit character evidence from her that would reinforce the charge of murder.

Blonde, pretty, petite, Taylor took the stand. Pistorius wore a wistful look. She had been seventeen when they started going out. He had been crazy about her. He used to call her 'Sam' and 'My little butterfly'. 'You're my dream, you're all I want and all I need,' he would say to her. 'You're the love of my life.' And here she was in court now, playing her part to get him sent to jail.

Pistorius remembered that Samantha's mother had posted a message on Facebook just after Reeva had died saying she was so glad 'Sammy' was 'out of his clutches' and that 'things could have gone wrong with her and his gun during the time they dated'. What Pistorius did not know was that a friend of Taylor's had been telling reporters over the previous year that one day, in the middle of one of his rages, he had held a gun to her head. This was the main reason the press were so excited. Would she recount this alleged incident in court? Would she deliver the prosecution's killer punch by saying that when she was with him she had feared for her life?

She did not. Had the story been true, Nel, it was assumed, would have got it out of her. She did testify in response to Nel's questions that Pistorius had fired that shot out of the car, and that he had laughed immediately afterwards. In so doing, she reinforced the image the prosecution wished to convey to the court of Pistorius as a reckless gun fanatic.

In cross-examination, Roux asked Taylor whether when Pistorius screamed and was really anxious he ever sounded like a woman. She could have offered him a lifeline by saying yes, or expressing some doubt. But she was categorical.

'No, my lady. That is not true. He sounds like a man. I've seen him be very anxious and he would shout at myself. It sounded like a man, my lady.'

Roux did get Taylor to concede that she had never heard him screaming in a life-threatening situation, but when he asked her a question that went to the core of the defense case, whether Pistorius was a person who seemed to her to be unusually scared of coming under criminal attack, she replied, 'Not necessarily.'

Pistorius, who made notes all the time that Taylor spoke, reacted stonily to that response. But his look changed, and a shadow of a smirk passed over his face, as she revealed under questioning from Roux that she was still sad that he had left her.

'He cheated on me. I was upset, my lady,' she said, and shed a tear. Taylor was the only person apart from Pistorius who wept on the witness stand during the trial, also forcing breaks in the proceedings, each time consoled by her sister, as he would be by his.

This evidence held little relevance for the case, either for the murder charge or the firearms charge, and was of value only to those sectors of the media whose public found the subject of infidelity endlessly entertaining. The one potential difficulty that Taylor's

testimony about her relationship with Pistorius presented for the defense was that it could portray him
in the judge's mind as a liar. Roux, seeking to refute
this perception, found himself in the undignified
and almost farcical position of having to debate with
Taylor who had cheated on whom first, his client's
contention being that she had cheated first, with
Quinton van der Burgh, in the middle of 2012, when
he was away at the London Games.

'I have never admitted to cheating on Oscar. I did not
cheat on Oscar,' she said in reply, explaining that they
had split up during that period but had got back together
again after London. It was then, she said, that he had
cheated on her, with Reeva. Roux replied that he had
e-mails demonstrating they had broken up, to which she
righteously retorted that they had not broken up 'officially'. Roux, as he would confess to his colleagues later,
might have pursued the matter further, but he risked
reducing the manifestly vulnerable and innocent Taylor
to a quivering wreck. He deliberately held back, figuring that a contest so unequal would not go down well
with the judge, whose gentler feelings he knew he had to
try and elicit if, when the time came for the judgment,
she was to give his client the benefit of the doubt.

The evening after Taylor completed her testimony
one of Pistorius's cousins, a daughter of Arnold's, asked

him how it was that he could have fallen for a woman so young and so naive. The cousin could not understand how the thoughtful, sensitive and worldly Pistorius that she knew could possibly have considered Taylor a fitting match. He was unable to offer his cousin an explanation.

Another figure from Pistorius's past, to whom he also thought he had been close, took the witness stand after Taylor. His name was Darren Fresco and again Pistorius's family were baffled, asking him later how on earth he could have made friends with someone who appeared so fickle. This time he had an answer. He had been away from South Africa for long stretches at a time, and when he came back he was lonely and had to find companions where he could. Fresco, like him, had time on his hands during the week to go out and have fun at places like Tasha's restaurant in Johannesburg, where the young and idle and well-off went to see and be seen.

Unfortunately for Pistorius, Fresco backed up Taylor's testimony regarding the shooting of the gun through the open sunroof, which Fresco said he had been driving. He also testified regarding the third count on which Pistorius had been charged, concerning the gun he had fired at Tasha's. Fresco was a key witness. The gun in question had belonged to him, and he testified that he had slipped it under the table to Pistorius, who had fiddled with it on his lap until it went off, the bullet grazing the leg of another friend at their table.

'Oscar said, "There is too much media attention around me, please take the blame," and like a good friend, I agreed,' Fresco testified.

No one at the time of the alleged incidents, either in the car or at the restaurant, had lodged a complaint with the police, and neither charge would ever have come to court had Pistorius not shot Reeva. Gerrie Nel had figured that, should Taylor's testimony in particular be believed by the judge, Pistorius's hair-trigger temper would enter into the equation and improve the chances that he would be found guilty of having killed Reeva Steenkamp in a rage.

Roux believed that Pistorius's rash behavior and wild outbursts served, in the context of the court case, as a double-edged weapon. They could be interpreted as reinforcing the thesis that he had killed Reeva Steenkamp in a rage, but, just as plausibly, they could be interpreted as reinforcing the thesis that he had reacted in a crazily fearful and disproportionate manner to an imagined threat. South African commentators, aware of all the stories in the media about his fast driving and his mania for guns, listened to the evidence about the bullet he had fired at Tasha's, about the other one he had allegedly shot from the car, saw the extremity of his emotions in court, and declared that there was a deep psychological problem rooted in what one of them called 'a loose Pistorius gene'. Roux did not necessarily disagree. Evidence of its existence, as he would try and show later in court, might prove beneficial to the defense case.

**So might** the private WhatsApp messages between Pistorius and Reeva, which the prosecution team went to great lengths to present as evidence in court.

Pistorius had complicated Captain Mike Van Aardt's life immensely by informing him, through his lawyers, that he had forgotten the master code for his iPhone. This alerted the detective, and Nel, to the possibility that the critical incriminating material that the murder case needed might lie within the phone. The problem was that there was only one way to break into it and access the messages, including deleted ones, which was to send it to Apple's headquarters in Cupertino, California. Legal permission had to be obtained before Apple would agree to this. A laborious process began in the second half of 2013 that involved appealing to courts in both South Africa and the United States, which ended with the contents of both Reeva's and

Pistorius's iPhones being recovered with just days to go before the trial.

The prosecution's hope was that a message from Reeva would be found that could have caused Pistorius to fly into a murderous rage before shooting her. Along with the prosecution, a large part of the general public had suspected from the start that the motive for the killing was jealousy. The most widespread version of the Othello theory was that the man with whom Reeva had had a relationship prior to Pistorius, the famous South African rugby player Francois Hougaard, had sent her a provocative or salacious Valentine's message – or perhaps some joke about her boyfriend's missing legs – to which she had replied with enthusiasm. Those who chose to believe in Pistorius's guilt invariably chose also to regard Reeva in a saintly light, but this inconsistency did not appear to loom large in their thinking. The unsubstantiated gossip surrounding Reeva and Hougaard, which only made a wide public impact after her death, was sufficient to persuade those who chose to believe it, that Hougaard was the reason behind the supposed argument that had led to her fleeing into the bathroom, locking herself inside the toilet cubicle, and dying in a blaze of gunfire. It was pure hypothesis, rendered all the more implausible by Hougaard himself having stated publicly before the trial that there had been no such messages between him and Reeva.

When the WhatsApp evidence was revealed in court, however, the phone messages did not turn out to be the smoking gun the prosecution was looking for. Their chief impact was on Pistorius himself, who found the experience of listening to them being read out to a worldwide audience of millions excruciatingly embarrassing.

Had he been on the outside looking in, he might have seen something funny in the spectacle. The person reading out the messages from the witness stand was a large, bluff police captain called Francois Moller who had accessed 1,709 communications between the couple. Captain Moller solemnly recited the love burblings that they contained.

The single incriminating shadow in the entire collection appeared in that line where Reeva had said, 'I'm scared of u sometimes and how u snap at me and of how u will react to me.' But then Barry Roux asked the captain to read the line that immediately followed. The captain duly did: 'You make me happy 90% of the time and I think we are amazing together.'

Roux maintained – and Nel did not contradict him – that close to 98 per cent of the messages the prosecution had unearthed contained not recriminations but endearments. To prove it, he asked Captain Moller to read out a representative, and lengthy, sample of messages Reeva had sent to his client. Moller duly deadpanned, 'I love sleeping next to you and never want to cramp your style', 'you are an amazing person and you are more than cared for . . . blessings', and – the final WhatsApp exchange between them on the afternoon before he shot her – 'Baby can I cook for you on Thursday?' 'I'd love that,' was the reply.

If Captain Moller felt some discomfort himself at being obliged to continue reciting a long and numbing litany of the 'my boos', 'my babas', 'my angels', 'babycakes', and variations on 'I miss you' and 'I miss you 1 more', contained in the lovers' exchanges, he did not show it, remaining gamely professional all the way through. But even he might have wondered what use this could be for the prosecution. Shedding all this light on the cooing intimacies between the man the prosecution was seeking to convict of premeditated murder and the victim he had evidently been besotted with, seemed unlikely, on balance, to lend much weight to their case. And less so when it emerged that not only had she not received any Valentine's messages from any previous lovers on the night she died, but that the last Twitter message she wrote, on the evening of February 13, read, 'What do you have up your sleeve for your love tomorrow?'

---

**More worthy** of the judge's consideration in her duty to arrive at the most 'reasonably possible' interpretation of what happened on the night Steenkamp died was the evidence of the sounds heard by the neighbors, three of whom would be produced by the defense team after the end of the prosecution case, which lasted fifteen days.

These three witnesses had been interviewed by the police, but Nel had chosen not to call them. The five he had called were all white; the three whom the defense would call were all black. They were Pistorius's next-door neighbors, living either side of his home.

The first was Michael Nhlengethwa, whose balcony was 11 meters (36 feet) from the bathroom where Reeva Steenkamp was shot. Nhlengethwa told Roux, who led his evidence, that he had been friendly with Pistorius, although they did not socialize, and had met Reeva, whom Pistorius had introduced to him as 'my fiancée'. Nhlengethwa, who worked in the construction business, said he had been very taken with the couple.

'Oscar is the type of person who if he sees me, he will stop, get out of his car and greet me.' As for Reeva, the first time Nhlengethwa met her, he recalled, he had stretched out a hand in greeting. 'But she just opened her arms, she came to hug me. I could see the person that she was.' Nhlengethwa said he had advised Pistorius not to let her go; she should be 'for keeps'.

Nhlengethwa testified that on the night of the incident he was woken by his wife, who had heard a loud noise. He worried at first that it might have come from inside his house and rushed to check on his daughter, whom he found to be asleep and safe. He realized the sound must have come from outside.

'Then we started hearing a man crying very loud . . . Something was wrong. We started panicking,' Nhlengethwa said. 'There is a difference between normal crying and crying when you are in danger, when you need help. We felt probably he was in danger. It was very loud.'

Roux asked him to describe the pitch of the voice. He replied that it was 'very high'. He said he could hear the man shouting, 'Please, please, no!'

Nhlengethwa rang the estate security guards at 3.16, he said, and the crying went on during the call and after. Suddenly he realized that the sounds were coming from his neighbor's house. 'The question for me was, is Oscar okay?' he said.

Gerrie Nel began his cross-examination of Nhlengethwa in a vein similar to the one Roux had pursued with Michelle Burger, suggesting his evidence had been contaminated by his reading of the news about the crime and, in particular, by following the trial on TV. Nhlengethwa did not deny he was taking a keen interest in the action in court. 'Oscar is my neighbor,' he said. 'There's no way I would turn a blind eye to the case.'

Nel, citing the evidence of the neighbors who had appeared for the prosecution, asked him if he had heard gunshots, or the sound of a cricket bat breaking down a door, or a woman's screams. 'I did not hear those things,' Nhlengethwa said, adding that it surprised him that neighbors much further away had heard both shots and screams.

Nel asked him if he had talked to the accused since the incident. He replied that he had not. With that, and with surprising swiftness, Nel announced that he had no further questions.

The next witness Roux presented was Nhlengethwa's wife, Eontle Nhlengethwa. She said she was awoken by 'a bang . . . a very loud sound'. Then she heard somebody crying, 'Help, help, help.' It was a male person's voice, she said. Roux asked her if she could make a sound that resembled the crying she had heard. Mrs Nhlengethwa obliged with a high-pitched wail and then immediately clarified, 'But it was in the voice of a man.'

Nel took over and asked if she had heard a woman screaming. She insisted that she had not and, without much further ado, Nel said he had nothing more to ask.

Rika Motshuane, Roux's next witness, was a psychologist working at the Ministry of Labor. She testified that she and her husband were not friends with the accused, but when they moved into their home in 2008 he had come round to welcome them. They were out at the time, but 'the next day', she said, 'we went to greet him and he asked us to come in for coffee, but we were in a hurry so we could not.'

She heard no shots or loud bangs, but was woken up by a man crying. 'To me, my lady,' she said, 'it was a cry of pain. I woke my husband up. I said, "Do you hear?" He said, "Yes, but I thought I was dreaming." I said, "The crying is real." I was panicking . . . I said it could be that one of the security guards has been shot. The crying was very loud and very close. I even thought it could be in the house.'

Roux asked her to try and imitate the cry she heard. She obliged, as Eontle Nhlengethwa had done, producing a long, eerily convincing howl that amazed and chilled those listening in court and following the action on TV.

Roux asked her if she had also heard a woman scream and she said that she had not.

Nel gave Mrs Motshuane short shrift, surprising the court once more by how quickly he completed his cross-examination. He asked her whether she had been following the case on television. She said she had, after the prosecution had told her they would not be calling her to give evidence. He asked her if she had heard gunshots. She said that she had not. Nel said, 'The state has nothing further'. The judge thanked her for her assistance and Mrs Motshuane was free to leave the witness stand.

Two theories were discussed in the public gallery as to why Nel had expended so much less time cross-examining the neighbors who appeared for the defense than Roux had spent on those who appeared for the prosecution. One was that he simply did not place much value on their testimony, because what they had heard had happened after the shots, or the sound of the cricket bat, meaning that they must have slept through the screams of a terrified woman that the prosecution witnesses said they had heard. The second theory was that he wished to try and minimize the significance of the male screams that they said they had heard.

The judge would need to establish whether the closer neighbors had heard a man's screams at the same time as the neighbors who appeared for the state had heard a woman's screams. If so, then the immediate neighbors' testimony would suddenly acquire great weight. The best clues as to the timing of the various cries would lie in the records of the phone calls the neighbors had made to security guards or the police. If the female screams heard by the neighbors who lived further away coincided with the time the nearest neighbors heard male cries, then the defense position would be reinforced. If Nel managed to persuade the judge that they had occurred at different times, that the female screams had happened before the next-door neighbors woke up, then he would be proved right and their testimony would indeed not count for very much. Both sides would attempt to fit the puzzle to suit their objectives, revealing their different conclusions towards the end of the trial when they would deliver their 'closing arguments', their respective summations and interpretations of all the evidence heard.

**The defense** team had one more card up their sleeve to try and shift the debate concerning the sounds heard that night in their favor. They produced a witness by the name of Ivan Lin, an electrical engineer and acoustics expert who had carried out research on how people perceive sounds. Lin, who was young and bespectacled, gave the impression – unlike the three neighbors who testified for the defense – that he had no personal stake whatsoever in the outcome of the trial. He conveyed little sense of knowing who the accused was, and even less of taking any interest in his predicament. Whether led by Roux or grilled by Nel, his demeanor remained unflappably scientific.

Lin, led initially in his evidence by Roux, began by saying that he had conducted a series of sound tests in the neighborhood of the accused's home to help apportion value to the evidence previously submitted. He testified that he had drawn up a report the previous week, measuring the sound levels generated in the bedroom, the bathroom and the balcony of the accused, and had then projected how they would be perceived at the distances of the homes of the neighbors who had testified for the state. He provided numerous and varying examples of how sound would carry at night from house to house – in decibels adjusted (dBA), the measure of the relative loudness of sounds as received by the human ear. Roux, as if seeking to blind the court with science, had Lin enumerate a wide range of possible registers – 50, 60, 90, 75, 110, 140 dBA – depending on how far away the listener was and whether doors or windows were open or closed.

'The act of listening is an intellectual event,' explained Lin, who said that the critical question to be decided here was whether, at a determined distance, sounds could be perceived 'intelligibly' as well as 'audibly', whether they could not just be heard but understood, analyzed and interpreted.

All of the science and all of the measurements Lin took boiled down to the one question Roux wished him to answer: whether, from the distance where Michelle Burger and her husband, Charl Johnson, lived – namely, 177 meters (580 feet) away – it would be possible to hear 'blood-curdling' screams and to identify the gender of the person uttering them.

Lin said it was not always possible to tell whether a scream was made by a man or a woman. Specifically, he said, 'It is unlikely that a scream from someone in a lavatory heard from 170 meters away would have been heard audibly and intelligibly.' Lin's proposition was that it would not have been possible for someone at that distance to distinguish with absolute certainty between a man's and a woman's screams.

In his cross-examination, Nel battled to compete with Lin on his specialist terrain – just as Roux had done in his attempts to undermine the credibility of the gun expert Captain Mangena.

The prosecutor's main objective was to try and discredit not so much Lin himself, as his impressively detailed scientific know-how. Nel put it to Lin that surely distinguishing between a man's and a woman's screams was a straightforward, everyday occurrence which hardly required the taking of complex acoustic measurements.

'One cannot be absolutely certain, reliably certain', Lin replied. But Nel insisted, 'We hear male voices, female voices . . . often we are able to identify that. It is common sense.'

'Often,' Lin agreed, 'it is.'

Nel proposed that a woman's screams would have a higher tonal character, 'almost like a musical note'. Lin agreed that this was a common perception. But he said that at 177 meters even a 'high-end' scream of 160dBA at source would be perceived as quieter than the ambient sound of the courtroom they were in, which was 40dBA.

Nel, who made little headway against Lin, concluded his cross-examination by asking him directly whether he questioned the truthfulness of his witnesses.

'You're not saying the witnesses who told us they heard a woman scream are lying, Mr Lin?' Nel asked.

'We're talking about a possible scenario from a scientific perspective,' responded a mildly affonted Lin. 'I'm not saying the witnesses are lying at all.'

Nel, having endeavored to portray Lin to the judge as an egghead blind to the obvious, called it a day there. The contest between them appeared to have ended as a muddled tie – muddle having been precisely what Barry Roux had sought in presenting Lin as a witness. The question that remained to be decided was how much clarity the judge had been able to glean from the confusing testimonies of the eight individuals who – save for Pistorius himself – would pass for the closest thing to material witnesses that the court would hear during the entirety of the trial.

**Legions of** pundits had submitted their opinions on South African television's 'Oscar Channel' and across numerous media outlets at home and abroad, evaluating the quality and credibility of the witnesses, offering blow-by-blow analyses of Roux's and Nel's strategies and tactics, seeking to second-guess the thought processes of the judge. Views differed widely, depending on the pundits' legal knowledge, or lack of it, or simply because some, like many members of the general public, had made up their minds before the trial began as to the guilt or innocence of the accused. Calmer heads pointed out just how implausible were both the prosecution's and the defense's versions of the events at Pistorius's home in the early hours of Valentine's Day. It was as hard to comprehend the 'tragic accident' version as it was to glimpse what possible motive he might have had for wanting to kill the woman whom he apparently loved, and who was apparently in love with him. Barring Estelle van der Merwe's vague and uncorroborated testimony, the prosecution had offered no evidence to support the theory of an argument having taken place prior to the shooting.

What all observers agreed upon, however, was that everything that would be heard from the start of the trial to its finish would dim in significance in comparison with the testimony of the only person alive who knew exactly what had happened that night. In the absence of decisively compelling facts, the outcome would turn on how coherent or incoherent the testimony of Oscar Pistorius would be, on how he would stand up to what everyone anticipated would be a merciless interrogation by Gerrie Nel, and on whether the judge would feel that he was lying or telling the truth.

# 17

*I am bound upon a wheel of fire that mine own*
*tears do scald like molten lead.*

SHAKESPEARE, *KING LEAR*

At 12.10 a.m. on April 7, 2014, Barry Roux said, 'I call Mr Pistorius.'

Pistorius stood up and strode briskly along the bench he occupied alone at the front of the court, towards the witness stand, looking neither left at the judge nor right at the public gallery, where June Steenkamp, Reeva's mother, sat. It was the moment for which he had been steeling himself for more than a year, the first time he would tell his story in his own words since the day he shot Reeva – but he could not have been in a more fragile state of mind.

Pistorius had not slept the night before, despite all the pills he took, and earlier that morning the first defense witness Roux had called, a pathologist named Jan Botha, had described in clinical detail the wound on Reeva's hip, the perforation of her skull, the spilling brain tissue. Then Nel, during his cross-examination, had flashed up on a screen, so that everyone in the court could see, close-up images of the blood-splattered bathroom and of the wounds themselves, including, for one harrowing instant, a photo of Reeva's dead face in profile, gray and bruised, her hair matted with blood, the entry point of the bullet to her head distinctly visible. Reeva's mother had put her hands to her face and gasps rose from the public gallery, but no one had responded with more visible dismay than Pistorius. He put a handkerchief to his mouth, pressed his thumbs to his ears and sobbed more loudly than he had at any point in the trial so far. It was impossible to carry on. Roux stood up and asked the judge for the 'courtesy' of a brief adjournment; she granted it, and once more Aimée, almost as distraught as her brother, rushed to his side.

The one faint comfort now, as he stood facing side-ways on to the judge, preparing to take the oath, was that his image was forbidden – by his own choice – from being shown on TV. But millions around the world could hear him on TV, radio, tablets or phones as a female court official instructed him to say after her, 'I swear that the evidence I shall give, shall be the truth, the whole truth and nothing but the truth, so help me God.' He struggled to get the words out. He would struggle still more a moment later when, still standing, he recited a rehearsed statement.

'I'd like to begin by tendering an apology,' Pistorius said. 'I want to take this opportunity to apologize to Mr and Mrs Steenkamp, to Reeva's family and friends, you who are here today.' His jaw was quivering, his soft voice cracking, barely audible. 'I can hardly hear you, Mr Pistorius,' the judge interrupted him.' I apologize, my lady,' he replied, and resumed his speech at a higher volume.

'There hasn't been a moment since this tragedy happened that I haven't thought about your family,' he said, turning his head in the direction of Mrs Steenkamp. 'I wake up every morning and you're the first people I think of. The first people I pray for. I can't imagine the pain and the sorrow and the emptiness that I've caused you and your family. I was simply trying to protect Reeva. I can promise you that when she went to bed that night she felt loved. I have tried to put my words on paper many times to write to you, but no words would ever suffice.'

Was it a ploy, suggested by his lawyers, aimed more at the judge? Was it a sincerely heartfelt appeal to Reeva's family? It was both – but June Steenkamp listened to him with her face as hard as stone, her lips puckered, acid the look in her eyes. A day later she would tell a British tabloid newspaper, the *Daily Mirror*, that Pistorius's apology had not had the desired effect. 'It left me unmoved,' she said. 'I knew it was coming. My lawyers had prepared me for it. I cried for the first time, yes, but not because he apologized, because of the suffering and agony that my darling daughter went through and because I will never have her again.'

Almost from the day Reeva died, it had been possible to find out what the Steenkamp family was thinking only from television broadcasts or from the publications of news organizations, like the *Mirror*, that had a policy of paying for interviews. Advised by the family lawyer, Advocate Dup de Bruyn, the Steenkamps chose to speak publicly about their daughter's death only in exchange for money. June Steenkamp and her husband, Barry, were poor, and especially so at the time Reeva died, Barry having been reduced to selling wood on country roadsides and June to selling home-made food at the local racecourse. During the brief period that Reeva was with Pistorius, they had depended on money from her to pay their basic bills. Their future had relied on Reeva having a successful career in modeling or else returning to the law, which she had studied at university. With her death, retirement appeared to promise only destitution. They had hoped initially to receive some money from a civil settlement with Pistorius, but it seemed likely that all of Pistorius's assets would be swallowed up by his legal fees. It was after receiving a deluge of requests for interviews from all over the world that they hit upon the idea, using De Bruyn as their intermediary, of charging the media handsome fees for their time. The Steenkamps grieved, but in a perverse and cruelly unexpected way their daughter did more to swell her family's fortunes in death than she ever had in life.

Two South African media outlets that had the money and the ethical inclination to make the required payments were the sister celebrity magazines *You*, in English, and *Huis Genoot*, in Afrikaans. De Bruyn revealed that for an interview with the Steenkamp parents they paid 500,000 rand, or US$50,000, and for the photographic rights to a ceremony in which the family scattered Reeva's ashes on the Indian Ocean another 250,000 rand, or US$25,000. Over the following year, then into the trial and beyond, the Steenkamp family gave interviews to London's *Mail on Sunday*, *Daily Mail*, *Daily Mirror* and *Hello* magazine, as well as to British TV's Channel Five.

Thus the public learned of what they described as their 'unbearable grief' at the loss of their adored daughter, of 'a space inside that could never be filled', and that Barry would often get out of bed at night and sit on his porch weeping, drink and cigarette in hand.

De Bruyn would routinely tell journalists who called him that the Steenkamps were 'indigent' – but that did not last long. Before the start of the trial, Barry and June moved to a new house in the countryside, near the Port Elizabeth racecourse. Barry stopped selling wood for a living and resumed training horses, making plans to build stables on the large plot, almost the size of half a football field, on which his new home stood. By November 2013, Barry Steenkamp was back at work, with as many as three horses competing on race days. Sometimes his jockey would be Wayne Agrella, Reeva's old boyfriend.

The Steenkamps also acquired a pub near the racecourse called the Barking Spider. June would continue to cook food for a living, but now she would be serving it in her own establishment. Journalists who arrived unannounced in search of free information were shooed away.

Early on in the trial, the Pistorius family, who sat throughout on the same long bench as June Steenkamp, made an attempt to make peace with her. Aimée walked across, with a sad and apologetic smile, and handed her a note. When a journalist from a South African Sunday newspaper asked June if she would reveal to him the contents of the note, she replied, 'You know the story. You know the story . . .' The journalist took her to mean that she might do so in exchange for payment.

The last interview the Steenkamps did before the trial began was published in the *Mail on Sunday*. June, always more loquacious with the media than her husband, said it would be torture for her to listen to the evidence of 'my lovely girl's last moments', but she had a need to know what she had gone through, and why Pistorius had done it. 'That is my obsession: the truth about why Oscar did what he did that night.'

Yet she was surprisingly generous towards the man who had killed her daughter. 'Whatever the court decides at the end of his trial, I will be ready to forgive him,' she said. 'I know many people in my position would want to see him dead or badly punished. But I believe in faith and justice and I don't have any hatred or revenge in my heart. That's not my way. I would rather pray for him and pray that my family can get through this terrible time. I want to look at Oscar, really look him in the eyes, and see for myself the truth about what he did to Reeva.'

Inside the High Court in Pretoria on March 7 she finally had her chance. It was the first time she would hear Pistorius speak in person, for Reeva had never introduced him to them. Unmoved by his personal plea to her, June Steenkamp listened expressionless as Barry Roux, standing across the court from Pistorius, began leading his client gently through his testimony, seeking first to extract from him a sense of his state of mind since the shooting, and then prodding him into recounting the salient moments of his life since childhood.

Pistorius said he had been on heavy medication since the third week of February, when he had moved from a police cell to his uncle's home. Yet the sleeping pills and antidepressants were of ambiguous value because he was scared to go to sleep. 'I have terrible nightmares about things that happened that night where I wake up and I can smell the blood, and I wake up terrified. I wake up just in a complete state of terror to a point that I'd rather not sleep than wake up like that. For many weeks I didn't sleep.'

He drew all the comfort that he could muster from his Christian faith. 'Religion is what has got me through this last year – I have been struggling a lot,' he said. But Reeva had been his refuge, too. 'I always wanted to have a girlfriend who was Christian. She would pray for me at night. We would pray before we would eat.'

Roux led Pistorius through a detailed exposition of his life from birth, highlighting not his triumphs and indomitable character but the emotional and physical trials he had endured, inverting the public narrative of his achievements prior to the shooting of Reeva. He began with a description of the congenital defect in his ankles and feet, his fibular hemimelia, and the choice that was made to amputate below the knee. The two words he repeated most often were 'my mother'. In a mournful and melancholic voice, so soft the judge repeatedly had to prompt him to speak up, he listed the areas of his life in which she had been the decisive influence.

'My mother grew up in an Anglican Church and a Methodist Church. My mother taught me to trust the Lord.'

'My mother wanted me to get over my physical limitations by trying several sports. She never wanted me to see my disability as something that would hold me back.'

'My mother taught me to stand up for myself. She always said don't come crying to your parents.'

'My mother owned a pistol that she kept in a padded bag under the pillow. My father was not around much. She often called the police at night. Often we were scared, and me and my brother and sister went to my mother's room and waited for the police to come.'

'My mother was very important to us. Everything I learned in life I learned from her.'

When he mentioned her death, his voice broke again. 'My mother passed away when I was fifteen,' he said, his grief evidently still fresh twelve years on. 'She died very unexpectedly. I had just started boarding school and she had just remarried. We did not know she was sick and then we were told she was in a coma . . . On the day she died, we rushed to the hospital and were there for ten minutes before she passed.'

Roux, eager to portray his client to the judge as a philanthropic-minded soul, got him to talk about the project he had worked on with Strathclyde University in Scotland to develop prosthetic legs for African amputees. The court learned of his charity work with landmine victims in Mozambique, and of a visit to a Mozambican coastal town where he had challenged the fastest people to run a race against him. He won the race, whereupon, he said, a group of amputees who had been watching were 'not ashamed anymore', and they pulled up their pants 'to show off' their prosthetic legs.

Yet, Pistorius confessed, he struggled to act in accordance with the example he set. His prostheses, he said, were an extension of his body. 'I don't really want to be seen without them . . . I get shy, embarrassed, when I don't have them on. They are a part of me.'

With that, his first day of testimony drew to a close, twenty minutes before schedule. 'Mr Pistorius is very tired,' Roux told the judge. She was not unsympathetic.

'He does look exhausted. He sounds exhausted', she said. She asked Nel if he had any objection, and he said he did not, 'so long as this is not a daily occurrence'.

Pistorius stood up, bowed before the judge as she got up to leave and, the moment she had left the chamber, collapsed in his chair, almost crumpling to the floor. His sister hurried across the courtroom to his aid.

Aimée was by her brother's side all day and every day during the trial, both in court and at home. In the morning she would lay out his clothes – always a dark suit and a white shirt and tie – and make him some breakfast. She sat in court unfailingly with him from the start to the end of every session; she had lunch with him in a room in the court building, the two of them invariably alone; she cooked for him in the evenings, sat next to him watching TV. Often she put him to bed and then slept on a couch alongside him, watching over him as if he were a sickly child, keeping an eye on him to make sure that he stayed true to the promise he had made his uncle Arnold months earlier that, yes, he saw a purpose in carrying on living.

**Day two** of Pistorius's testimony dawned with a message posted on Twitter by Samantha Taylor, which she evidently regretted for she quickly deleted it. The message read, 'Last lies you get to tell . . . You better make it worth your while.'

Roux, coincidentally, began proceedings by questioning Pistorius about the accusation that he had fired a gun through the sunroof of a car, and on the two other subsidiary firearms charges. He denied all guilt, flatly contradicting Taylor's and Darren Fresco's testimony about the gun in the car; blaming the incident with the gun at Tasha's restaurant partly on Fresco, whose gun it was, for passing it to him under the table when it was not safe to handle; and dismissing the charge concerning the unlicensed bullets found in his home, saying he had never claimed to own them, that he was just storing them for his father.

Roux asked him what his attitude was towards guns now. 'I don't ever want to hold a gun in my hand again,' Pistorius said.

Roux nodded, paused to retrieve a piece of paper from his desk and, deliberately calm, as if seeking to drain the tension from the moment, said, 'I am taking you, Mr Pistorius, to the events of the 13th of February'.

Seats shifted in the packed courtroom. Necks straightened. The drama's central act was about to begin.

Roux led him through the events of the evening before 'the incident'.

Reeva, Pistorius said, had come over to his home to spend the night. She was already there, preparing dinner, when he got home around six in the evening. He showered, changed his clothes and at seven they ate, chatting about the day – he telling her about a visit to the new home he meant to buy in Johannesburg, and the two of them discussing the details of a new contract she was about to sign. They went up to the bedroom at about eight and he opened a sliding door onto a balcony because the air conditioning was not working and it was a hot and muggy night. He placed two fans – one big, one small – by the balcony door. Ever cautious about security, he placed his gun under the left side of his bed and a cricket bat by a cabinet near the door to the bedroom.

He took off his prosthetic legs to air them, placing them between the bed and the sliding balcony door, then the two of them lay on the bed – he, unusually, choosing the left side, because of a pain in his shoulder for which he was receiving treatment. He trawled through the internet on his iPad; she got down from the bed to do some yoga exercises, pausing in her routine for an occasional kiss. She returned to the bed and they chatted for a while. He began to drift off. He asked her to remember to pull the curtains tight shut and close the balcony door before going to sleep. He fell asleep before she did, with his head on her stomach.

Breaking the tension in the courtroom, Roux asked him whether he and Reeva had made any plans for Valentine's Day. Pistorius said they had no plans to go out, but he had ordered a bracelet for her from a designer she liked and had meant to go and pick it up with her from a jewelry store during the course of the day. She, for her part, had wrapped a present for him addressed to 'Ozzie': four framed photos of the two of them and a Valentine's card.

The message Reeva had written on the card had read, 'I think today is a good day to tell you that I love you.'

Pistorius paused, sighed, wiped his eyes. She had not had a chance to give him the card before she died.

Roux returned to the night of the 13th. What had he been wearing? Pistorius said he had worn a pair of basketball shorts. This was Roux's cue to ask for 'a very short' adjournment. He said the defense would like to offer a demonstration for the benefit of the court, giving no warning what it would consist of.

The judge left the chamber and Roux nodded to Pistorius, who left the courtroom by a side entrance. Five minutes later, Pistorius reappeared in a long-sleeved white vest and baggy black shorts, exposing his skin-colored prosthetic legs, on the ends of which he wore a pair of running shoes.

The judge returned, everybody bowed, and Roux apologized to her 'for the informal dress of Mr Pistorius'. But there was a reason for it.

Roux instructed Pistorius to step down from the witness stand and position himself next to the wooden door with the bullet holes, which remained propped up in place at the side of the courtroom. Roux asked him if he would please remove his prostheses.

Pistorius sat down on a chair, swiftly removed his two artificial legs and stood up again. Everybody in the courtroom craned their necks for a clearer view. The judge leaned forward on her desk. 'Oooh,' gasped a woman in the public gallery.

Pistorius had shrunk nearly a foot in height. South Africa's 'hottest hunk', 'sexiest man', and national sporting hero stood transformed into a dwarfish indi-vidual, balancing with difficulty on a pair of thin, pale, wrinkled stumps. Judge Masipa leant forward and, her head stock-still, silently studied his calf-less half-legs. Thirty seconds later she relaxed her posture and sat back in her black orthopedic chair. Pistorius sat down again, slipped on his artificial legs, and returned to his place on the witness stand.

It had been a bold move by Barry Roux, another gambit in his quest 'to soften the judge's heart', under the legitimate pretext of allowing her to see what

Pistorius looked like when he got up in the middle of the night and fired the fatal shots. For Pistorius, baring his deformity before the court had been one more twist of the knife, but one to which he had grudgingly lent his consent.

A far worse torment awaited him in the afternoon session when, dressed again in suit and tie, Roux led him through his version of what happened when he woke up in the early hours of February 14.

'I sat up in bed and noticed that the fans were still running and that the door was still open,' Pistorius said, 'although the lights had been switched off. Reeva was still awake or obviously not sleeping. She rolled over to me and asked, "Can't you sleep, my baba?" I said, "No, I can't."'

The tone of his voice, melancholy throughout, became plaintive as he struggled to stop himself from crying.

'I got out of my side of the bed, walked around the foot of the bed, holding onto the foot of the bed with my left hand, and got to where the fans were and took the small fan, the floor fan, and placed it inside the room. I took the bigger fan and took it by the part underneath the fan and placed it in the bedroom. The fans were still running at the time. I then proceeded to close the sliding doors and lock them, I then drew the curtains.'

He was walking on his stumps. The lights were out. His bedroom's thick curtains were tight shut. It was pitch dark.

'I came into the room at this point. The only bit of light that was in the room was a little blue LED light on the amplifier . . . I could see a pair of jeans on the floor, Reeva's jeans . . .'

He paused, fighting to stop himself from falling apart.

'I picked her jeans up and was going to place them over the amplifier, over the light . . .' Another pause – dead silence in the courtroom, as if everybody had stopped breathing. He paused to take a deep breath and continued.

'It was at this point that I heard a window open in the bathroom, it sounded like the window sliding open. I could hear it hit the frame, as though it had hit a point where it couldn't slide anymore.'

'What did you think at the time, Mr Pistorius?' Roux asked.

'My lady,' he said, dissolving into tears, 'that was the moment that everything changed.'

He paused to collect himself. The eyes of the judge were riveted on his face. At Roux's prompting, he continued.

'I thought there was a burglar entering my home. I was on the side of the room where you first have to cross the passage that leads to the bathroom. I just froze. I heard this noise.' He paused, glanced down at the floor, continued, 'I interpreted it as someone climbing into the bathroom. I thought they could be there at any moment. The first thing I thought was I needed to arm myself, I needed to protect myself and Reeva, I needed to get my gun. I was looking down the passage scared that the person, people, were going to come out at that point. I rushed as fast as I could. I couldn't see anything in the room.'

He felt under his bed in the dark with his fingers, he said, took his 9mm gun out of its holster and moved towards the narrow passageway, seventeen feet long, linking the bedroom with the bathroom. Continually he paused for breath now, as if wishing to delay the terrible climax that lay ahead.

'I whispered for Reeva to get down and phone the police. At that point I just wanted to put myself between the person that had gained access to my house and Reeva. When I got just before the passage I slowed down because I was scared that that person could have possibly already been in the closet passage, so I slowed down and had my firearm extended in front of me. As I entered where the passage is to the bathroom I was overcome with fear and started screaming for the burglars to get out of my house. I shouted for Reeva to get on the floor . . .

'I slowly made my way down the passage, constantly aware that these people could come at me at any time . . . I didn't have my legs on.

'Just before I got to the wall where the tiles start in the bathroom I stopped shouting as I was worried the person would know exactly where I was. I could get shot.

'I heard a toilet door slam, what could only have been the toilet door . . . I couldn't see inside, but it confirmed for me there was a person or people inside.'

Roux called on a police official to put up a photo of the bathroom on the screen. Instead, apparently by mistake, a picture of Reeva Steenkamp's dead body flashed up for an instant, for the whole court to see. June Steenkamp covered her face in her hands. Pistorius gasped. A uniformed policeman hurried over with the green plastic bucket. Pistorius vomited. The judge called an adjournment for lunch. Arnold Pistorius strode angrily towards the policeman who had displayed the wrong photograph. Aimée left the courtroom in tears.

**An hour** later court resumed. Roux asked Pistorius to pick up where he had left off.

'I got to the entrance of the bathroom at the end of the passage, where I stopped screaming. At that point I was not shouting or screaming, I thought the intruders were going to come out or were in the bathroom at that time. With my pistol in my right hand I peered into the bathroom. I then made my way to where the carpet and tiles meet on the left-hand side. I had my shoulder against the wall and I had my pistol raised to my eye to the corner of the entrance of the bathroom. There was no light in the bathroom.'

There was another long pause. Roux coaxed him on gently. 'Please continue, Mr Pistorius.'

'As I peered in I could see that the window was open. I was with my back against the wall, with my hand against the wall for balance, slowly scuffling along the left-hand side wall.

'I wasn't sure if the intruders were in the toilet or on a ladder that they would have used to gain access or if they were round the corner at that point. I still had my firearm in front of me to look round the corner, to look at the shower.'

He stopped again for fully half a minute. There was not a sound in the courtroom. Roux stood statue-still.

'At that point I saw there was no one in the bathroom and the toilet door was closed and the window was open. I retreated a step or two back.

'At this point I started screaming again for Reeva to phone the police.

'My eyes were going between the window and the toilet, I must have stood there for some time. I wasn't sure if someone was going to come out of the toilet and attack me or come up the ladder and point a firearm in the house and start shooting. So I just stayed where I was and I kept on screaming.

'Then I heard a noise from inside the toilet that I perceived to be somebody coming out of the toilet. Before I knew it I had fired four shots at the door.

'My ears were ringing – I couldn't hear anything – so I shouted. I kept shouting for Reeva to phone the police. I was still scared to retreat because I wasn't sure if there was somebody on the ladder, I wasn't sure if there was somebody in the toilet. I don't know how long I stood there for.

'I shouted for Reeva.

'At some point I walked back to the bedroom, my ears were ringing, I couldn't tell if there was a response or not. I kept on shouting for Reeva. I didn't hear anything. At this point it hadn't occurred to me yet that it could be Reeva in the bathroom – I still thought that there could be intruders. I retreated to a point where I got to the corner of the bed. I tried to lift myself up. I was talking to Reeva. There was nobody. Nobody responded to me.

'I lifted myself onto the bed and placed my hand on the right hand side of the bed and felt if Reeva was there and couldn't feel anything. The first thing I thought was maybe she'd got down to the floor like I'd told her to, maybe she's just scared. I kept my firearm pointed at the passage.

'It was at that point, my lady, that it first dawned upon me it could be Reeva in the bathroom or the toilet.'

He jumped to the other side of the bed, he said, and ran his hand along the curtains covering the sliding balcony door to make sure she was not hiding there. He made his way back to the passage with his gun still in front of him.

'At this point I had mixed emotions,' he said. His jaw trembled. 'I did not know – I did not want to believe it could be Reeva in the toilet. And I was still scared somebody was coming to attack me, or us. I made my way back inside the bathroom and I tried to push the toilet door open but it was locked. I ran back to the bedroom and out to the balcony and shouted, help, help, help, for someone to help me. I went back in and I put my prostheses on and I ran as fast as I could back to the bathroom. I tried to kick the door but nothing happened. I ran back to the bedroom where the cricket bat was . . .'

'Were you still screaming at this stage,' Roux asked him.

'I was screaming and shouting the whole time. I don't think I've ever screamed like that, my lady. I was crying out to the Lord to help me. I was crying out for Reeva . . .'

The sobbing became more frequent now – the silences, too.

'I went back to the bathroom, I placed my firearm on the carpet. The light was on now . . . I kicked the door and then with the cricket bat I think I hit the door three times. The first time I felt a shock in my hand. Then I hit again and a small piece opened and then I hit again and there was a big plank. I broke it off with my hands and threw it into the bathroom . . .'

Choking again, gasping, his eyes red, Pistorius looked as haunted as a condemned man at the gallows.

'I then opened the little partition and I tried to open the door from the inside and I saw the key was on the floor at that point . . . I leant over the partition and I got the key and opened the door and threw it open . . .'

His shoulders were heaving, tears coursed down his cheeks. He bit his upper lip. Nobody in the courtroom moved. Having striven for fourteen months to banish this very image from his mind, an image that returned only in his nightmares and that he had never been able to bring himself to describe even to his family, he was reliving it now as if it were happening right there, then, for the first time.

'I now rolled down to the floor,' he said, dragging each word out. 'I sat over Reeva and I cried, I don't know how long . . .'

Another silence, then a sharp, deep breath and then, in a long drawn-out howl, he forced the words out, 'She wasn't breathing . . .'

Then the floodgates broke.

His head collapsed onto his lap as if his neck had snapped and a rasping sob tore out of his throat, then another, and another, as he gasped for oxygen like a drowning man. His face in his hands, he bawled like an infant, beyond shame or consolation, uncorking a lifetime of stored pain. Aimée was the mirror of her brother's anguish. Lois wept. Arnold, until now a monument of Afrikaner rigidity, padded an eye with a white handkerchief. June Steenkamp held her head in one hand. The North Gauteng High Court was too mean a stage for the emotion on display, and the judge knew it. Needing no prompting from Barry Roux, she stood up and, barely pausing for the ritual bow, with Aimée already on her feet running to comfort her brother, the judge hurried out of the back door as

Pistorius's cries echoed around the chamber's august wooden walls.

Five minutes later the judge returned and Roux rose to his feet. 'I cannot responsibly ask the court to carry on,' he told her. She could not disagree. Nor could Gerrie Nel. Court was dissolved for the day.

# 18

*When I use a word it means just*
*what I choose it to mean.*
LEWIS CARROLL, *THROUGH THE LOOKING-GLASS*

The next day, April 9, the nineteenth day of the trial, Gerrie Nel began his long-awaited cross-examination of Pistorius. The South African press had billed it as a duel between the Pit-Bull and the Blade Runner. The Johannesburg Star had already decided how it would end. 'Death Nel For Oscar' ran the headline that morning. But some reporters covering the case in court wondered whether the duel would take place at all. How could Pistorius possibly stand up to Nel if he could not face his own lawyer without breaking down? Might he be declared unfit to stand trial?

Or would he even show up at all? It was not entirely outlandish to ponder, as did some in the public gallery, whether he might have taken an overdose of sleeping pills the night before.

But the Pistorius family's mood an hour before the trial resumed was far less glum than might have been expected. If any of them had been on suicide watch, they did not show it. While gathered for breakfast at a cafe called Tribeca, two hundred yards along Madiba Street from the court building, Arnold and Lois, their pregnant daughter, Maria, and other uncles, aunts and cousins gave the impression of having shaken off the previous day's traumatic events. They smiled – wan smiles, but smiles nonetheless – and there seemed to be a greater resolve about them. 'We must get through this,' Lois explained. 'There's no stopping, there's no choice. So we must make the best of it.' Another aunt said that one good thing to have come out of the trial was that the family was more united than ever. They were a team, here to help 'Ozzie' shoulder the burden. The experience, she said, had brought out the best in them.

Pistorius himself wore no marks of his ordeal when he arrived in court just before 9 a.m., flanked, as he was every day, by Arnold's three sturdy sons-in-law. He strode past the camera crews and photographers with a stare as blank as if he were just another lawyer reporting for a day's work – he even wore something of the confident celebrity air of the old days, before the shooting. He sat down, bowed his head and prayed, but when he had finished he stood up and greeted his lawyers, looking almost refreshed. When Roux beckoned him to one side he listened like a boxer receiving instructions from his trainer before a fight, then gave a brisk nod and sat down again. Ampie Louw, his athletics coach since he was seventeen, was in court for the first time. Louw noted, approvingly, that Pistorius had his game face on, nerves taut but controlled.

Nel would see to it that he did not keep his composure for long.

The prosecutor believed that, short of forcing a confession, his best chance of securing a murder conviction rested on exposing Pistorius, the only living witness, as a liar. His strategy would be to plug away at every detail of what he believed to be Pistorius's improbably tailored version of events, to throw him off balance and lure him into a web of self-destructive contradictions. Nel's objective would be to persuade Judge Masipa that the only reasonable inference she could possibly draw was that there had been an argument between the accused and the deceased, after which Reeva Steenkamp ran screaming to the bathroom, where Pistorius intentionally shot her.

Nel came out blazing.

'You killed Reeva Steenkamp, Mr Pistorius. You shot and killed her. Is that correct?'

'I made a mistake,' Pistorius replied, 'a terrible mistake.'

'You made a mistake? You killed a person, that's what you did!

You still are one of the most recognized faces in the world . . . a model for both disabled and able-bodied sportsmen. Before you killed Reeva, people looked up to you and now you have a responsibility to tell the truth, and now you will not?'

'I have a responsibility to myself and Reeva to tell the truth,' he replied, his voice already beginning to crack.

'You killed her! You shot and killed her! Won't you take responsibility for that?'

'I did, my lady.'

'Say it! Say, "Yes, I shot and killed Reeva Steenkamp"!'

'Yes, my lady . . .' he whimpered.

Barely a minute into the cross-examination, Pistorius looked crushed.

Nel, having won the first flurry, declared that he would now be showing him a piece of video footage taken from Britain's Sky News channel. The video, projected before the whole court on a big screen, showed Pistorius at a shooting range, taking aim with a pistol at a watermelon. He pulled the trigger and the scene cut to a close-up of the watermelon at the moment of impact.

'You know the same happened to Reeva's head, Mr Pistorius: it exploded,' Nel said. Nel paused, letting the image sink in, then added, 'Now I am going to show you the exact same effect caused by the bullet that went into her head.'

The picture that had flashed up by accident the day before appeared again on screen for the whole courtroom to see. But this time it stayed there. Reeva had her face turned sideways, her blonde hair matted with blood, her skin turned a yellowy-grey, the top of her forehead spattered with brain tissue and white bone matter. The gallery responded with murmurs, gasps and one loud cry of shock. The Pistorius family members present looked down, shaking their heads, horrified and also disgusted by what they would later describe as Nel's brutal manipulations. No one in the courtroom would have found the picture more devastating than June Steenkamp, who would tell a newspaper that the image would remain carved in her mind for the rest of her life. But Nel had consulted with her, via her lawyer, beforehand, warning her of what he planned to do, and she had agreed that the picture should be shown. She wanted her daughter's killer to face up to the horror of what he had done.

'That's it, have a look, Mr Pistorius,' Nel snapped. 'I know you don't want to, because you don't want to take responsibility, but it's time that you looked at it. Take responsibility for what you've done, Mr Pistorius.'

'I've taken responsibility, my lady,' Pistorius replied, his eyes on the judge and not on Nel, as if he was afraid of what he might do if he looked his inquisitor in the face. 'But I will not look at a picture where I'm tormented.'

Nel insisted that he should. 'Take responsibility, Mr Pistorius.'

'I have been waiting for my time on this stand to tell my story,' Pistorius cried. 'I remember! I don't have to look at a picture where I am tormented by what I saw. I touched her head. I was there!'

Nel was not going to let go. 'Will you look at the picture?'

Unable to articulate a reply this time, Pistorius wept. Judge Masipa ordered the photograph to be removed and Nel showed some mercy at last, calling for an adjournment before Roux had time to stand up and do so himself. 'I'm giving the witness time to console himself,' Nel said, dryly. 'He is distressed.'

That first exchange set the tone for the five days of relentless cross-examination that followed. Nel was never quite as confrontational again, but he was rarely less than combative, and always blunt. He had set phrases, which he repeated throughout like jabs to the head.

'You are deceitful, Mr Pistorius.' 'Your version makes no sense.' 'You are lying, Mr Pistorius.' 'You never take responsibility, do you, Mr Pistorius?' 'It's all about you, isn't it, Mr Pistorius? It's all about Oscar.'

In breaks between sessions the Pistorius family expressed growing outrage at Nel, complaining that he was acting as if he had some personal score to settle. But they were mistaken. Nel had come to the Pistorius trial with a well-established reputation for conducting harsh, *ad hominem* cross-examinations – as Jackie Selebi, the former commissioner of police, whom he had sent to jail in 2008, would have been the first to attest. Nel had carried the nickname 'Pit-Bull' – some also called him 'Bulldog' – for a long time. A lawyer who had known Nel for nearly thirty years said that he had always been like this, even at the start of his career, in the late 1980s, when one of his jobs as a junior prosecutor had been to send stone-throwing anti-apartheid militants to jail. Mike van Aardt, the chief police investigator, said Nel was just doing his job. The accused had pleaded not guilty and so he had to face the music.

'Gerrie is not a persecutor, as some say he is,' Van Aardt said. 'He is a prosecutor.'

Nel, as if he were deploying his tactics as an amateur wrestler in his professional arena, kept his opponent continually off guard, unable to anticipate what his next line of questioning would be. He would shift abruptly from a harrowing examination of the events of February 14 to the relatively trite matter of the firearm Pistorius had discharged at Tasha's restaurant and then back again, with no warning, to the fan Pistorius said he had brought in from the terrace before grabbing his gun from his bedside and rushing to the bathroom to fire it. The whole case boiled down to what Pistorius was thinking when he fired the four bullets, and the more contradictions or ambiguities Nel could find in Pistorius's version of what happened, the greater the chance the judge would find him guilty as charged.

Pistorius, for his part, had understood from his lawyers that the issue was not just whether he had known he was shooting at Reeva, but whether he had knowingly intended to kill a human being – any human being – which would still leave him vulnerable to a *dolus eventualis* murder verdict.

**Pistorius was** not always distraught during Nel's cross-examination. Much of the time he was articulate and composed, but Nel caught him in one tangle after another.

'I didn't intend to kill Reeva, or anyone else,' Pistorius said. 'I never intended to shoot anybody. It was an accident. I shot out of fear. I didn't want to shoot anyone. I didn't intend to kill anyone.'

'You just don't take responsibility, Mr Pistorius! You just don't do anything wrong, do you?'

'That is not true, my lady,' he said. 'I do take responsibility for what happened, but it was an accident. I didn't have time to think about what I was doing. I fired before I could think.'

Nel dripped disbelief at his repeated mention of the word 'accident'. Seeming almost to enjoy the unevenness of the contest, he bounced with ever more vigor on the balls of his feet.

'What was the "accident", Mr Pistorius? Did your gun go off accidentally, or not?'

'When I fired I believed someone was coming out of the toilet to attack me, my lady,' he replied. 'I don't know what the implications are of what Mr Nel is asking me, whether it was accidentally or not accidentally . . . My firearm was in position. I had my finger on the trigger . . . I didn't have time to think about what was happening . . . I thought that somebody was coming out . . . It's easy for me to think back to that day and what I would have done or what I could have done if I had all the time in the world, but at that time I didn't. I had to deal with the situation and I believed I was going to be attacked, that my life was in danger. Many thoughts were going through my mind of what could have happened to Reeva . . . I can say that when I heard a noise inside the toilet, before thinking, out of fear, I fired four shots. When I realized the scale of what was happening I stopped firing. I was in shock . . .'

At that he sobbed again. Nel reacted with exasperation. 'Why are you emotional now? Now that the questions are difficult . . . why are you emotional? What happened now?'

'Now hold on, hold on, Mr Nel,' interjected the judge, this time unprompted by Barry Roux.

'He is emotional my lady,' Nel said. 'May I just ask why . . .?'

The judge cut him off. 'It's fine,' she said. 'He may be emotional. I don't think you can ask him why now. He has been emotional throughout.'

It was an important moment, because it showed that Judge Masipa did not share the view, held by some members of the press and the public, that all of Pistorius's weeping and retching had been faked. A debate had arisen on social media and in some newspapers as to whether the previous day's breakdown had been a dramatically calculated show of remorse.

Few who had sat in court watching Pistorius had any doubt that his anguish was real, including the judge. She gave him license to express his emotions, and the pugnacious prosecutor had no option but to display some rare meekness and respond, 'I will abide by the court's ruling, my lady.'

Nel, however, was not going to be persuaded by the judge, or anybody else, to ease up on Pistorius. He was going to do his job as he best saw fit, and that meant menacing and terrorizing on the witness stand a man who, he believed, had menaced and terrorized Reeva Steenkamp in his home the night he killed her. As Nel said, with very deliberate menace, at the end of one particularly bruising exchange, 'I am not going away, Mr Pistorius.'

Neither was he going to stop pummeling away at the question on which everything turned: what was going through Pistorius's mind when he pulled the trigger? In Nel's view, all he had received in response was lies. One moment Pistorius said he had fired in what he imagined to be self-defense, the next he said he had succumbed to an inexplicable and involuntary action. He claimed he had thought 'somebody was coming out', that he 'was going to be attacked', that his life was 'in danger', but almost in the same breath he said, 'I didn't have time to think about what was happening.' Which, Nel reminded him, was much the explanation he had given for that 'miracle' at Tasha's when the gun 'went off by itself'.

Which was it? Nel wanted to know. What did his defense truly consist of?

'My defense is, my lady, that I heard the noise and I didn't have time to think and I fired my firearm out of fear,' Pistorius said. Nel said that meant he had two different defense arguments: he was pleading that he had acted in self-defense, and, at the same time, that he had reacted out of blind instinct.

'Which was it?' Nel kept on asking, reminding Pistorius that in his recent testimony with Barry Roux he had said, 'Before I knew it I had fired four shots at the door.' Did that mean, Nel asked, that he 'never purposely fired shots into the door'?

'No, my lady, I didn't.'

Nel, unable to repress a smirk, paused for a moment to look around the courtroom, as if to confirm that everybody present must share his bemusement.

'"I never meant to pull the trigger." Is that what you said?' Nel asked.

'That's correct.'

'You didn't want to shoot at intruders?'

'That's correct . . . I heard a noise and I discharged the firearm My eyes were going between the window and the toilet door. It was an accident.'

Nel looked almost gleeful.

'Well, unfortunately, Mr Pistorius, I will have to show you something. I will be referring to the bail application . . . There, you said, "I felt trapped, the bedroom door was locked, I had limited mobility on my stumps. I fired shots at the toilet door." Why did you say then that you shot at the door and today you say you never did?'

'I think it's obvious, my lady, that I shot at the door. I do not deny shooting at the toilet door, my lady. I fired shots at the toilet door. That is what I did.'

'You cannot get away with it, Mr Pistorius. I said, did you deliberately shoot at the door and you said no, then I read out your words in the bail application and now your story changes. Why?'

'I never said I didn't do it.'

'But you said you shot at the door because it's "obvious".'

'No. Because it's the truth.'

Pistorius tried standing up to Nel. He tried engaging him in verbal battle, but this was Nel's terrain, not his. And he repeatedly got caught out.

'Are you thinking of the implications of what you are saying, Mr Pistorius?'

'My lady, if I was sitting here and I wasn't thinking of every implication of what I say it would be reckless. My life is on the line.'

'Reeva doesn't have her life anymore because of what you've done,' Nel shot back. 'She's not alive anymore. So please listen to the questions and give us the truth, and not just the implications for you, Mr Pistorius.'

As Nel did not tire of reminding the judge, the accused's notion of the truth was too contradictory to be credible. One moment he said he had not meant to shoot at the door, the next he said he had shot at a door behind which he heard an imagined attacker, yet he never meant to shoot anyone, let alone the woman whose life he had ended. He even said at one point that he had not fired at the shower because he feared a bullet would ricochet from the tiles, which in turn suggested to Nel that Pistorius was admitting to having engaged in some forethought after all.

**Whether Pistorius** was genuinely confused by Nel's cleverly choreographed attempts to unsettle him, or whether he was tired, as he said several times that he was, what was clear to most people in the court was that he was talking too much for his own good, arguing too much, volunteering too much needless information. That, certainly, was Roux's opinion.

Roux had warned him not to fall into the trap of becoming over-combative with Nel, but to limit himself to short answers or, when appropriate, to a simple 'I don't know' or 'I don't remember'. But, as Roux found to his exasperation, his client's competitive vanity was getting the better of him. Suddenly he was behaving as if he imagined he had found an opportunity to recover his shattered dignity. He could not resist trying to go toe to toe with the prosecutor. And, as Roux revealed in a rare moment during Nel's cross-examination, when he put his hand to his brow and shook his head, it was folly for his client to engage as an equal in a battle he could not hope to win.

Roux had faced a decisive question before the trial began: whether to put Pistorius on the witness stand or not. To do so would inevitably be self-incriminating, for he had no choice but to confess to firing the fatal shots. But not to do so would also incriminate him, because it would indicate a lack of faith in his ability to defend his core claim, that he mistook Reeva Steenkamp for an intruder. Roux had opted for what he considered to be the lesser of two evils.

As the cross-examination wound on into a third, fourth and then a fifth day, Roux had reason to re-examine that decision.

He would not have failed to notice that things did not improve for Pistorius when Nel examined the detail of his actions just prior to the shooting, dwelling at length on the fans that he said he had retrieved from the balcony. When Pistorius told Nel he was so absorbed in the task that he had failed to notice that Reeva had got out of bed and gone to the bathroom, Nel's response was, 'Keep trying Mr Pistorius. It's not working. Your version is so improbable that nobody will ever think it's reasonable.'

Nel pursued this seam. He knew it was a profitable one for him. From the very beginning, when the news broke of the shooting and word got round that Pistorius had believed there was an intruder in his home, the question in many people's minds was how could he not have noticed that Reeva had gone to the bathroom?

Did he not hear her get out of bed? Nel asked

'No. I had the fans blowing in my face,' he replied.

Nel could not resist laughing out loud. The judge stepped in.

'You possibly think this is entertainment. It is not,' she told him. 'So please restrain yourself.'

'I apologize, my lady, for laughing,' Nel said. 'It won't happen again. I was surprised.'

The judge's rebuke obliged Nel to recover his professional poise. Soberly, he took up his next theme, a

minute examination of the items in Pistorius's bedroom that had been photographed by the police after
the shooting. Nel initiated a debate that his opponent
would have been wise to avoid entering. It concerned
the position of a duvet and a pair of jeans which he
claimed the police had moved after they arrived on
the scene. Pistorius remembered them having been
elsewhere in the bedroom at the time of the incident.
Nel wanted to know why the police would have moved
them. Pistorius did not have an answer, but insisted
that they had done so. His stubbornness gained him
little and lost him more. His claim to an exact recollection of where those items had been did not help him,
for, as Nel pointed out, it indicated a degree of lucid-
ity on his part that was entirely at odds with the state
of terrified befuddlement he said he was in. Again, as
Roux would lament, Pistorius was too clever for his
own good. Or maybe, as his family would suggest, too
honest. It would have been better for his case, because
it would have been better for his credibility, to have
said he had no recollection of where the duvet and
jeans were.

As it was, Pistorius was providing ammunition for
Nel to argue that he was lying.

'I'm not trying to lie,' he replied. 'I can't change the
truth.'

Nel said the truth was the last thing on Pistorius's mind. His testimony, he repeated over and over, was an invention.

'You are just adapting as you go,' he said. 'It's improbable.' 'You concocted it.' 'You tailored your version.'

At one point Nel exclaimed, 'Your version is a lie. When you got up you had an argument, which is why she ran away screaming.'

'That is not true, my lady.'

'You fired at Reeva.'

'I did not fire at Reeva!'

Whether Nel's feelings were running away with him or he was seeking deliberately to provoke a rash reaction was hard to tell, but he kept on insisting that all he was hearing was lies until he said it once too often, prompting the judge to intervene again.

'Watch your language, Mr Nel,' she said. 'You don't call the witness a liar, not while he is in the witness box.'

Tea-leaf readers in the public gallery pondered whether the judge's intervention on the accused's behalf once more signaled her willingness to be sympathetic towards him, despite the hole he seemed to be digging for himself. Pistorius seemed to sense an opportunity.

'My lady, if I was tailoring my evidence, I would tailor it to suit me,' he complained, revealing some clarity of mind. It appeared to have dawned on him that the confusion and inconsistencies in his testimony, even if he regarded each individual statement as true, were not doing his case much good. 'I understand it doesn't sound rational,' he continued, 'but I did not have a rational frame of mind at the time.'

Nel restrained himself from laughing at that and, despite the judge's rebuke, proceeded on his next line of attack with his confidence undimmed.

A question people following the case from afar had been puzzled by was why, if it was pitch-dark, Reeva Steenkamp had not turned on the lights on the way to the bathroom. Nel wanted to know, too. On this occasion, the explanation seemed a plausible one, not least as it also helped resolve another troubling question – namely, why had she taken her mobile phone, as all sides agreed she had, to the bathroom?

Pistorius's answer was that it might well have been that she used the light on her mobile phone to guide her. People did that. It was not such an unlikely possibility.

But Nel, it turned out, had set a trap.

'That is what I was waiting for you to say!' he cried. 'That is devastating for you, Mr Pistorius. If it was pitch-dark, you would have seen the light from the phone in your peripheral vision!'

Pistorius, however, seemed to have an answer to that, and he delivered it with some composure.

'Peripheral vision doesn't mean you can see behind you. If my back was towards her, I wouldn't have seen. I had my back to the bathroom.'

Nel was unimpressed.

'Mr Pistorius,' he said, 'this is not good for you. If you are facing away from the bed, and you just put the fan down, if you then turn your head to the right you would look down the passageway . . . Being pitch-dark, a cellphone screen light would have been in your peripheral vision. So why didn't you see it?'

He had no answer this time.

'I don't know,' he said.

Nor did he have an answer when Nel asked him, 'Before you ventured into the passage, if you fired a warning shot into that passage, that would scare anybody, wouldn't it? Why did you not do that?'

'I don't know why not,' he replied.

If he was very scared, why did he just fire four shots? Why not empty the magazine? Why did he not fire at the open window in the bathroom, given that he seemed to think there might have been someone outside on a ladder?

He said he did not know why he fired four times. He wasn't thinking.

'"I wasn't thinking" isn't good for you, Mr Pistorius. It's also reckless,' Nel said.

Did he aim and then fire, or did the gun just go off accidentally in his hand?

He said he did not aim, he merely fired.

'So you were just lucky that you hit the door?'

'How would that be lucky?' Pistorius cried, in outraged tears. 'She lost her life!'

'There is no need for that,' Nel tut-tutted, as if reproving an overwrought child.

**Roux had** been sarcastic at times during his earlier cross-examinations. He had been confrontational, skeptical, combative. But for the most part, he had kept his emotions in check. Nel exhibited a wider and more histrionic range of feeling. He was condescending, he was sneering, he was contemptuous, he was mocking, he was shocked, he was outraged, he was indignant, he was angry and, that one time, he laughed out loud. Yet he brought the long interrogation to its conclusion with surprising restraint. He did not end the way he had begun, with a clatter and a bang. He felt he did not need to. He might not have landed a knock-out blow – there had been no single overwhelmingly damning piece of evidence in the accused's testimony – but, by a wide margin, he had won on points. He had achieved his chief objective, which was to damage his opponent's credibility. The judge had seen how self-contradictory and evasive Pistorius had been, how agitated and confused at times. He had rambled and over-explained. Judge Masipa might yet conclude that Nel had failed to show beyond reasonable doubt that the accused's version was false, but she did hear him offer Nel two different explanations as to why he had fired the lethal shots: that it had been an instinctive reaction, an accident provoked by a rush of fear and a twitchy trigger finger; and that it had been a deliberate and rational act of self-defense, intended to protect both himself and the woman he loved from what turned out to be a tragically imaginary attack.

Nel, wishing to believe the judge had reached the same conclusions as he had, brought the trial's decisive act to a calm finale, drily reiterating his claim that the accused's version made no sense and that the only possible inference to be drawn was that the screams the neighbors heard were the victim's, not his own, as she ran away from him in terror for her life following an argument.

'Your version is so improbable that it cannot possibly be reasonably true,' Nel said. The truth was, rather, that 'You shot four shots through that door whilst knowing that she was standing there. You knew that she was talking to you . . . You armed yourself for the sole purpose of shooting and killing her, and that's what you did.'

'That is not true, my lady,' Pistorius replied.

Nel turned to the judge and announced that he had no further questions. The Pistorius family let out a collective exhalation of breath. Aimée wept and, in the break that followed, Arnold Pistorius went up to his nephew and, in a public display of affection that was unusual for him, held him in a long embrace. 'He may have a difficult time,' Arnold remarked to an acquaintance in the public gallery, 'but there is one thing I can tell you for sure: Oscar is not a criminal.'

Roux judged that, by a narrow margin, he had made the right choice in advising Pistorius to testify. Roux had been irritated by his client's insistence on debating with Nel, on over-explaining, on not answering more questions with a simple yes or no. Pistorius had been a poor witness, self-contradictory and muddled. But under South African law that was not proof of guilt; it still left scope for the judge to detect reasonable doubt. Besides, Roux's worst fears had not materialized. Pistorius had not broken down beyond repair; he had kept answering the questions thrown at him, however inconsistently at times; and he had resisted what might have been a dangerous impulse to tell Nel what he really thought of him.

Fifteen minutes after the end of Nel's cross-examination the court resumed, and Roux stood up to question Pistorius one last time, hoping to turn the judge's attention away from the muddle of his client's testimony and towards the prosecution's failure either to give any substance to the theory that there had been an argument prior to the shooting, or to come up with any motive for murder. The signs were, rather, that at the time of the shooting his client and the deceased were very much in love, indicating no reason for a violent argument, much less a motive for murder. As evidence, Roux produced an envelope with a card inside. Pistorius had already made mention of this when Roux had led him through his testimony six days earlier, but Roux calculated that this piece of evidence was so central to his case that he should seek to imprint it as indelibly as possible in Judge Masipa's mind.

Roux asked Pistorius if he knew what it was that he held in his hand. Pistorius replied that it was the Valentine's Day card he had received from Reeva 'on the day the accident happened'. Roux asked him to describe the envelope in which the card was contained. It was addressed to 'Ozzie', he replied, and was covered with hearts and squiggles. Roux asked him to read the card. Pistorius, in tears, did so. Alongside a printed 'Happy Valentine's Day' message she had written, in her own hand, 'I think today is a good day to tell you that . . . I love you.'

Roux turned to the judge and said he had nothing further to add.

At 11.48 on the morning of April 15, 2014, the twenty-third day of the trial, Judge Masipa politely thanked 'Mr Pistorius' for his assistance and told him he could stand down. He had been on the witness stand for seven days, five of them in direct confrontation with Gerrie Nel.

Outside the court building that afternoon, when the day's proceedings had ended, a dozen teenagers in school uniform waited to catch a glimpse of Pistorius. All of them were black. One of them, a girl of about fifteen, spoke for all of them. 'Oscar shall always be our hero,' she said, to nods of assent from her schoolmates. 'What he did was very terrible, of course. And he may have to spend some years in jail. But we shall never forget what he did for our pride as South Africans.'

On a nearby bus shelter one of the students had scrawled, 'We will honor always U.R. talent. Prison is not the end!'

# 19

*We are often strong out of weakness,*
*and bold out of timidity.*
FRANÇOIS DE LA ROCHEFOUCAULD, *MAXIMS*

Gerard Labuschagne, the police colonel who had accompanied Pistorius to the hospital for medical tests on the morning after the shooting, had rightly surmised from the very start that his defense would be in part a psychological one. If Pistorius could convincingly be portrayed as mentally damaged, prey to all manner of phobias and insecurities, it might add credence to his story; it might help explain why he had reacted with such disproportionate terror to the noise he said he had heard in the bathroom. But now, as the defense case neared its conclusion, there was a second imperative to present him as damaged mentally: it would offer some mitigating explanation for his befuddled and confused testimony during the cross-examination by Gerrie Nel. It might help undercut Nel's contention that he had told a pack of lies.

On the advice of his lawyers, in a move they had not planned at the start of the trial, Pistorius submitted himself in the first week of May 2014 to an evaluation by Dr Merryl Vorster, a distinguished professor of psychiatry at Johannesburg's University of the Witwatersrand. She interviewed him over two days, and spoke also to Aimée, Carl and Pistorius's agent, Peet van Zyl. On May 12, day thirty of the trial, Dr Vorster took the witness stand, offering the court an interpretation of Pistorius's character based on the information she had gleaned about his life up until the time of the shooting and in the fifteen months since.

Dr Vorster, led by Barry Roux, began at the beginning. She noted that the amputation of Pistorius's legs when he was eleven months old had happened at the pre-language stage, and that he would not have been able to understand what was being done to him. But the emotional impact had been enduring.

'There would have been pain, perceived by an infant as a traumatic assault,' she said. 'He would not have been able to be soothed by his mother.'

To help him cope with his loss, his parents encouraged him to behave as normally as possible. 'He was never allowed to perceive himself as being abnormal.'

But, Dr Vorster explained, there was a downside to this.

The obligation continually to appear normal when he was not, when at primary school the children reminded him of his condition by teasing him about his prosthetic legs, established a pattern of 'anxiety and stress', expressed partly in chronic headaches, that never went away.

For Pistorius, to sit and listen to the implacably authoritative Dr Vorster dissect his personality was a new form of torture. She peeled away, layer by layer, the personality he and his parents had sought so assiduously to construct for him, exposing him to the world as a man who had lived a lie – or, at any rate, a half-truth. The picture he had been projecting of himself as, successively, a plucky little boy, a regular 'one of the boys' teenager, a champion sportsman, a seducer of beautiful women, 'the king of the London Games', was only a part of the story. The other part, which he tried to keep from himself and from others, was timorous, child-like, painfully self-conscious, afraid of being pitied or laughed at. Unable to reconcile the contradictions of his dual nature, he had endured life, Dr Vorster said, in a state of perpetual stress.

Pistorius had striven to deny these verities and now not only was he being obliged to confront them, but the whole world was learning about them, too. There were no more secrets. He might just as well have been standing in a public square, pilloried by a jeering mob.

Dr Vorster spoke about Pistorius's mother, Sheila, whom she identified as his life's 'primary attachment figure', but who was ultimately exposed as having fallen short of the image of saintliness he had projected of her. He did not mind the psychiatrist describing his father as 'absent and irresponsible', but when she revealed the family secret that his ostensibly cheerful, devoutly Christian mother had been a heavy drinker, it was another nail in his cross. It was a measure of how low he had sunk and how urgent his predicament had become that his defense required the betrayal of the image he had built up not just of himself, but also of his mother, the person to whom he had always publicly attributed all the good things that had happened in his life.

'Sheila Pistorius,' Vorster coldly informed the court, 'was a very anxious person who abused alcohol intermittently.'

It was not a gratuitous revelation. Armed with this information, Dr Vorster exposed the ghastly truth that his mother's influence on Pistorius had not, after all, been entirely positive – to the point that she even made an implicit connection between Sheila and Reeva's death. Describing Sheila as someone 'whose importance in his life cannot be overstated', Dr Vorster reminded the court the other secret that had only been known within the family until the trial: that she used to sleep with a firearm under her pillow, which had had detrimental effects on her children's mental well-being.

'It appears that the children were not soothed by their mother, but rather that they all developed features of anxiety,' Vorster said. When Roux asked her to elaborate, she replied, 'The children were reared to see their external environment as threatening.'

Pistorius, sitting with his jaw clenched, could do nothing but listen, swallow his sorrow and shame, and try to remind himself that Dr Vorster was on his side.

Urged on by Roux, she continued, explaining how Pistorius's growing public stature after he took up running at the age of seventeen had generated ever greater stress, as 'he worked hard to control his environment', battling to keep 'the external facets of his life' separate from the twisted and vulnerable individual within. Famous as he became, and as admirably polite a person as Dr Vorster said he seemed to be, he was more sad and more socially uncomfortable than he let on. While he always remained close to his two siblings, frequent foreign travel caused him to experience loneliness and deprived him of the ability to form lasting friendships or to forge strong emotional ties. He had trouble with sexual relations, Dr Vorster said, and shied away from revealing his disability, which in turn made him 'less able to access emotional support'.

Running was a refuge, Vorster said. The strict training regime to which Pistorius submitted himself was another mechanism to which he resorted in the ceaseless task of trying to keep his anxiety in check. As for the high fear of crime she had detected in him, it was exacerbated by the fact that he was a double-amputee, which meant he would react to perceived threats in a different way from other people. He was not paranoid, but 'hypervigilant', always alert to danger; and faced with a choice between fight or flight in response to a threat, he was obliged to opt to fight because his capacity for flight on his stumps was limited.

It was against this background that Pistorius's reaction to the noise he said he had heard in his bathroom on the night of February 14 should be understood.

'In my opinion,' Dr Vorster said, 'Oscar Pistorius's reaction to the perceived threat should be considered in the light of his physical disability and his anxiety disorder.'

This disorder had a clinical name, she said. It was called Generalized Anxiety Disorder, a condition that she believed afflicted as many as 6 per cent of the South African population. It led people to see threats where there were none, often went hand in hand with sleep disorders, and generated 'high levels of free-floating anxiety'. Generalized Anxiety Disorder was 'pervasive and affected all aspects of life'.

'If he was afraid that there was an intruder,' Dr Vorster said, 'then certainly having a Generalized Anxiety Disorder would have affected the way he reacted to that fear.'

Roux made a special point of questioning Dr Vorster about Pistorius's present mental state, the lawyer's notion being that it would shed useful light on his fraught emotions and rambling inconsistencies when under interrogation by Gerrie Nel. She replied that since the shooting Pistorius had been suffering from depression, fed by guilt and remorse, and from Post-Traumatic Stress Disorder. Roux sought more in this vein, asking Dr Vorster how Pistorius had appeared to her when he talked about the events of the night the incident took place.

'As he described the events, he was distressed, crying and retching,' she replied. Roux asked her if she believed those emotions had been real. 'In my opinion they were genuine,' she replied. 'You cannot feign retching. If one had to feign retching one would develop a hoarse voice, red in the face. He was pale and sweating. This is difficult to feign.'

**Nel, as** Roux had expected, appeared restless during Dr Vorster's testimony, concerned that his good work in cross-examining Pistorius might be undermined. Nel needed advice on how to address this unexpected contingency, and when the first adjournment came he engaged in animated discussion with Gerard Labuschange, who remained head of the South African police service's forensic psychology section and had been present throughout the trial. Nel was unhappy with Dr Vorster's testimony for precisely the reasons that Barry Roux wanted him to be unhappy. She was offering, first, what the judge might interpret as scientifically plausible excuses for Pistorius's poor performance on the witness stand; and, second, she was opening up the possibility that the legal notion of what constituted 'reasonable' behavior at the time of the shooting might be broadened to accommodate the unusual levels of anxiety deriving from Pistorius's disability and the childhood complications that had gone with it. Roux was angling for the judge to accept Dr Vorster's premise and agree that a response to a perceived threat that might be considered criminally disproportionate in an ordinary, able-bodied person might be regarded as reasonable in a disabled one.

This, for Nel, was poison. For the prosecution case to succeed, he needed Pistorius to be regarded by the judge as he had always portrayed himself prior to the trial – more able than disabled, a strong-minded athlete capable of competing against the world's fastest men at the Olympic Games. Nel needed Oscar Pistorius the myth, not Oscar Pistorius the man, to be the person in the dock. To prove that Pistorius had knowingly killed Reeva Steenkamp, Nel had to portray him as a champion whose feats rested on free will, not as a man at the mercy of fate or of motivations he only faintly understood and over which he had limited control. Nel had to deny the existence of the secretly vulnerable and fear-plagued amputee as vigorously as the Blade Runner himself had sought to do all his life until the night of the shooting.

Following his consultation with Colonel Labuschagne, Nel hatched a plan, but he did not reveal it until the end of what turned out to be a dispiriting cross-examination of Dr Vorster. She was a model witness. She spoke in crisply formed sentences and was confident enough in her expert knowledge to answer with a simple 'yes' or 'no', or even 'I am not certain', when that was what the questions required. She also made it clear that she was not tailoring her evidence to suit Pistorius, by agreeing that he would be a person especially anxious about losing a relationship and therefore especially prone to jealousy, and that for a person with Generalized Anxiety Disorder to own firearms represented a danger to society.

But Dr Vorster would not budge on her core contention that special circumstances – notably, the amputation at eleven months old and his mother's anxiety and alcohol abuse – had decisively shaped Pistorius's character, rendering him more fearful and insecure than most other people in all areas of life. Whether these factors should be taken into account in judging the guilt or innocence of the accused was, she said, for the court to decide. But, in sum, she said, her opinion was this: 'As one is increasingly anxious, one feels more and more insecure about one's personal safety, even though factually one's safety may not be threatened. By having increased levels of anxiety, you perceive your surroundings as being threatening, when maybe they are not.'

In other words, yes, it could reasonably possibly be – in the legal language pertinent to the case – that Pistorius was telling the truth when he said he thought there had been a dangerous intruder lurking behind the bathroom door.

Alarm bells were ringing in Nel's head. He would never look more flustered during the defense case than when Dr Vorster was on the witness stand. So much so, that before resuming his cross-examination of her after an adjournment, he neglected to turn off his mobile phone before the judge made her entrance. To Nel's acute embarrassment, his phone rang as he was in the middle of questioning Dr Vorster, prompting another rebuke from the judge and profuse apologies from him.

Nel understood that the trial had suddenly entered a critical phase. It was imperative for the success of his case that the accused's disability and its psychological ramifications should be deemed to be irrelevant and not, as the defense were seeking to propose, the heart of the matter. In order for this to happen, he had to discredit Dr Vorster's evidence. The problem, as he was shrewd enough to understand, was that he was bashing at a brick wall. Recognizing that he lacked the scientific wherewithal to expose holes in the psychiatrist's evidence, he sought outside help.

That was where the plan he had devised with Colonel Labuschagne came in.

Nel made an application to the judge for Pistorius to be referred for external psychiatric evaluation. Suddenly it was Roux and the defense team who looked flustered. Nel had turned the tables on them with what turned out to be not an unreasonable or unusual request. As he said, psychiatric referral was common procedure in cases where the accused claimed diminished responsibility due to mental incapacity. If the judge were to accept the application, Pistorius would be sent for observation before a panel of experts at a state psychiatric facility in Pretoria known as Weskoppies. Nel's hope was that these experts would discredit Dr Vorster's testimony in a way that he could not.

Roux objected bitterly. 'This is just a ruse by the state to get a second opinion,' he told Judge Masipa. 'There is no merit in the application.' Nel's move was merely a recognition of the fact that his cross-examination of Dr Vorster had been 'not good enough'.

Nel, rather than take offence, looked pleased with himself. 'Mr Roux,' he said, addressing the judge, 'is being too emotional. I would also be if I had called a witness and that witness opened the door for the referral of my client.' To which Roux, collecting himself, replied that Dr Vorster was not saying that his client was delusional or incapable of distinguishing right from wrong. 'The witness,' Roux said, 'is simply saying that the court must take his condition into account.'

Nel, who had no intention of backing down, revealed that he understood perfectly the reasons why Roux had called on Dr Vorster to make her evaluation after his client had testified in court – on the one hand, to try and compensate for the weakness of his 'unimpressive' testimony by claiming he was in some way unbalanced; on the other, because the defense was placing his mental state at the center of the murder case. Nel said he was aware of the practical implications should the judge accept his application, and that an already long-delayed trial would be delayed even further. But Nel said that the accused had to be referred for observation because otherwise, in the event that he was found guilty of murder, his mental fitness to stand trial might be raised on appeal. The judge, he recommended, 'should err on the side of caution'.

Judge Masipa, adjourning proceedings, said she would ponder the matter overnight and deliver her ruling the next morning. Curiously, heated as the debate had been between Roux and Nel, both lawyers left the courtroom that afternoon wondering whether they might have been mistaken on the position they had taken. If the referral were to go ahead, the findings of the expert panel would have to be accepted by all parties. The judge would take them as gospel. This meant that if the panel found Pistorius of sound mind in every respect, Nel would be the victor and the psychological defense would be deprived of all validity. But if the panel agreed with Dr Vorster and found him to be a deeply damaged individual, Roux would be able to claim victory. Nel understood, on colder reflection, that he was taking a risk. Roux wondered whether it might, after all, prove to have been a risk worth taking.

The following morning Judge Masipa ruled in favor of Nel. As if she had tapped into Roux's ambivalence, she noted that the defense had 'strangely' opposed the prosecution's application. The effect of the evidence of Dr Vorster, she said, was that 'doubt is created regarding possibly diminished criminal responsibility', which, she implied, could work in the defense's favor. The sum of her ruling was that neither she, nor the defense, nor the state, were in a position to reach a satisfactory understanding of these psychiatric and psychological matters without, as Nel had demanded, objective outside assistance.

'This court,' she declared, 'is ill equipped to deal with Dr Vorster's evidence . . . A proper inquiry in my view is needed so that the accused can get a fair trial.' Stressing that her aim was 'not to punish the accused twice', she said it would be 'preferable' if it could be ensured that he would not be confined in a state facility, but treated as an outpatient.

The judge's wish was respected and Pistorius was assigned to undergo a month of tests under the supervision of three psychiatrists and a psychologist at the

Weskoppies clinic, where he would report every day but would otherwise be free to carry on living at his uncle's home.

On the face of this, it was a blow for the defense, but Barry Roux did not look displeased when the judge announced her decision. Having slept on it, he had decided to look on the bright side and trust that the outcome of the evaluation would be favorable to the defense. Apart from Aimée, whose eyes seemed continually on the verge of watering up, the Pistorius family did not appear downcast either. Arnold, briefly addressing the news media later that morning, said they were all 'comforted by the thoroughness and detail of this judgment'. He did not publicly reveal his nephew's full feelings on the matter, but the word from family members was that Pistorius still retained sufficient vestiges of his pride to regard Nel's application as a sick and vindictive joke.

As to the Steenkamp family, June, who attended the trial every day, continued to give away nothing in the courtroom. But she did give an interview to Britain's *Daily Mirror* from which it appeared that she was finding it hard to retain the equanimity she had displayed before the trial began. Before, she had said that she wanted the truth and was prepared, if need be, to forgive Pistorius. Now, she began by telling the Mirror, 'I don't care what happens to Oscar . . . I don't even care if he goes free . . . I'm not a person who wants to punish him. I want my daughter back, but it's never going to happen.'

But while her husband, who sat in on the interview but had not yet been to court, stuck to his position that he did not seek revenge, there came a point when she could contain her fury no longer.

'He has an aggressive persona,' June Steenkamp said. 'He's used to having people adore him, so it must be pretty different for him now. He's been spoilt by other people, that's why he struts around and looks superior. He's gone from hero to devil.'

June's daughter and Reeva's half-sister, Simone, who would accompany her mother to court, was even more forthright in an interview published two days later in the *Mail on Sunday*.

'He killed my sister and yet he still seems to be enjoying his celebrity status,' she said. 'He is trying to convince the court that they were really close and that he cared for her. It's not true. He is a disgusting liar.'

**On June 30, 2014,** the court resumed. The Weskoppies team had submitted two reports: one a psychiatric assessment, an evaluation of the medical condition of Pistorius's mind; the other a psychological one, based on observation of the circumstances that shaped his behavior and character. The reports were filed away by Masipa, who would take their conclusions into account when making her final judgment. Both the prosecution and the defense said they would abide by the findings, which were not read out in court but were made available to the news media.

At first sight, the outcome of the month-long examination did not look encouraging for the defense. Dr Vorster's opinion that Pistorius suffered from Generalized Anxiety Disorder had been overruled. The opinion of most journalists covering the case was that the defense's decision to call Dr Vorster had back-fired. Closer inspection of the reports yielded more complex conclusions, however, and they could, on balance, even be interpreted as favorable to the defense. That, certainly, was what Barry Roux chose to believe. In private, he was telling colleagues that 80 per cent of the findings favored his client's cause.

The difference between Dr Vorster's opinion and that of the three psychiatrists who did the evaluation at Weskoppies was more of degree than of substance. They did detect symptoms of Generalized Anxiety Disorder, but not quite enough to define the condition as 'clinically significant'. Yet they did find that Pistorius suffered from 'clinically significant depression' and

Post-Traumatic Stress Disorder, and that he suffered from 'high social phobia', including an acute fear of being ridiculed or embarrassed. They also found that he was able to distinguish right from wrong and that – somewhat undercutting Nel's depiction of him under cross-examination as callously self-obsessed – he was not a narcissist. The reports also said that he had an elevated risk of suicide but his strong religious beliefs and family ties mitigated this possibility.

The psychological report, compiled by the head of psychology at Weskoppies, Professor Jonathan Scholtz, was of particular value to the defense. Scholtz made the telling observation that Pistorius's 'biggest dream was to race against able-bodied athletes, perhaps in an attempt to give psychological credence to his mother's position that he was not disabled'; but more importantly, and substantially reinforcing Dr Vorster's opinion, he reached the conclusion that there were, as he put it, 'two Oscars'.

One Oscar was 'an international superstar, more confident and feeling more in control at 1.84 meters (six feet) tall'; the other Oscar was 'a vulnerable and fearful disabled person, at less than 1.5 meters (4 feet 11 inches) once his prostheses were removed and he was alone at night'.

Scholtz added that Pistorius's vulnerability without his prostheses heightened his fear of crime, and actions that might have seemed extraordinary in an able-bodied person could be classed as 'normal in the context of a disabled person with his history'.

Scholtz said, however, that Pistorius was 'gentle, respectful and conflict-avoidant' and he had found no evidence of 'abnormal aggression or explosive violence' in him; neither did he display 'the personality characteristics of narcissism and/or psychopathy that are mostly associated with men in abusive relationships and have been linked to rage-type murders in intimate relationships'.

But what Nel took from the Weskoppies reports was not insignificant either. He could savor the satisfaction of knowing that they did not offer the defense the help they had sought from Dr Vorster in terms of providing an excuse for what would remain – along with the screams the neighbors testified they heard – the strongest element of the state's case: Pistorius's woeful performance under cross-examination.

In sum, the month-long psychiatric and psychological evaluation had been of value for both the prosecution and the defense. The prosecution was able to say that Pistorius's mental condition was not so grave as to exclude him from assuming criminal responsibility for his actions in the early morning of Valentine's Day 2014; the defense could persist in the argument that the phobias and stresses he endured reinforced their case that he had fired the shots that killed Reeva not out of rage, but out of fear. In order to try and tilt the balance further in favor of this latter interpretation, Roux called as his next witness the surgeon who had performed the amputation on the infant Pistorius, Dr Gerry Versfeld.

Versfeld's purpose was to explain to the court the physical difficulties, pain and vulnerability experienced by a person obliged to walk on two stumps. Roux calculated that it would help his case if the judge were given a second opportunity to see for herself what Pistorius's stumps looked like. Early on in Versfeld's testimony, Roux asked Pistorius to leave his seat, move to the front of the court, by the witness stand and next to the bullet-holed door which still remained in place, and remove his prostheses. He did as Roux asked. This time the judge came down from the bench to take a closer look. It did not escape the attention of anyone in court that she walked with great difficulty. Unsteady on her feet, she made her way slowly down from the raised platform where she sat and around the front of the courtroom to where Pistorius had been asked to stand, all the while holding onto the hand of a policeman.

But if her arthritis was causing her pain, she did not show it. Her ankle-length red robes looked as if they were too big for her small frame, but she did not lose her dignity, paying studious attention as Dr Versfeld explained the procedure he had carried out on Pistorius's legs twenty-seven years earlier. He informed the judge that he had positioned the heel cushions of Pistorius's mangled feet onto the base of his stumps, but, with time, one of them had moved up the side of his leg, rendering it more painful for him to walk now than when he was a child. The judge did not shy away from looking at Pistorius's stumps. Nel did. He pointedly ignored a spectacle that generated a keen, if morbid, interest in everyone else in the courtroom. He sat with his back turned to the spectacle Roux had staged, as if it were beneath his dignity to take part in it. There were two other possible reasons why Nel refused to look: that he found the defense maneuver not only manipulative and distasteful but of dubious legal value; or that, just as the comedian Nik Rabinowitz had not wanted to engage personally with the man who was the butt of his jokes, he did not want to run the risk of feeling pity for the man he was professionally required to try and send to jail.

The last defense witness was Wayne Derman, a sports medicine professor at the University of Cape Town who had been the team doctor for South Africa's Paralympic team at the Beijing and London Games in 2008 and 2012. Derman's role was to back up both the psychiatric arguments put forward by Dr Vorster and the 'two Oscars' split-personality theory put forward by Professor Scholtz. But Derman had a weakness as a witness of which he made no secret – his friendship with, and affection for, the accused. Nel targeted that weakness and also, with some success, Derman's authority to testify about the psychological factors that might be at play in Pistorius's response to a perceived threat.

But through Derman, Roux was nevertheless able to persist with his deeper strategic objective of seeking to soften the judge's heart.

'You've got a paradox,' Derman said. 'You've got an individual who is supremely able and an individual who is significantly disabled . . . Although he loathes to be pitied in any way, the hard truth is that he does not have lower legs.'

Derman, who was familiar with the daily hardships endured by people with disabilities, added, 'The saddest thing I have learned through my six years of working with athletes with disability is that disability never sleeps. It's there when you go to sleep at night, and it's there when you wake up in the morning. It affects nearly every aspect of your life.'

Roux, who could only hope that Judge Masipa heard some echo of her own affliction in those words, declared at the end of Derman's testimony that the defense case rested. The date was July 8. The court had sat for thirty-nine days, but, due to the various long and unexpected adjournments, the trial had been running for four months and five days, since March 3. No further evidence would be heard in the trial. On August 7 and 8, Nel and Roux delivered their closing arguments. Then Judge Masipa announced the date for the verdict: September 11.

# 20

*Doubt is disagreeable, but certainty is ridiculous.*

VOLTAIRE

At 9.33 in the morning of Thursday, September 11, 2014, Judge Masipa entered the courtroom to deliver her judgment. Every seat was taken; even the gap between the family and friends of Pistorius and the family and friends of Reeva Steenkamp had disappeared, the bench they sat on swelled by the presence of Henke Pistorius and Barry Steenkamp. They had both made their first appearance at the trial during closing arguments a month earlier, but had not greeted each other and neither did they do so now.

Carl Pistorius had not been able to make it for the closing arguments because six days earlier, on

August 1, he had been in a head-on collision between a car he was driving and another vehicle. His two legs had been crushed below the knees. Reported to be in critical condition when he arrived in hospital, it was not clear initially whether he would live or, if he did, whether he would be able to walk normally again. But he had made a surprisingly strong recovery and doctors said he would be on his feet again before the end of the year, and here he was now in court, in a wheelchair, to listen to the verdict. The other driver in the collision was badly injured too, and the police had opened an investigation into negligent and reckless driving, though Carl denied all blame. Press reports of the incident recalled that in May 2013 he had been acquitted of culpable homicide after another car accident in which he had been the driver and a woman had died. Today in court Carl was praying, along with the rest of the Pistorius family, that culpable homicide would be the verdict pronounced on Oscar.

When Judge Masipa sat down, Pistorius alone remained standing, as court rules required. But the judge, signaling that it would be some time before she announced the final verdict, turned towards him and said: 'Mr Pistorius, you may remain seated. I will tell you when to rise.'

Masipa adjusted her glasses, held with two hands the top page of a thick sheaf of papers on her desk – the judgment would turn out to contain a total of seventy-two pages – and began reading.

She named the four counts on which Pistorius was charged, count one being murder; she quoted extracts from the explanation plea that Kenny Oldwadge had read out on Pistorius's behalf at the trial's start, detailing the defense's version of the 'tragic incident' at his home in the early hours of February 14, 2013; and then she stated the prosecution case: 'that the accused and the deceased had had an argument and that the accused had then intentionally shot and killed the deceased who had locked herself in the toilet'.

The judge offered a brief summary of the main evidence put before her, then listed the facts that were not disputed – among them, that Pistorius had fired the shots while on his stumps, that the toilet door had been locked from the inside, that Pistorius had called for help, that he had used a cricket bat to break down the door, that he was very emotional after the incident and that he was seen trying to resuscitate the deceased.

'It is clear, therefore,' she said, 'that the issues are limited to whether at the time the accused shot and killed the deceased he had the requisite intention, and if so, whether there was any premeditation.' She dismissed as insignificant the claim raised by the defense that the police had contaminated the crime scene and declared, 'I proceed to analyze the evidence. I deal first with count one.'

Masipa read through the judgment in a steady, clear voice, never deviating from her prepared text. Millions of people were hanging on her words, which were being broadcast live around the world, but she betrayed no suggestion of stage nerves and neither did she reveal any inclination to indulge in theatrics. Pistorius's eyes did not deviate from the judge and, initially, his face revealed no emotion.

The record of the evidence, the judge continued, ran into thousands of pages. 'Thankfully, the nub of what is at issue can be divided into three neat categories as set out hereunder: gunshots, sounds made by a cricket bat striking against the door, and screams in the early hours of the morning.' All three were 'inextricably linked', she said, and would be examined together in the context of the testimony provided by Pistorius's neighbors, the five who had been called by the prosecution and the three who had been called by the defense.

Overall, the judge said it was clear that some of the sounds had been misinterpreted by the witnesses, who had not been able clearly to distinguish between the four gunshots and the smacks of the cricket bat against the door.

The judge first addressed the evidence of Michelle Burger and her husband, Charl Johnson, who lived 177 meters (580 feet) from Pistorius's home. Noting that this distance put the couple 'at a distinct disadvantage', she said their evidence had not been dishonest, as Barry Roux had suggested, but had been 'correctly criticized, in my view, as unreliable'. One indication of this had been Burger's refusal to concede to Roux that the sounds she thought were gunshots could have been made by the bat.

The testimony of Johan Stipp, who lived 80 meters (260 feet) from Pistorius's home, had also been 'unreliable', in his case in terms of 'the times when different events in this matter unfolded'. But the judge criticized Roux for suggesting Stipp had colored his evidence to fit the state case, noting that Stipp had shown no bias against Pistorius, whom he described as 'destroyed' when he found him at his home 'attempting to resuscitate the deceased'.

On the critical question of whether the screams heard by the witnesses were made by a man or by a woman, Judge Masipa noted that distinguishing intelligibly between the two was a 'tricky' matter.

'None of the witnesses had ever heard the accused cry or scream, let alone when he was anxious. That in itself poses a challenge, as the witnesses had no prior knowledge or a model against which they could compare what they had heard that morning. Even Ms Samantha

Taylor, who confidently stated that when the accused was anxious or agitated he sounded like a man and not like a woman, had to concede that she had never heard him scream when he was facing a life-threatening situation. In any event, the evidence of Mr Lin, an acoustic engineer, cast serious doubt on whether witnesses who were 80 meters and 177 meters away, respectively, from the accused's house would be able to differentiate between a man and a woman's screams, if the screams were from a toilet with closed windows.'

Barry Roux, who during earlier phases of the trial would recline almost languidly on the back of his chair, sat up straight, alert to every inflection in the judge's voice. Gerrie Nel listened with his head bent.

**Things so** far were going Pistorius's way, but when the judge began describing Reeva's injuries he responded with the same display of distress as he had done each time they were described earlier in the trial. 'The injury to the arm was particularly devastating,' the judge said, causing Pistorius's face to redden. 'A person sustaining a wound of that nature would be almost immediately incapable of voluntary action of any kind. He or she would probably also be immediately unconscious.' Pistorius closed his eyes tight shut and a muscle began to quiver on the back of his neck.

'There was also damage to the brain as well as substantial fracturing of the base of the skull, but minimal blood in the airways. This suggests that the deceased probably did not breathe more than a few seconds after sustaining this wound.'

Tears seeped out of Pistorius's eyes and once more he was battling to stop himself from breaking down. He continued to battle on even as Judge Masipa began a summary of the debate surrounding the screams that clearly suggested that, on this critical aspect of the case, she was about to rule in his favor.

'The shots were fired in quick succession,' Judge Masipa said. 'In my view, this means that the deceased would have been unable to shout or scream, at least not in the manner described by those witnesses who were adamant that they had heard a woman scream repeatedly. The only other person who could have screamed is the accused.'

Pistorius's rational response should have been relief, or outright joy, but he was unable to suppress his now customary reflex response to descriptions of the wounds he had inflicted on Reeva. Tears stained his cheeks and he strained to hold himself together, at one point moving the green plastic bucket, which still stood near his feet, closer to him for fear that he would vomit. His family would say later, however, that there had been more to it than a physical reflex. The tears had also expressed a huge release of tension as, for the first time in nineteen months, Pistorius dared to believe that he might be absolved of the chief crime of which he had been charged. When the first break in the proceedings came, after an hour, Aimée once more went to his side and embraced him, but this time she did not look sad.

Court resumed and Judge Masipa turned to what she considered to be evidence more trustworthy than that provided by the 'fallible' neighbors.

'Thankfully, as shall be clear from the chronology of the events, this court is in a fortunate position in that it has objective evidence in the form of technology which is more reliable than human perception and human memory and against which all the other evidence can be tested.

'Phone records which tell us exactly who made the call, from which cellphone to which cellphone, and at what time, were made available to this court and we took full advantage of that. There is also a record of the duration of each call. It is significant that although most of the timelines were initially introduced into evidence by the state, it was the defense which analyzed the timelines as set out hereunder and addressed the court on each.'

Judge Masipa was alluding to what had been the centerpiece of Barry Roux's closing arguments a month earlier: a detailed time chronology of the events of the

early morning of February 14, 2013, which the defense
team had labored over to exhaustion – going over it
thirty-eight times, as one of Pistorius's lawyers would
later confide – before hitting upon their definitive version. It was significant, the judge said, that while the
times of the phone calls were submitted by the prosecution, it was the defense that came up with the final
breakdown. More significant still, the prosecution had
not challenged the defense's timeline.

The judge made a point of noting that when she
had asked Nel whether he agreed with the defense's
sequence of events, Nel had replied that he did so in
so far as the recorded times of the phone calls were
concerned, initially suggesting to her that he disputed
the rest. However, she added, Nel had not come up
with an alternative chronology of his own, leading
her to conclude that 'there was no address forthcoming from the state to disturb the timelines as set out
hereunder'.

'In any event,' the judge continued, 'one can safely
use the phone records which were made between
03.15.51 and 03.17 as a base to arrive at the approximate
times when the shots were fired, and when the screams
were heard as well as when the sounds of the cricket bat
was striking against the door were heard. In addition,
the accused's phone records are also available.'

Judge Masipa proceeded to list twenty-three episodes in the timeline, starting at 02.20 when a Silver Woods security guard passed by Pistorius's house and reported nothing amiss, and ending at 03.55 when the police arrived. The most important evidence concerned what had happened in the approximately five minutes between the shots being fired and Pistorius's first phone call for help. This was the sequence in which they appeared on the judge's list:

— Approximately between 03:12 and 03:14 first sounds were heard. These were shots.
— Approximately 03.14–15 accused was heard shouting for help.
— Between approximately 03.12 and 03.17 screams or screaming were heard.
— Approximately 03.15, the accused was seen walking in the bathroom.
— 03.15.51, the duration was 16 seconds, Dr Stipp telephoned Silver Lakes security.
— 03.16, the duration was 58 seconds, Mr Johnson called and spoke to Strubenkop security.
— 03.16.13 Mr Michael Nhlengethwa made his first call to security. This call did not go through.
— 03.16.36, the duration was 44 seconds, Mr Michael Nhlengethwa made his second call to security.

— 03.17 Dr Stipp attempted to make a call to 10111.
— 03.17 second sounds were heard. These were cricket bat striking against the door.
— 03.19.03, the duration was 24 seconds, the accused called Johan Stander.

'The chronology above,' the judge said, 'gives a feel of where various witnesses corroborate one another's evidence and where they contradict one another. An analysis of the evidence using the timelines as a basis will also assist this court to determine whether the state has proved beyond reasonable doubt that the accused had direct intention and premeditation to kill the deceased.'

A core point in the case for premeditated murder made by Gerrie Nel, based on the evidence of the neighbors he brought to the stand, had been that Reeeva Steenkamp had screamed in terror – 'blood-curdingly', in Michelle Burger's words – prior to her death. Therefore Pistorius had to have known he was shooting at her. Judge Masipa dealt Nel's case a double blow when she said, first, that the first sounds heard by the neighbors had been the shots and not the screams, and, second, 'What is also clear is that the screams that were heard shortly after the shots were fired and before the second sounds, which turned out to be the sounds of the cricket bat striking against the door, could not have been those of the deceased as she had then suffered devastating injuries.'

In other words, there was no reliable evidence that Reeva had screamed at any point. This conclusion was further bolstered, the judge said, by the testimony of Mr and Ms Nhlengethwa, Pistorius's next-door neighbors, who both said they heard a man screaming after the shots. 'This version,' the judge said, 'has a ring of truth.'

Pistorius's version of the events that ended with him striking the cricket bat against the toilet door also convinced the judge.

'The number of these loud bangs or thud sounds, as well as the time, is consistent with the version of the accused that soon after he had realized that the person behind the toilet door might have been the deceased, he ran to the balcony from where he screamed for help, took the cricket bat and proceeded to the bathroom where he struck the toilet door three times with the cricket bat.'

**Roux continued** to sit alert as a hound at a hunt. Nel, who was looking down or to the side, seemed to be struggling to look at the judge. Pistorius, no longer weeping, sat expressionless, even though so far he had heard nothing but good news.

But a question still remained as to whether, as the prosecution contended, there had been an argument between Pistorius and Steenkamp prior to the shooting. The prosecution case supporting this 'theory', as the judge called it, rested on four different pieces of evidence: that the deceased had taken a mobile phone with her to the toilet, which she then locked from the inside; the WhatsApp messages between the deceased and the accused; the partially digested food in the deceased's body found in the post-mortem, indicating to the prosecution that the accused had lied when he said she had not got up again after going to bed with him at 9 p.m. the previous night; and the specific argument Estelle van der Merwe said she had heard after being woken at 1.56 a.m., approximately one and a quarter hours before the shots were fired.

Many people around the world who had been watching the case keenly from the beginning argued that Reeva's decisions to take the phone with her to the toilet and then to lock the door offered clear indications that she had fled from Pistorius. She must have taken the phone with her to call for help; she must have locked the door to prevent him from physically attacking her. As to Pistorius's contention that she had remained silent throughout, even after he asked her to call the police, it seemed to make little sense.

Months before the trial, the defense team had come up with a possible explanation as to why she had locked the door and why she did not identify herself to Pistorius, but they had chosen not to bring this up in court. It concerned the incident five years before Reeva died, when she was alone at home with her mother in Port Elizabeth and thieves had broken in, remaining in the house for fifteen minutes as the two terrified women hid inside a locked bedroom. Pistorius's lawyers believed that the recollection of this trauma might have influenced Reeva's actions and state of mind after Pistorius warned her that there were intruders in the house. It would have been of value to the defense case to raise the incident as evidence in court – but Barry Roux calculated that, on balance, it would be best not to. They would have had to call either June Steenkamp or Reeva's boyfriend at the time as witnesses. Neither would have taken the stand willingly; both would have been 'hostile witnesses', and Nel might have elicited additional evidence from them that would have been detrimental to the defense case.

Judge Masipa was therefore in no position to rule in her judgment as to why Reeva had locked the door or why, according to Pistorius's version, she had kept silent. These and a number of other questions raised by the case would have to remain, she said, 'in the realm of speculation'.

But she did note that there might be 'a number of reasons', as suggested to her by the defense, why Reeva had taken the phone with her to the toilet. 'One of the possible reasons,' the judge said, 'is that the deceased needed to use her cellphone for lighting purposes as the light in the toilet was not working.'

As to the evidence of the WhatsApp messages that both prosecution and defense had presented, Masipa gave it short shrift.

'The purpose of such evidence was to demonstrate to this court that the relationship between the accused and the deceased was on the rocks and that the accused had a good reason to want to kill the deceased,' the judge said. 'In a bid to persuade this court otherwise, the defendant or the defense placed on record more WhatsApp messages that painted a picture of a loving couple.

'In my view, none of this evidence from the state or from the defense proves anything. Normal relationships are dynamic and unpredictable most of the time, while human beings are fickle. Neither the evidence of a loving relationship, nor of a relationship turned sour, can assist this court to determine whether the accused had the requisite intention to kill the deceased. For that reason this court refrains from making inferences one way or the other in this regard.'

Judge Masipa dealt with the evidence of the partially digested food in Reeva's stomach and the argument Estelle van der Merwe said she had heard in summary fashion, too.

Noting that expert witnesses had agreed that 'gastric emptying was not an exact science', Masipa said that even if she were to accept that the deceased had eaten something shortly before she was killed, it would not lead to 'the only possible inference' that the accused had been lying. 'She might have left the bedroom while the accused was asleep to get something to eat.'

In bringing forward the evidence of Van der Merwe concerning the alleged argument, the judge said that the prosecution had lost sight of the fact that she 'had no idea where the voice came from, what language was being spoken or what was being said'. 'Accordingly,' the judge ruled, 'there is nothing in the evidence of Ms van der Merwe that links what sounded like an argument to her to the incident at the house of the accused.'

**That was** the end of Judge Masipa's dissection of the prosecution case, and it pointed to the conclusion that she would be finding Pistorius not guilty of intentionally killing Reeva Steenkamp. The judge had found no proof that there had been an argument, that Reeva had screamed before the shots were fired, or that problems in their relationship had provided Pistorius with a motive for killing her.

She now turned her attention to the defense case, which centered overwhelmingly, as she made clear, on the testimony Pistorius had given. Gerrie Nel's closing arguments had also identified Pistorius's testimony as the crux of the defense case, and Nel had savaged it accordingly. Nel had said that Pistorius had been 'an appalling witness', 'a deceitful witness', 'one of the worst witnesses ever encountered', that his testimony had been full of 'glaring contradictions' and 'devoid of any truth'. Giving full flight to his rhetoric, Nel had compared the trial to a relay race in which Pistorius 'had dropped the baton of truth', and described his evidence as a 'snowball' of lies.

Judge Masipa agreed with Nel to the extent that Pistorius had been 'a poor witness' and that his testimony had contained many inconsistencies. Quoting extensively from Pistorius's testimony, the judge pointed out that he had said, 'I fired before I could think'; that he had said 'I shot because . . . I believed someone was coming out to attack me'; and that, in reply to a question from Nel as to whether the discharge had been accidental, he had replied, 'The discharge was accidental, my lady. I believed that somebody was coming out. I believed the noise that I heard inside the toilet was somebody coming out to attack me or take my life.'

Pistorius had testified later that he had not shot to kill, otherwise he would have shot higher up, which was conclusive proof to the judge that he was contradicting himself. 'This assertion,' she said, 'is inconsistent with that of someone who shot without thinking.'

The judge proceeded gently to mock Barry Roux's repetition of the very same contradiction in his closing arguments when he had said that Pistorius had 'not consciously discharged his firearm in the direction of the toilet door', and yet, 'in the same breath', had 'submitted that the fact that when the accused approached the toilet, he had the intention to shoot to protect himself did not imply that the accused intended to shoot without reason'.

Alert to the fact that the defense had submitted Pistorius to assessment by Dr Merryl Vorster not before but after he had testified, the judge addressed herself to the psychiatric and psychological arguments produced to account for the accused's 'strange conduct' on the witness stand.

The question raised by Dr Vorster's testimony, by the month-long examination Pistorius had undergone at Weskoppies psychiatric hospital, and by the testimony of Dr Wayne Derman, was whether Pistorius's criminal culpability was in some way diminished by his mental state. The specific point the defense had sought to make was that firing the shots that killed Reeva had been an uncontrollable reflex response, and that accordingly he could not be found guilty of murder, or even of culpable homicide.

Judge Masipa disagreed.

'There was no lapse of memory or any confusion on the part of the accused,' she said. 'On his own version, he froze, then decided to arm himself and go to the bathroom. In other words, he took a conscious decision. He knew where he kept his firearm and he knew where his bathroom was. He noticed that the bathroom window was open, which is something that confirmed his correctness about having heard the window open earlier. This is inconsistent with lack of criminal capacity.'

Masipa was undermining the defense's psychiatric and psychological case as thoroughly as she had the part of the prosecution's case built on the sounds the neighbors had heard. She also turned out not to be as impressed as Roux had hoped by the argument that Pistorius's disability should afford him a special latitude in terms of the legal interpretation of what constituted reasonable behavior.

'It is understandable', the judge said, 'that a person with a disability such as that of the accused would certainly feel vulnerable when faced with danger. I hasten to add, however, that the accused is not unique in this respect. Women, children, the elderly and all those with limited mobility would fall under the same category. But would it be reasonable if, without further ado, they armed themselves with a firearm when threatened with danger? I do not think so, as every case would depend on its own merits.'

The judge had settled this particular question in favor of the prosecution. Pistorius's behavior had not been reasonable, which spelled the end of any faint notion he might have harbored in the depths of his mind that he might somehow be found innocent on all charges relating to Reeva's death. He had consciously, deliberately fired his gun, and that would not go without punishment. He would be found guilty – if not of premeditated murder, then of one of the two lesser charges.

'The intention to shoot,' she said, 'does not necessarily include the intention to kill. Depending on the circumstances of each case, an accused may be found guilty of *dolus eventualis* or culpable homicide.'

In other words, intention to shoot was culpable homicide; intention to kill, *dolus eventualis*. The question now, two hours into the reading of the judgment, was whether Judge Masipa would find that Pistorius had intended to shoot to kill.

'In this case there is only one essential point of dispute,' the judge said, 'and it is this: Did the accused have the required *mens rea* to kill the deceased when he pulled the trigger? In other words, was there intention? The essential question is whether on the basis of all the evidence presented, there is a reasonable doubt concerning the accused's guilt.'

Judge Masipa returned to Pistorius's testimony, reiterating that he had been 'a very poor witness' and adding that he had been an 'evasive' one.

'The accused was clearly not candid with the court when he said that he had no intention to shoot at anyone, as he had a loaded firearm in his hand, ready to shoot,' she said.

However, the judge added, 'untruthful evidence does not always justify the conclusion that the accused is guilty'. And although several aspects of the case did 'not make sense' and would remain 'a matter of conjecture' – among them, why Reeva did not respond when Pistorius asked her to call the police, why Pistorius did not ascertain where she was before pulling the trigger, and why he had fired not one but four shots – the law said that if there was any possibility of Pistorius's version being true he should be found not guilty of murder.

'The onus is on the state throughout to prove beyond reasonable doubt that the accused is guilty of the offense with which he has been charged,' the judge said. 'Should the accused's version or evidence be found to be reasonably possibly true, he would be entitled to his acquittal.'

This brought the judge to examine whether he was entitled to an acquittal on count one, premeditated murder. She was categorical in her findings.

'In respect of this charge the evidence is purely circumstantial . . . Viewed in its totality, the evidence failed to establish that the accused had the requisite intention to kill the deceased, let alone with premeditation. I am here talking about direct intention. The state clearly has not proved beyond reasonable doubt that the accused is guilty of premeditated murder. There are just not enough facts to support such a finding.'

In the space of two hours Judge Masipa had lain to rest the question that had been on the lips of everyone, everywhere, who had been following the case since Valentine's Day 2013: had Pistorus killed Reeva intentionally or not? Many would continue to believe that he had, but legally that opinion was worthless. It was a blow to the prosecution, but not an unexpected one. Members of Nel's team had confided prior to the judgment that they were reconciled to the possibility that Masipa would not find Pistorius guilty of premeditated murder. The evidence, all circumstantial, lacked the credibility to prove the charge beyond reasonable doubt. The suspense now centered on which of the remaining two possible charges had convinced the judge more.

*Dolus eventualis* was the verdict on which Nel had pinned, if not his hopes, then his highest expectations. Within the prosecution team they believed that the case for *dolus eventualis*, that Pistorius had intended to kill the person behind the locked toilet door, was almost watertight. So much so, that one senior member of the prosecution team confided that he believed Barry Roux had been irresponsible in not persuading Pistorius to plead guilty to *dolus eventualis* – a plea that the prosecution would in all likelihood have accepted, avoiding the necessity for a trial. Had Roux succeeded in persuading him, Pistorius would have received a more lenient sentence than he was likely to receive from Judge Masipa if she found him guilty. That individual had gone so far as to attribute the decision that Pistorius should face trial to Roux's desire to milk as much money as he could from his client.

That a member of the prosecution should have said such a thing, without any foundation, offered a measure of the bad blood that had developed between the rival legal teams. The antagonism was mutual. The word from the defense was that Gerrie Nel was a flawed glory-seeker whose ambition had blinded him to the weakness of his case for premeditated murder. He had overreached himself and was now suffering a blow to his pride, in which the defense team rejoiced. But, as to the charge that Roux should have opted for a *dolus eventualis* guilty plea, the individual who made this point had failed to grasp one crucial aspect of Pistorius's character. Even in his moment of deepest sorrow and disgrace, he held onto the maternal admonition that had shaped every important decision in his life: 'The real loser is the person who sits on the side, the person who does not even try to compete.' It would have been impossible for Roux to persuade Pistorius to plead guilty to murder of any kind. It would even have been difficult for him to persuade Pistorius to plead guilty even to culpable homicide. That would have been Roux's preferred option, but the problem there was that Nel would never have accepted it.

**The question** now, as the lunch break approached on September 11, was whether the judge would rule out *dolus eventualis*, too. She did, starkly declaring, 'The evidence before this court does not support the state's contention that this could be a case of *dolus eventualis.*'

Pistorius's reaction was not as might have been expected. No description of Reeva's wounds had passed the judge's lips for an hour and a half, yet once more he was shaking, biting his lower lip. But this time he was fighting back tears of relief and joy.

Roux did not move a muscle, though inside he was elated. Nel had remained impassive throughout the judgment, but not any longer. He shook his head vigorously.

As if responding to the prosecutor's dismay, the judge analyzed her own finding. It rested to a significant degree on Pistorius's reaction immediately after the shooting.

'The evidence shows that from the outset the accused believed that, at the time he fired the shots into the toilet door, the deceased was in the bedroom while the intruders were in the toilet. This belief was communicated to a number of people shortly after the incident.'

Among these people, the first had been the Silver Woods estate manager, Johan Stander, at 3.19 a.m., five to seven minutes after Pistorius had fired the shots; Stander's daughter, Clarice, three minutes later; a few minutes after that, Dr Johan Stipp; and at about 4 a.m., the police.

'Counsel for the defense correctly argued that it was highly improbable that the accused would have made this up so quickly and been consistent in his version even at the bail application before he had access to the police docket and before he was privy to the evidence on behalf of the state at the bail application.

'The question is: Did the accused foresee the possibility of the resultant death, yet persisted in his deed reckless whether death ensued or not? In the circumstances of this case the answer has to be no.

'How could the accused reasonably have foreseen that the shots he fired would kill the deceased? Clearly he did not subjectively foresee this as a possibility, that he would kill the person behind the door, let alone the deceased, as he thought she was in the bedroom at the time.

'To find otherwise would be tantamount to saying that the accused's reaction after he realized that he had shot the deceased was faked, that he was play-acting merely to delude the onlookers at the time.

'Doctor Stipp, an independent witness who was at the accused's house minutes after the incident had occurred, stated that the accused looked genuinely distraught, as he prayed to God and as he pleaded with him to help the deceased. There was nothing to gainsay that observation, and this court has not been given any reason to reject it, and we accept it as true and reliable.'

The lunch break came and the judge left the chamber. June Steenkamp shook her head. Barry Steenkamp revealed no emotion at all. A female cousin of Reeva's broke into sobs, as did Reeva's best friend, Gina Myers. Pistorius, sitting perfectly still, wept too. The tears he had been containing welled up, as if he were not quite ready to digest the enormity of the judge's words. Aimée ran forward to his side, smiling as she had never done since the trial began, put her arms around him and kissed him.

Nel left the courtroom devastated, members of the prosecution team said. The supposition among observers in the public gallery was that in due course he would lodge an appeal, but meanwhile the irony could not have failed to strike him that a witness he had brought to the stand had turned out to be the best witness for the defense. Johan Stipp had not only undermined the state's case when he testified about the sounds that he had heard, effectively confirming Pistorius's version of the sequence of events, but he had drawn attention to Pistorius's frantic pleas to try and save Reeva, barely fifteen minutes after shooting her

Roux, who had warned his legal team the night before the judgment to brace themselves for the possibility of a *dolus eventualis* verdict, was a picture of barely contained euphoria. 'It's going to be "culp"! It's going to be "culp"!' he smiled to his confidants.

Roux and Nel found themselves together in a back passage of the courtroom building, by the judge's chamber, for fifteen minutes during the lunch break. They did not talk to each other.

Court resumed at 14.16.

'I now deal with negligence in culpable homicide cases,' Judge Masipa began. 'In determining whether the accused was negligent in causing the death of the deceased, this court has to use the test of the reasonable man.'

The judge provided a hypothetical example of a possibly reasonable response to a perceived threat. 'If the accused, for example, had awoken in the middle of the night and in darkness saw a silhouette hovering next to his bed and had in a panic grabbed his firearm and shot at that figure, only to find that it was the deceased, his conduct would have been understandable and perhaps excusable.'

Seeking excuses had been Roux's purpose in providing ample evidence of Pistorius's troubled childhood and, in particular, the influence his mother had had in shaping his perception of crime. The judge dispensed with this line of defense in less than a minute.

'Growing up in a crime-ridden environment, and in a home where the mother was paranoid and always carried a firearm, placed the accused in a unique category of people. This would explain the conduct of the accused that morning, when he fired shots at what he thought was an intruder, it was argued.

'I agree that the conduct of the accused may be better understood by looking at his background. However, the explanation of the conduct of the accused is just that: an explanation. It does not excuse the conduct of the accused. Many people in this country experience crime, or the effects thereof, directly or indirectly, at some time or another. Many have been victims of violent crime, but they have not resorted to sleeping with firearms under their pillows.'

Neither was the judge persuaded by the disability argument, noting that 'millions' of South Africans felt as vulnerable as Pistorius did in the face of crime.

'The accused had reasonable time to reflect, to think and to conduct himself reasonably. On the facts of this case, I am not persuaded that a reasonable person with the accused's disabilities in the same circumstances would have fired four shots into that small toilet cubicle. Having regard to the size of the toilet and the caliber of the ammunition used in the firearm, a reasonable person with the accused's disability and in his position would have foreseen that if he fired shots at the door, the person inside the toilet might be struck and might die as a result.'

Inexorably, the judge's findings were leading her to one conclusion, and it came in the last act of the day's drama.

'I now revert to the relevant questions.

'First, would a reasonable person in the same circumstances as the accused have foreseen the reasonable possibility that, if he fired four shots at the door of the toilet, whoever was behind the door might be struck by a bullet and die as a result? The second question is: Would a reasonable person have taken steps to guard against that possibility?

'The answer to both questions is, yes.

'The last question is: Did the accused fail to take steps which he should reasonably have taken to guard against the consequence?

'Again the answer is, yes. He failed to take any step to avoid the resultant death.

'I am of the view that the accused acted too hastily and used excessive force. In the circumstances it is clear that his conduct was negligent.'

With that, Judge Masipa declared the day's proceedings over. She would deliver the formal verdict the following morning, once she had completed her examination of the three firearms charges against Pistorius. But there was no room left for doubt as to the main charge. Culpable homicide would be the verdict.

Rarely would a man found guilty on a criminal charge, possibly liable to a jail sentence, have felt such satisfaction. Pistorius, no longer tearful, stood up for the judge's departure from the room and remained standing as Aimée, Arnold, Carl and other family members took turns to hug him. The Steenkamp family left the courtroom saying nothing and revealing nothing, but Pistorius did have something to say to Barry Roux.

'I don't give a shit about the sentence,' Pistorius told Roux. 'I am not a murderer.'

Pistorius might find that he cared more about the sentence when the time came for Judge Masipa to pronounce it, still some weeks hence, but at that moment what he felt most was a sense of vindication. He had said from the very beginning, within seven minutes of shooting Reeva, that it had been an accident, that he had not intended to kill her, and a high-court judge had determined that he had spoken the truth. A vast weight had been taken off his shoulders, and that night, at a barbecue with friends, it showed. There were moments during the evening when he withdrew into himself, a shadow fell over his features, but for the most part he chatted amiably, even taking it upon himself to turn over the meat on the fire, in a more carefree frame of mind than at any time over the previous nineteen months. He left early, with the party still underway, but before going he said that, at long last, he would be taking to his bed with some measure of peace.

**Judge Masipa** began proceedings at 9.35 on the morning of September 12, launching straight into count two, the charge concerning the shot Pistorius had allegedly fired through the sunroof of a car in September 2010. Here it had been one word against two: Pistorius on the one side, his former friend Darren Fresco and his ex-girlfriend, Samantha Taylor, on the other. He denied the charge; they said they had seen him fire the gun.

But the judge found Fresco's evidence to be damningly unreliable. She described him as 'not an impressive witness at all', as a 'dishonest' witness who had told lies. She said that he had failed to point out convincingly the spot on the road where the alleged incident had happened, even though he, Fresco, had been driving, and she described as 'an unlikely story' his claim that Pistorius had fired a shot through the open sunroof without warning.

Fresco's evidence having been discounted, the verdict now came down to Pistorius's word against Taylor's.

The judge did not accuse Taylor of dishonesty, but did say she saw some relevance in the fact that her relationship with Pistorius had not ended amicably. 'It was clear from the evidence of Taylor that she had been hurt by the manner in which the relationship had terminated.'

This, the judge hastened to add, did not 'necessarily mean that she was out to falsely implicate the accused'. But it did mean Taylor's evidence should be approached 'with a degree of caution'. While acknowledging that there was more of a ring of truth in her evidence than Fresco's, providing the additional detail he had omitted that Pistorius had fired the alleged shot after first joking with Fresco that he wanted to shoot at a traffic light, the problem was that Taylor's evidence was at odds with Fresco's claim that the shot had come out of the blue. Yet she found Taylor to be 'a poor witness', which meant that – including Pistorius, whom she had already described in such terms – the court had been faced 'with three poor witnesses'. But, as with the murder charge, the onus was not on Pistorius to prove his innocence, the judge said, but on the prosecution to prove his guilt. They had not done so.

'The state witnesses contradicted each other on crucial aspects – namely, the circumstances under which the shot was fired, and when and where exactly the shot was fired. The evidence placed before the court falls short of the required standard for a conviction in a criminal matter. This court's conclusion is that the state has failed to establish that the accused is guilty beyond reasonable doubt on this count, and has to be acquitted.'

Count three concerned the pistol Pistorius had accidentally fired in a crowded restaurant, Tasha's, in Johannesburg, in January 2013. The judge noted that no one had contended that Pistorius had fired the bullet intentionally. This, she said, did not matter. The question was whether the accused had acted negligently.

'What is relevant,' the judge said, 'is that the accused asked for a firearm in a restaurant full of patrons and that while it was in his possession, it discharged. He may not have intentionally pulled the trigger. However, that in itself does not absolve him of the crime of negligently handling a firearm in circumstances where it created a risk to the safety of people and property, and not taking reasonable precautions to avoid the danger.'

The judge did not absolve him. She ruled that the prosecution had proved beyond reasonable doubt that Pistorius had contravened the relevant firearms law in asking for the pistol in a crowded place, as he admitted he had, and then handling it under a restaurant table.

Count four was the most innocuous of the charges Pistorius faced – namely, that he had had bullets in his possession at his home for which he did not have a lawful permit, but which he claimed he had been holding in safekeeping for his father. The judge recalled that Pistorius had said he had had no intention of 'possessing' the ammunition, a claim that was not corroborated. But neither did the state come up with evidence to the contrary. The judge swiftly reached her conclusion.

'The state has failed to prove that the accused had the necessary *animus* to possess the ammunition. He therefore cannot be found guilty on this count.'

At 10.19, forty-four minutes after the morning session had begun, Judge Masipa turned towards Pistorius.

'Mr Pistorius, please stand up,' she said. He did so, with his hands folded in front of him, his eyes on the judge. 'The unanimous decision of this court,' she said, 'is the following.'

By 'unanimous decision' she meant that the two assessors who had sat silently by her side during the whole of the trial, Janet Henzen-du Toit and Themba Mazibuko, both agreed with her verdicts.

On count one, the judge said: 'Murder, read with Section 51(1) of the Criminal Law Amendment Act, 105 of 1997, the accused is found not guilty and is discharged. Instead, he is found guilty of culpable homicide.'

On count two, Pistorius was found 'not guilty and discharged'; on count three, 'guilty'; on count four, 'not guilty and discharged'.

---

**While the** judge remained in her chair, the solemn protocols of the court allowed for no manifestations of the triumph and disappointment the defense and prosecution teams felt. The climax of the trial delivered the most anticlimactic of responses. Barry Roux stood up and said, almost matter-of-factly, 'As the court pleases.' Gerrie Nel, subdued, echoed Roux's words.

# 21

*One's personality is only a ridiculous and aimless*
*masquerade of something hopelessly unknown.*
JOSEPH CONRAD, FROM A LETTER TO A FRIEND

The verdict was not quite the end of the matter. After delivering it, Judge Masipa did not stand up and exit the courtroom. Pistorius had been found guilty of a serious crime and sentence still had to be passed. That would not be done today. But an urgent question remained and it had to be attended to straightaway – would Pistorius be ordered to spend the time between the verdict and sentencing behind bars? Gerrie Nel had no doubt as to what the answer to that question should be. He gave the judge a number of reasons why she should rescind Pistorius's bail.

The first was that 'a lengthy imprisonment was probable'. The second reason, more unexpected, offered a glimpse of the kind of evidence Nel might have wished to introduce earlier in the trial but could not, because it had not been strictly germane to the case. It concerned an incident two months earlier, after the end of the defense case but before closing arguments, when Pistorius appeared to have revealed how short his temper was – a side of his personality of which the court had heard relatively little. It had happened at a night club called The VIP Room, in the affluent Johannesburg suburb of Sandton, where he had gone late at night on Saturday, July 12, with a cousin. According to various press reports, Pistorius, 'drunk and aggressive', had got into an altercation with a South African racing driver, whom he had not previously met, called Jared Mortimer. Mortimer said there had been an argument and Pistorius had poked him in the chest and pulled him around the neck, causing bouncers to intervene. Mortimer also said Pistorius had insulted the South African president, Jacob Zuma. According to Nel in his statement to Judge Masipa, Pistorius was asked to leave the nightclub.

Once more, though, the truth of what had happened in an incident involving Pistorius was to remain hazy. The nightclub's manager was quoted in the press as saying that everything had been blown out of proportion and that Pistorius had left, 'like any other normal patron', of his own free will.

But evidence that an altercation of some sort had occurred, that Pistorius was worried about the consequences and that he felt the need to exercise some damage control, came the next day when he broke what had been a five-month silence on Twitter with three posts in quick succession. The first was a passage from the Bible that read, 'The Lord is close to the broken-hearted'. The second, against the background of a photograph of Pistorius with disabled children, read, 'You have the ability to make a difference in someone's life. Sometimes it's the simple things you say or do that can make someone feel better or inspire them.' The third tweet was an extract from a book called *Man's Search for Meaning* by Victor Frankl, a survivor of the Holocaust. It read, 'I understood how a man who has nothing left in this world still may know bliss, be it only for a brief moment, in the contemplation of his beloved.'

Two days later, the Pistorius family had issued a statement that gave further credence to the allegation that there had been an altercation of some kind at The VIP Room. 'Whilst Oscar, venturing out in a public space with his cousin in the current climate and whilst his court case is still underway, was unwise, those of us closest to him have been witnesses to his escalating sense of loneliness and alienation,' the family statement read. 'This, we believe, is underlying some of his self-harming behavior. As a family we are counselling Oscar to find ways of dealing with his feelings of isolation.'

Now, at the trial, with Nel's latest application to rescind bail underway, the Pistorius family regretted their choice of language. Nel had seized on the term 'self-harming' to suggest to the judge that unless Pistorius were kept in custody he might attempt suicide. It also offered Nel an opportunity he did not wish to let pass by of depicting Pistorius in a reckless light.

Roux's response to Nel was, first, that he disputed the facts of the nightclub incident as presented by Nel, but would not enter that debate now. The term 'self-harming', as used by the family, had not had a physical connotation, Roux said, but referred more to their awareness that for Pistorius to go out in public was to invite potential problems. Roux's main reply to Nel, however, concerned not the nightclub incident but the fact that Pistorius had been released on bail a year and a half earlier, when charged with murder, 'a far more serious allegation than culpable homicide', and that he had complied with the bail terms. Judge Masipa withdrew from the chamber for two hours to decide her ruling, during which time, at Nel's insistence, Pistorius was kept in a holding cell in the court building, where he sat with his lawyer, Kenny Oldwadge, for company.

Judge Masipa returned to her chair and, in familiar vein, said the onus was on the prosecution to persuade the court that 'in the interest of justice' bail should not be extended. She found that the prosecution had failed in this regard. As to events at the nightclub, her only comment was that should there be any future incident that might bring into question Pistorius's right to continue to be free on bail, the state would be free to re-examine the question. However, she said, 'I have used my discretion in favor of the accused. I grant the application to extend the bail of the accused on the same conditions.'

One last matter remained. The date for sentencing. Under South African law this would not be a straightforward matter. The defense would have an opportunity to submit arguments, to which the prosecution would have the opportunity to reply, in mitigation of sentence. In other words, the defense would seek to advance reasons, chiefly related to Pistorius's character, why the judge should exercise leniency. A culpable homicide conviction allowed the judge wide discretion in terms of sentencing: everything was possible, from community service, to a suspended sentence, to a maximum of fifteen years in jail. Roux would be bidding for the lowest possible sentence, Nel for the highest.

The judge set the date for October 13, with the expectation being that the matter would be addressed over three or four days, after which she would take an as yet unspecified amount of time before delivering her final ruling.

Judge Masipa stood up, bowed, left the chamber and Pistorius was at last able to celebrate. Aimée rushed to embrace him, as his uncles, aunts and cousins waited in line to embrace him, too. The last to do so was Henke Pistorius. Father and son had been estranged for six years and when they had met in court a month earlier their body language had been awkward. But not this time. The embrace, tight and heartfelt, smacked of a well-timed family reconciliation.

Pistorius was cheered by a crowd of young men and women when he left the court building, but, as soon became evident on social media, a large section of the general public refused to reconcile themselves to Judge Masipa's verdict. No matter what the judge had concluded, many continued to believe that he was a murderer. Among them, the Steenkamp family, who gave an interview to America's NBC television on the very day the judgment was delivered. 'I just don't feel that this is right,' June Steenkamp said. 'They believe his story and I don't believe that story . . . He shot through the door and I can't believe that they believe that it was an accident.' Barry Steenkamp said their disbelief was shared 'by everyone in the world'.

**Not everyone** in the world, but some of the South African newspaper headlines – 'Oscar Dodges Bullet', 'Oscar's Great Escape' – and the responses on Twitter certainly indicated that the Steenkamps' dismay was widespread. Typical examples were: 'Speechless. Rest in peace, Reeva, sorry there is no justice and no closure for your family'; 'If I feel completely depressed about #OscarPistoriusJudgement I cannot imagine how Reeva's parents must feel'; 'Oscar Pistorius has been found NOT guilty? He killed his girlfriend! Is this is a sick joke?! #JusticeForReeva'. Trevor Noah, a well-known South African comedian, tweeted simply: 'O. J. Pistorius'.

Judge Masipa came under especially heavy attack, not least from the American billionaire Donald Trump who, getting the spelling of Pistorius's name wrong, saw a parallel with the controversial O. J. Simpson case. Trump entered the spirit of Twitter mob justice by posting a message that read, 'The judge in the Oscar Pistorious case is a total moron. She said he didn't act like a killer. This is another O. J. disaster!'

Masipa was abused on social media not only on account of what people like Trump considered to be her mental and physical deficiencies – 'she is blind and deaf' – but also because she was black and a woman. She even received threats. One Twitter posting carried a photograph of youths with axes and spears in their hands and a message that read: 'Outside Masipa's house tonight. #OscarTrial. We just wanna clear a few things.' As a consequence of other messages in a similarly menacing vein, police officers were stationed outside her home.

Three respected South African legal organizations – the Legal Resources Centre, Section27 and the Centre for Child Law – issued a statement two days after the judgment in response to the abuse hurled at Masipa.

'Due to the high-profile nature of the Pistorius case, it was inevitable that many people, both within South Africa and internationally, would form strong opinions regarding the judgment that should have been reached in the matter,' the statement said. But there was a difference between criticizing the judgment and criticizing the judge, which the statement 'strongly condemned'. 'Attacking and threatening Judge Masipa because she is black or because she is female is simply unacceptable and should not be tolerated in our current constitutional framework, where equality and non-discrimination are of paramount importance.'

The personal attacks and the threats, like much of the criticism of the judgment, came from individuals with little understanding of the law and whose sense of how the trial should end had been shaped in large measure by a South African news media that was generally so blinded by bias against Pistorius that few noticed at the time just how contradictory or insubstantial had been the evidence of the sounds the neighbors heard, the ballistic evidence, and the WhatsApp messages.

But various legal experts, often ones who had been offering running commentaries on the trial for the press or for the 'Oscar Channel', also weighed in against the judge. Martin Hood, an attorney who specializes in criminal firearms offences, was much quoted in the South African and international press. Hood said he was 'disappointed and shocked' by the verdict. 'I think the judge has made some incorrect factual findings and applied the wrong legal tests,' said Hood – who, two months before the verdict, had been telling the press that he thought Reeva's killing had been 'an intentional crime of passion'. 'She should have found legal intent and found him guilty of murder,' he said, adding condescendingly, 'She got mixed up, unfortunately.'

Some of the opinions offered by the commentators revealed a need to explain away their failure to anticipate the trial's outcome. But that did not mean that the arguments against Judge Masipa's verdict were all driven by bias or vanity. Her decision not to find

Pistorius guilty of *dolus eventualis* murder did offer grounds for legitimate debate. As Pierre de Vos, a constitutional law professor at the University of Cape Town, wrote in his blog, 'Given all the evidence presented in court about Pistorius's knowledge of guns and what the bullets he used would do to a person, it is unlikely in the extreme that Pistorius did not foresee that the person behind the door (who he might have thought was an intruder) would be killed.' Vos acknowledged that the prosecution had not made its case for premeditated murder, but expressed his opinion that *dolus eventualis* would have been the correct judgment. 'To my mind,' De Vos wtote, 'the judge did not engage with this issue in sufficient detail to explain convincingly why she found that Pistorius did not have the *dolus eventualis* to kill an unknown person behind the toilet door.'

De Vos's position was widely shared among the South African legal community, where many had held the view since long before the trial began that, even on Pistorius's own version, it was evident that he had shot to kill.

But Judge Masipa did have her supporters in the legal world. One of them was Kelly Phelps, a senior lecturer in criminal law at the University of Cape Town, who said in a radio interview that the South African media, guilty of spreading 'utter misinformation', had set up unrealistic expectations regarding the judgment. She blamed this in part on legal commentators who were not criminal law specialists but had 'pegged their names to the trial in order to get publicity', and in part on the prosecution, whom she accused of leaking allegations to journalists that turned out to have no substance in fact. Among these were the reports that appeared in the press soon after Steenkamp's death claiming Pistorius had killed her in a testosterone-fueled rage. The upshot, Phelps said, had been 'a massive build of misperception within the public'. 'It set up a convenient situation for [the prosecution],' said Phelps, 'that when they lost the case it was not the state that lost the case, but it was the judge who messed up the verdict.'

In Phelps's view the culpable homicide verdict was not only 'predictable', but 'correct'. 'It is the reason why all similar cases to this one generally get prosecuted as culpable homicide,' she said. 'They are not actually prosecuted as murder and I suspect that if in this case an offer of culpable homicide had been made from the state from the beginning, we probably would have avoided this trial, we wouldn't have spent millions of rands of state resources on this trial.'

One point Phelps made, on which most legal experts agreed irrespective of their views on the verdict, was that Judge Masipa had been courageous. To have opted for *dolus eventualis* would have calmed the more vociferous anti-Pistorius wing of public opinion and would probably have spared her the need for police protection at her home. The outcry may have been far greater, however, if the judge who delivered the culpable homicide verdict had been male and white. Aware of the accusations of racial favoritism that would have rained down upon him, a white, male judge might have been more inclined to tilt the balance in favor of murder. Whatever the case, having Thokozile Masipa presiding over his trial had turned out not to be a disadvantage for Pistorius, as his defense team had initially feared, but of significant benefit to him. Coming from a black woman, the judgment arguably had a degree of credibility it would not have had from a white man, thereby improving Pistorius's chances of one day rehabilitating his public image. For some of his detractors, however, rehabilitation of any sort would always remain an impossibility.

The absence of controversy over Judge Masipa's more dramatic conclusion that no evidence had been supplied to back the contention that Pistorius had intentionally killed Reeva did not deter those who had convinced themselves from the start that the crime fell into the category of gender violence. The president of

the ANC Women's League, government minister Angie
Motshekga, said the verdict had been 'extremely disappointing' and had failed ordinary women, who would
now feel that the law was not there to protect them.
The disappointment of the ANC Women's League and
other women's organizations had its origins in their
faith that Judge Masipa would use the Pistorius trial to
send a message to society about the unacceptability of
gender violence.

Ranjeni Munusamy, of the online South African
newspaper the *Daily Maverick*, wrote, 'Because Judge
Masipa was a black woman, there were assumptions
that she would have more of an understanding of the
imbalance of power relations between men and women,
and the scourge of violence against women.'

This line of criticism against Masipa revealed the
degree to which people had presumed Pistorius to
be guilty of the premeditated murder charge before
he was proved innocent. So deeply ingrained had the
belief become that it remained immune to the most
incontrovertible part of her judgment – namely, that
the evidence put forward alleging that he knew it was
his girlfriend behind the door was extremely weak.
It followed that the most likely conclusion was that
the intruder Pistorius thought he was shooting at was
a man. In previous trials, Masipa had been harsh on

men who attacked women – notably in May 2013, three months after Pistorius had killed Steenkamp, when she handed down a life sentence to a man she found guilty of three rape charges. Even if she had convicted Pistorius of *dolus eventualis* murder, the verdict the vast majority of her critics clamored for, the issue of gender violence would have remained irrelevant and she would have been in no position to send the cautionary message that so many demanded.

But controversy, whatever Masipa's verdict, was inevitable. Pistorius was the only person who knew whether he had intended to kill Reeva or not, and while no meaningful evidence was forthcoming to show that he did know it was her behind the door, the suspicion would always remain in some people's minds that he was lying. But on the much finer point to which the outcome of the trial was reduced, perhaps not even Pistorius knew – either at the time, or a year and a half later, or at any point in the future – whether in those split seconds when he had fired four bullets in quick succession he had had the unequivocal intention of putting an end to the life of a human being. Judge Masipa was faced with the necessarily subjective, and ultimately impossible, task of interpreting Pistorius's thought processes in those moments – as the evidence left her no choice but to conclude – of fear and stress.

Barry Roux had said privately months before the trial that in a case like this, on the evidence heard a judge could arrive plausibly at two entirely different verdicts. He would have been disappointed, but not amazed, had Masipa gone for *dolus eventualis* murder. Roux would have lodged an appeal, just as Gerrie Nel was expected now to appeal the culpable homicide verdict. The point was so finely balanced that it was entirely possible the Appeal Court would overturn Masipa's judgment. They, like she, would offer their explanations in terms of legal precedent and all manner of technical interpretations of the evidence. But whatever verdict they might reach, it would still generate controversy because in this matter there could be no god-like final word.

**The sentencing** hearing began, as scheduled, on the morning of October 13, with the usual cast of Steenkamp and Pistorius family members present. This time Barry Roux went first, leading the case for mitigation of sentence, seeking to persuade Judge Masipa to opt for the gentler of the wide range of possible sentences she had the discretion to impose. Roux's mission in this trial within a trial was to save Pistorius from jail.

Roux called his first witness, a psychologist called Lore Hartzenberg who had been seeing

Pistorius for therapy sessions on a regular basis since February 25, 2013, acting, she told the court, as his grief and trauma counselor. Her role in the defense case was to demonstrate that the sorrow and remorse Pistorius had displayed in court had been genuine and, throughout the therapy sessions she had conducted with him, had remained unabated. Reading from a report she had prepared, Hartzenberg said that Pistorius lived in a permanent state of guilt; he felt worthless; he longed for the woman whose life he had ended. The 'malevolent' reports about him in the press had made his state of mind worse.

Hartzenberg went on to describe the symptoms of Pistorius's depression and post-traumatic stress disorder: 'acute stress', 'flashbacks and mental images he will always carry with him', and an irretrievable sense of loss. He had had big plans with Reeva, Hartzenberg said; he wanted to share a new home with her, to build a future together. 'I see no healing yet,' Hartzenberg said. 'We are left with a broken man who has lost everything.'

Pistorius, listening to his therapist reveal the secrets of their sessions together, looked the part. Once more, he looked bereft – head down, fighting tears.

Roux's purpose in bringing Hartzenberg to the stand was to try and persuade the judge that Pistorius

had already suffered enough, and that he would continue to suffer for the rest of his days, in or out of
jail. Gerrie Nel, cross-examining her, sought to demonstrate that, far from being broken, Pistorius cherished the idea of avoiding jail and picking up his old
life where he had left it before killing Reeva. His
intention, Nel suggested, was to resume athletic competition. Hartzenberg said she knew nothing of that,
and that what she had heard from Pistorius, rather,
was that what he would like to do should he obtain
his freedom was to go and work at a rural school his
uncle Arnold was involved with in Mozambique. Nel
also tried to get Hartzenberg to concede that Pistorius's
love for Reeva had been only skin-deep, far from the
intense and enduring dream of love he claimed to have
found with her. But Hartzenberg would not budge.

'He felt he had met the right person,' she said in
reply to Nel. 'There has been a void after her. In his
heart and mind, she was the one.'

Nel's tone was continually skeptical, at times sarcastic, but he made little headway with the woman
who, with the possible exception of Aimée, had
delved deeper into Pistorius's mind than anyone else
since the shooting. Hartzenberg stood her ground as
her cross-examination came to an end, Judge Masipa
busily making notes throughout. The sense in the

courtroom was that round one of the hearing had gone Pistorius's way.

The second witness Roux called was a social worker at the Department of Correctional Services – the prisons department – called Joel Maringa. Maringa was, like Nel, an employee of the state. He had studied Pistorius's case, he said, and had written up a report in which he argued that Pistorius should not spend one day in jail. Maringa's recommendation was that Pistorius, a first-time offender, should be placed under house arrest – or 'correctional supervision', as Maringa described it – for three years. Maringa recommended that Pistorius should be required to perform sixteen hours of community work each month, but that he should be free to return to training and even to resume his participation in athletics competitions. This last suggestion raised some eyebrows in the courtroom. Barry Steenkamp, who had been listening intently, leaning forward with his arms on the back of the bench in front of him, looked dumbfounded. He and his wife sat with their jaws clenched as Maringa explained his reasoning: 'Not only retribution is to be considered. We are also looking at reforming the accused.'

When Nel's turn came to cross-examine Maringa, he gave voice to what were clearly the Steenkamps' feelings, describing the social worker's recommendations for sentence as 'shockingly inappropriate'. To the distress of Barry Roux, it soon turned out that Maringa had prepared himself poorly for his appearance in court. Although he said in answer to a question from Nel that he had read the trial judgment, he did not seem to have understood it. Maringa's interpretation of the judgment was that Pistorius's frightened reaction to the noise he had heard behind the toilet door had been 'understandable', which was not what Judge Masipa had said. Worse still, Maringa had read her words to mean that he had not intended to fire his gun. Pressed by Nel, Maringa was insistent. 'The accused had not intended to shoot.'

This, Nel informed him, was plain wrong. 'How,' Nel asked Maringa, 'can you base your report on a misreading of the judgment?' Maringa mumbled that he had not misread the judgment, but – as even the Pistorius family had to agree – this time Nel was right. Maringa handed Nel another gift when he argued that Pistorius's life should not be 'destroyed'. Nel shot back that the Steenkamp family's lives had been destroyed. Should he not take that into account, too?

When Nel had finished with Maringa, Roux wisely let pass the opportunity to re-examine him.

The next witness Roux called was Peet van Zyl, Pistorius's agent. The service Van Zyl was called on to perform for his client now was to portray him as a philanthropically minded individual, who had it in him still to do good for the unfortunate of the earth. Prompted by Roux, Van Zyl listed a multitude of charities in South Africa and abroad – Unicef, the United Nations children's organization, for example – to which Pistorius had dedicated his time free of charge. Van Zyl spoke of his plans, cut short after February 2013, to set up his own charitable foundation and to work with the World Food Programme, as well as with war veterans who had lost limbs in Iraq and Afghanistan. It was not, however, immediately clear what impact Pistorius's good works would have on Judge Masipa. More relevant to the question at issue was the evidence presented on the second day of the hearing by the defense's fourth and final witness, Annette Vergeer.

Vergeer was a probation officer with twenty-eight years' experience, who worked both privately and for the state. She handled twenty-five cases of convicted criminals each month. Commissioned by the defense team, she had prepared a long report on the punishment she believed would best fit Pistorius's crime. Roux asked her to read it.

Unlike Joel Maringa, Vergeer had followed the trial attentively, and in compiling her report had even consulted with Gerrie Nel, who had told her that Pistorius's disability should not be used as an excuse and that he should be sent to jail. Vergeer disagreed. She noted in her report that Pistorius felt remorse and guilt, that he endured depression and had been 'publicly humiliated' during the trial.

Vergeer proceeded to paint a portrait of the typical South African prison. 'The facilities of prison will not cater to his physical or psychological needs,' she said – which turned out to be an understatement in the light of the overcrowding, gang violence, widespread disease and sexual abuse that she described as characteristic of prison conditions. Besides, she claimed, prison offered no facilities for disabled people.

It would be extremely difficult, she said, for Pistorius to walk on his stumps on the slippery cement floors of a prison. There were no baths and the showers had no rails for him to hold onto. He would be unable to protect himself from attack in prison and would be vulnerable to sexual assault in an environment where HIV/AIDS was prevalent.

'He would have to survive in very difficult circumstances, made more difficult by his disability and anxiety,' Vergeer said. 'The impact of imprisonment would be devastating. To be in prison would break the accused even further. It would be excessive punishment.'

Given that, additionally, Pistorius possessed the skills to be a productive member of society and was in a position to help people with disabilities, Vergeer recommended, as Joel Maringa had done, that house arrest would be the most appropriate punishment. 'He should be brought back into society,' she declared.

That was Vergeer's message to the judge. But in the course of her testimony she let slip a startling detail, hitherto unknown to the public, concerning a deal struck between Pistorius and the Steenkamp family. Under questioning by Roux, she revealed that Pistorius had been paying the Steenkamps 6,000 rand (US$550) per month since the death of their daughter. The announcement of the deal caused discomfort to Barry and June Steenkamp, who were seen shifting uneasily in their seats. Roux did not dwell on the matter, but Nel did when his turn came to cross-examine Vergeer. He had some news of his own concerning dealings between Pistorius and the Steenkamps. Shifting attention away from the fact that the 6,000 rand payments had indeed been made – every month between March 2013 and September 2014, as it turned out – Nel revealed that Pistorius had offered the Steenkamp parents a lump-sum compensation payment of 375,000 rand (US$34,000), which would have come from the proceeds of the sale of a car he owned. Nel informed the court that June and Barry Steenkamp had rejected the lump-sum offer, dismissing it as 'blood money'.

Those two words duly made it into the headlines of the news media the world over, prompting a number of journalists to ask whether the secret 6,000 rand the Steenkamps had uncomplainingly accepted from Pistorius over a period of twenty months might be described as 'blood money', too? As if anticipating the question, Nel announced in court that the Steenkamps had taken the decision to repay Pistorius the monthly sums he had given them 'in full, every cent'. He also said, after consulting with the Steenkamp parents and their lawyer, Advocate Dup de Bruyn, that they had resolved not to pursue a civil case they had initiated against Pistorius in 2013. In short, the Steenkamps sought no more financial compensation from Pistorius and intended, rather, to repay the total of 120,000 rand (US$11,000) they had already received from him.

As late as November 2013 De Bruyn had been telling reporters seeking to interview the Steenkamps that the couple were 'indigent' and would only talk in exchange for cash. When De Bruyn spoke to reporters now, outside the courtroom, he said that the Steenkamps had reached a point where they were 'reasonably comfortable'. The reporters, who knew that the Steenkamps had made more money than they ever had before in their lives thanks to interviews sold to the news media, disingenuously asked De Bruyn how they had achieved these new levels of comfort. To which he curtly replied, 'I have done deals for them.'

Whether the 'blood money' story would remain a media sideshow or would be taken into Judge Masipa's calculations on sentencing was not apparent. Of more urgent importance to Nel in his cross-examination of Vergeer was to address her core contention that Pistorius would be neither safe nor adequately cared for in prison. Nel thus returned to a theme familiar since the trial's beginning, endeavoring to portray Pistorius as he had depicted himself before he shot Reeva, as the near-mythical Blade Runner rather than an insecure, limbless man plagued by fears of nocturnal attack. Nel's line of argument was that Pistorius would be perfectly capable of looking after himself in prison – which, besides, was not nearly as dark and dangerous a hell-hole as Vergeer had made it out to be. Describing the house-arrest recommendation once more as 'shockingly inappropriate', Nel proceeded to fluster Vergeer by showing that a number of the views on prison conditions set out in her report had their source not in her own experience but in texts of dubious or biased provenance which she had obtained from the internet. But Vergeer did not shift from her position that prison would represent an excessive punishment for Pistorius. Sentence should be determined not only on Pistorius's actions on the night of Reeva's killing, she said, but 'on the totality' of his life and character.

That, in a nutshell, was the point that Roux was seeking to get across to Judge Masipa – and that Nel was seeking to exclude from her calculations.

Vergeer left the stand at noon on the third day of the hearing, concluding the defense's case for mitigation of sentence. Up first for the prosecution after the lunch break was Kim Martin, a first cousin of Reeva Steenkamp's. Martin was twelve years older than Reeva and had been close to her from her early childhood to her death. Martin said she had received the blessing of both Barry and June Steenkamp to testify in court. Neither of the two parents had felt they were up to the ordeal of appearing themselves – 'Uncle Barry told me he'd lose it,' Martin said – and had effectively left it to her to act as the family's spokesperson. It would be the first time since the trial began that Nel would opt for Barry Roux's tactic of seeking to soften the judge's heart.

Martin, led by Nel, described Reeva as a kind, considerate person, whose parents had always battled financially but had managed, through hard work, to obtain the bursary she needed to pay for her law studies at Nelson Mandela University in Port Elizabeth. She mentioned what she described as the 'emotionally abusive' relationship Reeva had had with her first serious boyfriend, the jockey Wayne Agrella. Martin intimated, too, that there had been problems in Reeva's relationship with Pistorius.

She said she had met Pistorius once, over breakfast with Reeva in Cape Town on January 2, 2013. Martin's teenage daughter was also at the breakfast. Noting in passing that Reeva called him 'Oz', Martin said Pistorius had come across as shy at first, but after watching him talking to her young daughter about boarding school she had formed the opinion that he was 'a very nice person'. But then Pistorius walked away from the table to take a phone call. Martin seized the opportunity to ask Reeva if she was happy in the relationship. In reply, Martin said, 'She pulled up her shoulders and said, "Yes, but we need to talk . . ."'

Martin said she never got a chance to find out what, if anything, was wrong.

That particular piece of testimony was unlikely to have any more impact on Judge Masipa's thinking than the earlier WhatsApp messages that the prosecution had gone to such lengths to provide as evidence of troubled relations between Reeva and Pistorius. Far more dramatic and emotionally compelling was Martin's description of her family's response to the news of the shooting on Valentine's Day morning, 2013.

Weeping, Martin recalled the moment. 'Everyone was running around screaming and shouting... We were all asking "Why? Why? Why Reeva?"' In the courtroom June Steenkamp looked pointedly across at Pistorius. He was weeping, too.

Martin said she went to Port Elizabeth from Cape Town, where she lived, to see Uncle Barry and Aunt June. 'Aunt June was very medicated, but she was hysterical. Uncle Barry was in a corner, crying, crying. Reeva was everything to them.'

Aimée wiped a tear from her eye as Martin continued with her testimony, leaving it to the court to see that it had been not only Pistorius who had sought psychological assistance in the aftermath of the killing. Martin said that she herself had gone for trauma counseling, and her children, who, she said, had adored Reeva, had also been in therapy.

With half an hour of scheduled proceedings remaining on the third day of the hearing, Nel asked for an adjournment, saying he had to consult with Martin regarding the last part of her testimony. Judge Masipa, clearly impatient to bring the long trial to an end, grudgingly gave her approval and the next morning, October 16, at 9.30 a.m. Martin resumed the stand. But before Nel began questioning her there was another matter he wished to attend to. Turning to face the judge, with a smile on his face and with a graciousness he had rarely displayed in court hitherto, he said, 'Just before we start, I am honored to be in a position to offer you congratulations on your birthday. We will do our best to make your day as enjoyable as possible.'

Enjoyment would not turn out to be high on the day's agenda, but Judge Masipa beamed back at Nel and thanked him very much. The public in the courtroom responded to the news – she had turned sixty-seven – with a spontaneous burst of applause. Masipa might have made enemies outside the courtroom, but among those who had followed the trial inside from start to finish the consensus was that she had acquitted herself with elegance, dignity and due gravity. The applause, one sensed, was as much in tribute to the calm authority she had exercised over the court, as for her birthday.

The remaining part of Martin's testimony consisted of her – and, by implication, the rest of her family's – position on the sentence Pistorius should receive. It was the most important thing she would say on the witness stand, as it was sure to carry weight with the judge.

First, Nel asked Martin what her response had been to the apology Pistorius had made to the

Steenkamp family upon first taking the witness stand six months earlier. Martin's response was straightforward and unequivocal. 'I did not feel it was genuine,' she said.

What, Nel asked her next, were her feelings towards the accused now?

'I am very fearful of the accused,' Martin replied. 'I have tried very hard to put him out of my mind and do not mention his name in my house. I don't want to expend energy thinking about him.'

And what, Nel wanted to know, did Martin consider to be a fitting punishment for Pistorius?

'I really believe Mr Pistorius needs to pay for what he has done,' she replied. 'My family are not people who are seeking revenge. We just feel that to shoot someone behind a door who is unarmed and is harmless needs sufficient punishment. I can say I honestly feel that Mr Pistorius should pay for what he's done by taking Reeva's life, for what he has done to my uncle and my aunt and to the rest of my family.'

Martin added that the sentence Pistorius received should send a message to society that one cannot do what he did and get away with it. As to the suggestion made in court that he should be placed under house arrest instead of being sent to jail, Martin's position was clear: 'It would not fit the crime.'

Roux, alert to the potency of Martin's testimony, did not keep her long on the witness stand. Cross-examination lasted less than five minutes, the chief purpose of the exercise being to allow Roux the opportunity to put it on record that Pistorius 'desperately' wanted an opportunity to apologize privately to the Steenkamps, 'at whatever time and date'.

Like much of what was heard in evidence at the sentencing hearing, this gesture was aimed more at public opinion than at the judge. What would not have escaped the judge, however, was that Martin had provided the most emotionally compelling evidence of the hearing.

The second and final prosecution witness was Zach Modise, the acting national director of the Department of Correctional Services. He began his testimony with what seemed to amount to a propaganda exercise on behalf of the South African prison system. Placed on the stand by Nel to refute Annette Vergeer's apocalyptic portrayal of conditions in jail, Modise went to the other extreme and painted South African prison life as an experience more akin to a vacation camp. Enthusing about the sports facilities – notably the abundance of gyms – and the quality of hygiene and health care enjoyed by prisoners, as well as the spiritual ministrations offered by visiting psychologists and pastors of the church, Modise said that, contrary to Vergeer's claims, the Kgosi Mampuru prison in Pretoria where Pistorius would be incarcerated if he were sentenced to jail catered amply for the needs of people with every type of disability, providing baths, showers with rails to hold onto, and single cells.

Roux, in his cross-examination, did not give Modise an easy ride, pointing to official statistics that showed an increase in torture and violent assaults inside South African prisons over the previous year. Roux, highlighting the well-publicized influence of criminal gangs in prison, mentioned the case of a prisoner at Kgosi Mampuru called Khalil Subjee but known to inmates as 'the General'. According to press reports, Subjee had made it known that he intended to 'take out' Pistorius, Roux told Modise, who said he knew nothing of this. Roux insisted, but Modise continued to plead ignorance, putting himself in an increasingly uncomfortable position.

If Roux was laying a trap, it worked. So defensive did Modise become under Roux's questioning that when Roux put it to him that, in the event of his going to jail, Pistorius should receive special treatment, Modise did not disagree. As if accepting that prison was, after all, a dangerous place not well fitted to accommodating disabled inmates, Modise was pushed into declaring that Pistorius should be kept not with the rest of the common criminals but in a hospital wing. Roux, who wanted the judge to hear that loud and clear, reiterated the point. Was the national director of prisons saying, then, that the hospital section would be the appropriate place to incarcerate Pistorius? 'Yes,' Modise replied. 'That would be a fair summary.'

That was quite a coup by Roux. In the worst of cases his client would find himself in the prison equivalent of the hotel suites Pistorius used to frequent in his days of international athletics competition.

**When closing** arguments began five days into the hearing, on Friday, October 17, however, Roux pressed on with his request that Pistorius should be spared jail and placed under house arrest.

In an emotional appeal to the judge, Roux recalled that the court had concurred with Pistorius that the shooting of Reeva Steenkamp had not been a conscious act. His client, he said, had already suffered enough, both on account of the remorse he had endured and the unfair public pillorying he had withstood.

'It is our respectful submission,' Roux said, 'that never in history before has any accused been denigrated, humiliated and ridiculed on false and irresponsible allegations, to the extent that the actual punishment for the crime would do little to alleviate the ill effects caused by the uninformed in their striving for sensation.'

Pistorius's fall from grace had been as abject as it had been spectacular, Roux continued. 'He was an icon in the eyes of South Africans for what he has achieved. He's lost everything.' Everything, Roux said, included 'the person he loved', 'his self-image, self-respect and dignity', 'his career', 'his reputation' and 'all of his money'. 'There is nothing left of this man,' Roux said. 'He's not only broke, but he's broken. He hasn't even the money to pay for legal expenses. He has nothing left.'

And yet, Roux said, the charitable works Pistorius had done showed that he had it in him to be valuable to society. 'He wants to make good as far as possible,' Roux concluded. 'Serious regard should be given to a community-based sentence so something good can come out of this.'

Nel, replying to Roux, repeated for the third time in the week his charge that house arrest would be a 'shockingly inappropriate' response to Pistorius's crime. Yet he stopped short of asking for the fifteen-year sentence which was typically the maximum available in cases of culpable homicide.

'The minimum term that society will be happy with will be ten years' imprisonment,' Nel said. 'This is a serious matter. The negligence borders on intent. Ten years is the minimum.'

Once again, Pistorius wept as Nel conjured up a picture of the crime he had committed. 'The deceased died in a small cubicle behind a closed door,' Nel said. 'Three bullets ripped through her body . . . it must have been horrific.'

Nel noted that some witnesses had said, 'Please don't break the accused'; yet what the court should not forget was that Pistorius had broken an entire family. As to Roux's point that Pistorius had endured excessively negative media coverage, Nel was not sympathetic, offering instead a whining parody of Pistorius's complaint: 'I'm a victim, feel sorry for me, the media victimized me. When I wanted the media to capture my brilliant athletic performance, I loved them; when the media write about my trial, it's unfair.'

Nel also attacked Pistorius for falling back on his disability as a reason to be spared the punishment he deserved. 'I find it disturbing,' Nel said, 'that a person who fought to compete with able-bodied athletes now shamelessly uses disability in mitigation.'

Arguing strongly for a jail sentence, confessing that he battled to keep his own emotions in check, Nel declared, 'We shouldn't fail the parents. We shouldn't fail society. Society may lose its trust in the court.'

Nel ended his appeal to the judge, who adjourned proceedings for four days until Tuesday, October 21, the date on which she would at long last deliver her sentence.

**The Pistorius** family arrived in court just after 9 a.m. on what would be the forty-ninth and final day of the trial, with Aimée and Carl telling reporters sitting behind them that they would stand by their brother no matter what – and that whatever punishment he received from the judge, he would never get over what he had done. June and Barry Steenkamp said they would never get over their daughter's death either. Pistorius walked in wearing his customary dark suit, white shirt and black tie, but this time carrying a bunch of white roses he had received from a supporter outside the court. The green plastic bucket remained at his feet, but this time he looked as if he would not need it. He sat down alone in quiet contemplation, his face revealing nothing, even though he knew the chances were high that he would not be spending that night in his comfortable bed at the plush cottage in the grounds of his uncle Arnold's large home – that for the first time in twenty months he might be back in a jail cell, to remain there alone with his demons but side by side with other criminals, for who knew how long?

Judge Masipa walked in, listed Pistorius's two convictions – culpable homicide and discharging a firearm in a public place – and declared: 'The decision on sentence is mine, and mine alone.' The views of the two assessors who had sat next to her during the trial did not come into it. It was up to her to take into account the chief factors determining the appropriate legal response: punishment, retribution, deterrence and rehabilitation. The task she faced in sentencing also concerned finding 'the right balance' in the interests of society. But she acknowledged that the process of sentencing was 'unscientific', allowing for reasonable people to arrive at different conclusions.

Pistorius sat bolt upright, staring straight ahead at the judge, still betraying no emotion, as if steeling himself to take on the chin whatever sentence she handed down.

The further Judge Masipa went into the reading of her judgment, the more it seemed Pistorius should prepare for the worst. Twenty minutes into the court session she delivered what sounded like a terminal blow to the argument made in favor of house arrest by Annette Vergeer. 'Her evidence,' the judge said, 'was slapdash, disappointing and had a negative impact on her credibility as a witness'. By contrast, the evidence put forward by Zach Modise on behalf of the Department of

Prisons had been convincing. Modise had been a good witness, the judge said, and while it was evident that the prison system was not perfect, it was 'progressive and professional'.

'I am satisfied,' Judge Masipa declared, 'that the Correctional Services Department is suitably equipped to deal with inmates with special needs.' Noting that she felt 'unease' at what she called 'the overemphasis' on Pistorius's vulnerability in the evidence put forward by the defense, she believed him to have 'excellent coping skills'. Making it clear that she did not believe Pistorius merited exceptionally lenient treatment, she added, 'It would be a sad day for this country if an impression was created that there is one law for the poor and disadvantaged and another for the rich and famous.'

Still more ominously for Pistorius, the judge said that the prosecution had been correct in characterizing his crime on the night he shot Reeva as 'grossly negligent', so much so that 'it bordered on *dolus eventualis*'. In acknowledging the fine line in this case between manslaughter and murder, the judge was all but preempting the nature – if not the length – of the sentence she meant to pass. Pistorius's facial expression began to alter. Shifting his eyes away from the judge and down onto the floor, he looked anxious and increasingly woebegone.

Judge Masipa did acknowledge that Pistorius's remorse was genuine, that his conduct immediately after the incident in particular had shown 'he wanted the deceased to live', and she did say that she would take his disability and vulnerability into account. Yet she said that the sentence proposed by Vergeer and the social worker Joel Maringa 'would not be appropriate in this matter'.

'I am of the view that a non-custodial sentence would send a wrong message to the community,' the judge said.

Jail it would be, then, and all that remained to be known was how long the sentence would be. Before getting there, she made a point of addressing the Steenkamp family's sorrow.

'Young, vivacious and full of life . . . a promising young woman who cared deeply for family, who was full of hope for the future, and lived life to the full. The loss of life cannot be reversed. Nothing I do or say today can reverse what happened to the deceased and to her family. Hopefully this sentence shall provide some sort of closure to the family . . . so they can move on with their lives.'

Then Judge Masipa instructed Pistorius to stand up and delivered her sentence. On the firearms charge: three years in jail, suspended for five years. On the conviction for culpable homicide: five years in prison.

There were no gasps, no shaking of heads, no sound or detectable movement at all in the courtroom. Not even from Pistorius himself, who seemed to have turned to stone, his face revealing no emotion at all as the judge left the courtroom, slowly and haltingly, for the last time. He sat down, knowing now that he would not be going back to his safe and comfortable cottage for a long time. He turned and, just before two policemen led him down into a holding cell below the court, he reached out both hands to his uncle Arnold and his aunt Lois, his eyes cast down. All that was left for him now was to do as he would at his mother's or his older brother's bidding when he was at school and he was teased by the other children, or when his blisters were so sore when he woke up in the morning that the pain was too great for him to stand up, or when, early on in his time at Pretoria Boys High, he had kept going on that trek across the bush on a blazing summer's day, even though his legs were chafed and bleeding at the point where the stumps and the prosthetics met – he had to 'man up'.

**There would** be no appeal. Barry Roux, who all in all had done mightily well by his client, confirmed as much. Pistorius would begin on the long road towards social rehabilitation – if rehabilitation were possible – by sending a message to the public that he accepted his punishment without complaint, Roux said. But, added Roux – who was owed legal fees by his client but, as he had indicated earlier, had little expectation that they would be fully paid – there was some good news for Pistorius. By his estimate, Pistorius would be eligible for release into house arrest after ten months in prison.

Speaking on the street outside the courtroom, Arnold Pistorius read out a statement expressing his family's feelings now that the long ordeal was over.

'Today a new season starts for us as a family,' he said. 'Not just the Pistorius family alone, but the Steenkamp family. It has been a harrowing twenty months. We are all emotionally drained and exhausted.

'We accept the judgment. Oscar will embrace this opportunity to pay back to society.

'I want to say something as an uncle. I hope Oscar will start his own healing process as we walk down the path of restoration. As a family we are ready to support and guide Oscar as he serves his sentence.'

The question now remaining was how the Steenkamps would react. If they reacted as negatively as they had to the culpable homicide verdict six weeks earlier, public controversy would continue to rage on their behalf, and Nel might find himself under pressure to lodge an appeal

As the courtroom emptied, and all that remained of Pistorius's presence were the white roses on the bench where he had sat and the empty green bucket beneath it, the Steenkamps' lawyer, Dup de Bruyn, provided reporters with an answer. Reeva's parents, he said, were 'satisfied' with the sentence. Barry Steenkamp then confirmed what De Bruyn had said, declaring himself to be 'very satisfied'. June Steenkamp, smiling wanly, said, 'It's right.' She added that the sentence had given her 'a sort of closure', but there would be no final closure without Reeva, 'unless you can magic her back'.

Possible further cause for satisfaction, if not comfort, for the Steenkamp family came later in the day in the form of a statement from the International Paralympic Committee saying that Pistorius would not be allowed to return to competition until 2019, the year his sentence would officially end. By that time he would be thirty-three years old, which meant that his athletics career was well and truly over. Over, too, was any possibility that his contracts with Nike and other commercial sponsors would ever be resumed. The punishment he had received in court could have been much worse – and it was certainly far more benign than he had feared, or than most people had expected when the trial had begun seven months and eighteen days

earlier – yet Barry Roux had been right in his closing arguments the Friday before when he had said that
Pistorius was 'broke and broken', that there was 'nothing left' of the icon he had once been.

An hour after Judge Masipa had passed her sentence
Pistorius was seen exiting the court building by a side
entrance, surrounded by police, before being led into
a yellow and white armored vehicle and taken away to
begin his new life at Kgosi Mampuru prison – twenty
minutes' drive from the house he no longer owned at
Silver Woods Estate, where, in the early morning of
Valentine's Day 2013, in a moment of criminal recklessness, he had sealed his own and Reeva Steenkamp's
fates.

Millions of people had been gripped by the case from
the morning the shooting happened. Most had made
up their minds from the beginning as to why Pistorius
did it, and then proceeded to follow the trial having
taken one side or the other. A very few had personal
reasons for wanting to believe one version or another.
Among these were Pistorius's family and friends like
Ebba Guðmundsdóttir and her mother, Sigga Hanna
Jóhannesdóttir. On the other side were the Steenkamp
family and friends of Reeva's, whose understandable
need it was to seek comfort for their loss in the punishment of the individual who had occasioned it. For

the majority who had no personal stake in the trial's outcome, each chose to believe the version that best accommodated their need to find some justice and sense in the chaos of life. For some, making sense of Reeva Steenkamp's death meant seeing Pistorius as a murderer; for others, it meant seeing him as a hero who had succumbed to one tragic error of judgment.

**South Africa** itself provokes similarly contradictory responses. It is a country that many people around the world have watched with interest, seeing in its political evolution an experiment with lessons and repercussions for humanity as a whole. During apartheid, the South African drama was regarded as a morality play in which the parties representing good and evil were clearly defined. Even the opposing sides in the Cold War were in agreement that apartheid was 'a crime against humanity'. In that morality play Mandela had played the role of the prince-redeemer. He was the larger-than-life figure who had set up the expectation when he assumed power in 1994 that South Africa would live happily ever after, overcoming the legacy of racial injustice and building the foundations of an exemplary democracy. But that was South Africa's heroic age, a time of forgiveness and reconciliation the likes of which the world had rarely seen. Mandela's successors did not live up to his exalted image. Corruption set in, both moral and financial. People of meaner minds took power. The old idealism gave way to self-interest and greed. And thus for many people, inside South Africa and beyond, the experiment had failed. It turned out to be a great disappointment.

Just like Pistorius. He had been a fairy-tale prince, handsome and charming. His story was one of the most unlikely in the history of sport. He had had his legs amputated at eleven months old and had run in the Olympic Games. South Africans of all races, weary of their political leaders, sought in him a hero to fill Mandela's boots. Feted around the globe, he made them proud to be South African once again, as they had been proud when Mandela was head of state.

After Pistorius killed Reeva Steenkamp, it became tempting to see him as a symbol not of South Africa at its best but at its violent, criminal, worst. That, as Judge Masipa's verdict helped indicate, was to oversimplify. Pistorius did remain a symbol of South Africa, but of a South Africa that was complex, ambiguous and could no longer claim to play a heroic role on the world stage. In 2014, Pistorius offered a more faithful mirror of the country than did Mandela.

The trial had heard from a defense witnesses that there were 'two Oscars'. There were two South Africas.

One was uplifting; the other was frightening. One was made up of people who were unusually polite, who were generous, indomitable, forgiving and brave; the other, of people who were reckless, volatile, violent and hot-headed. South Africans' politeness towards strangers was in part a self-defense mechanism, a response to an awareness that people might turn angry without obvious provocation.

But if Pistorius were to have offered only a portrait of the country in which he was born, the story of his rise and fall would not have proved so compelling to the rest of the world. As hero and anti-hero, he offers an archetype to which all people can relate. He is an extreme case of an individual who has made the best of the cards that life has dealt him, but he has revealed himself to possess to an equally extreme degree the insecurities that all are prey to.

His life story is archetypal, too, in its striking vulnerability to the random and the haphazard. He was cursed with cruel luck, but also blessed with immense good luck. His destiny at birth was never to be able to walk, or to do so haltingly at best. But because of a decision by his parents, which they might easily not have taken, and because of the uniquely driven mother it fell upon him to have, and because one day his grandmother dialed a number that led him to meet a young

prosthetics specialist – who should have been a farmer –
Pistorius ended up becoming one of the most celebrated
athletes in the world. On the other hand, after his
mother died there was no one around in his life with
the authority or the wisdom to ground him, to see that
he was a victim of his own success and that he needed
help to come to terms honestly with his disability, with
the limitations his mother had taught him to deny. He
remained trapped in a floundering adolescence, too
unfinished to stop the fame and the money from going
to his head. He was a teenager in an adult's body, prone
to foolish infatuations with women in whom he imagined he saw the image of his mother, irresponsibly sus-
ceptible to the allure of guns and fast cars.

Yet that was not the whole story either, for he was
impressively polished in his public presentation of himself and he could also be extraordinarily kind, considerate and empathetic – as the little Icelandic boy Haflidi,
the Paralympic swimmer Tadhg Slattery, Samkelo
Radebe, and his friends and admirers in Gemona del
Friuli would attest.

Early on in the Pistorius trial, a talk-show host
on a Johannesburg radio station said he had recently
talked to a retired judge who had told him there were
two kinds of truth: 'Legal truth, and truth truth'.
The legal truth was narrow, selective and exclusive of

both the good and the bad in Pistorius. Samkelo, who phoned Pistorius to congratulate him on the day he was acquitted of murder, was the one who said it was unjust to define his whole life in terms of the legal truth of the fatal crime he had committed in a few seconds of delirium. The 'truth truth' was that Pistorius was an enigma, a man of many masks. Jail, as one of his teenage fans had scrawled on the bus shelter outside the Pretoria High Court, did not have to be the end. In the silence of his cell he might find the time and mental space to ponder at last who he was, who he wanted to be and which mask fitted him best.

# Acknowledgments

This book is the outcome of many people's time, effort and kindness. So many individuals have I talked to in the task of assembling *Chase Your Shadow* that it would be an impossible act of memory to recall every single one. Thank you to all and apologies to those I omit to mention here.

First, I must express my gratitude to my old friend Paul Greengrass. It was Paul who suggested to me the idea of writing this book in the first place and it was he who coached and encouraged me along the way, offering invaluable input on structure, point of view and what he calls 'narrative pulse'. I cannot thank him enough.

My editor at HarperCollins, David Hirshey, can never be thanked enough either. His attention to style, eye for detail and hard toil generally provided immeasurable added value.

My agent, Anne Edelstein, went, as ever, far beyond the call of duty, both with her finely critical readings of my first drafts and with the therapy she was ever on hand to provide when I despaired, moaned or flagged.

Shelagh Frawley read through everything too and, with her meticulous eye for grammatical detail, taught me long overdue lessons on the use of the pluperfect, among other things. Many thanks also to Lauren Jacobson, whose reading of the text provided legal comfort and general reassurance.

Sue Edelstein, my rock, was another diligent reader – ever enthusiastic, encouraging and supportive on all fronts.

Devon Koen delivered a wealth of essential documentary research. Always swift to respond, he was a delight to work with.

Hannia, Tracey, Bella and Frans provided a warm and welcoming home from home at Ilali, the best bed-and-breakfast in Johannesburg. Thank you to my excellent friends Aspasia Karras and Mark Phillips, who also housed and fed me, while providing plenty of ideas for the book; likewise the no less excellent Indra De Lanerolle and Nicola Galombik.

Debora Patta made some key introductions for me, was a constantly valuable sounding board, great friend and – not least – speedily reliable Johannesburg–Pretoria chauffeur.

I won't go through all the people who helped me in South Africa, the US, Italy, Iceland or the UK but hopefully the mention of many of their names in the book will serve as acknowledgement of their generosity. Huge thanks to all. I will, however, single out Samkelo Radebe, who provided a measure of wisdom and insight that I alone could never have mustered. Samkelo also gave me the title of the book.

Also thank you to Greg Nott, Leila Amanpour, Reine Malan and family, Anneliese Burgess, Antony Altbeker, Riaan Labuschagne, Leon van Niekerk, Carolyn Raphaely and Natalie Holland. Natalie was the first person I interviewed for the book and painter of a most eloquent unfinished portrait of Oscar Pistorius.

Finally, thank you to all those involved in this enterprise who work for the publishing houses around the world that have acquired this book. Most of their names I do not know, though hopefully I will get to meet several of them in due course. The heroic translators of the book into various languages deserve special recognition. As does James Nightingale, my patient and admirably organized editor at Atlantic Books. Big thanks also to Margaret Stead, Fran Owen and David Atkinson at Atlantic, the indomitable Sydney Pierce at HarperCollins, David Figueras at Planeta and Nathalie Fiszman at Seuil. I am not forgetting Toby Mundy, either.

October 2014

# About the Author

John Carlin grew up in Argentina and in the UK and spent 1989–95 in South Africa as the *Independent*'s correspondent there. He has also lived in Spain, Nicaragua, Mexico and Washington, writing for *The Times*, the *Observer*, the *Sunday Times*, the *New York Times*, among other papers, and working for the BBC. His previous books include, *Playing the Enemy* (2008), the basis of the film *Invictus*, directed by Clint Eastwood, which earned Oscar nominations for both Matt Damon and Morgan Freeman, and *Knowing Mandela* (2013).

# HARPER LUXE

## THE NEW LUXURY IN READING

We hope you enjoyed reading
our new, comfortable print size and found it
an experience you would like to repeat.

**Well – you're in luck!**

HarperLuxe offers the finest in fiction and
nonfiction books in this same larger print size and
paperback format. Light and easy to read, HarperLuxe
paperbacks are for book lovers who want to see
what they are reading without the strain.

For a full listing of titles and
new releases to come, please visit our website:

**www.HarperLuxe.com**